LOST

Feast

Feast

CULINARY

EXTINCTION

AND

THE FUTURE

OF FOOD

LENORE NEWMAN

Published by ECW Press
665 Gerrard Street East
Toronto, Ontario, Canada M4M 1Y2
416-694-3348 / info@ecwpress.com

Editor for the Press: Susan Renouf
Cover design: Michel Vrana
Interior illustrations: © Pearson Scott Foresman/public domain and © Trees for Long Island/public domain

LIBRARY AND ARCHIVES CANADA CATALOGUING
IN PUBLICATION

Title: Lost feast : culinary extinction and the future of food / Lenore Newman.

Names: Newman, Lenore, 1973– author.

Description: Includes bibliographical references and index.

Identifiers: Canadiana (print) 20190120126
Canadiana (ebook) 20190120134

ISBN 978-1-77041-435-8 (hardcover)
ISBN 978-1-77305-407-0 (PDF)
ISBN 978-1-77305-406-3 (EPUB)

Subjects: LCSH: Food supply. | LCSH: Food—Social aspects. | LCSH: Food—History. | LCSH: Food habits. | LCSH: Gastronomy.

Classification: LCC TX353 .N49 2019
DDC 363.8—dc23

The publication of *Lost Feast* has been generously supported by the Canada Council for the Arts which last year invested $153 million to bring the arts to Canadians throughout the country and is funded in part by the Government of Canada. *Nous remercions le Conseil des arts du Canada de son soutien. L'an dernier, le Conseil a investi 153 millions de dollars pour mettre de l'art dans la vie des Canadiennes et des Canadiens de tout le pays. Ce livre est financé en partie par le gouvernement du Canada.* We acknowledge the support of the Ontario Arts Council (OAC), an agency of the Government of Ontario, which last year funded 1,737 individual artists and 1,095 organizations in 223 communities across Ontario for a total of $52.1 million. We also acknowledge the contribution of the Government of Ontario through the Ontario Book Publishing Tax Credit, and through Ontario Creates for the marketing of this book.

  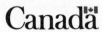

PRINTED AND BOUND IN CANADA   PRINTING: FRIESENS 5 4 3 2 1

MIX
Paper from
responsible sources
FSC® C016245

For Kitty.
Your support and encouragement
made this book possible.

Contents

Acknowledgments

A number of people helped bring this book to life. I would like to give special thanks to my editor Susan Renouf and the entire team at ECW Press for making this book a reality. I would also like to thank Trena White and the team at Page Two Strategies for the long brainstorming sessions needed to turn a handful of ideas into a book. I also want to thank Shannon Blatt and Kitty Newman for the hours of copyediting, and to Dr. Adrienne Chan for her patience and guidance. The research for this book was supported in part by the University of the Fraser Valley and the Canada Research Chair Program. Special thanks go to "Dan" (you know who you are). Lastly I want to thank William Newman for providing slices of pear pie whenever my motivation flagged. I owe all of you a dinner.

Section One

THE BEGINNING OF ENDINGS

Chapter One

SILPHIUM

It began with butter, a surreal amount of butter, glistening with tiny pinpricks of fat. It was studded with fragments of fresh herbs and whipped nearly to a foam. There was bread as well, but it was a supporting character. It too was excellent, a dark rye loosely stacked in rough slices on the right-hand side of a plate-sized slab of black lava rock. The butter was mounded up on the left side, a lump the size of a Christmas orange, melting gently where it lounged against the warm stone slab. The stone itself was of the same sort found in the walls of the restaurant and rimming the pool of steaming azure water outside the window. This stone played hide and seek among the drifting snow from here to Reykjavík. I took a moment to gaze out on the falling flakes and on the tall blond bathers reveling in the shimmering water. Some perched on the rocks, and others floated in the pool's volcanic embrace. I'd spent the morning there, and after the meal, and perhaps a short period of digestion, I would return. But for now, there was butter.

I plucked another slice of bread from the slab and spread it liberally with butter. The fresh herbs, tiny leaves and twigs I couldn't recognize, gave off the smell of a summer mountaintop. My grandmother liked butter, I thought to myself, my mind rambling in the manner of the solitary diner. My grandmother would have approved of this excess. I settled into my chair and took a slow bite, savoring the flavor and texture. I had a long lunch ahead of me and yet I was probably going to eat the whole lump of glorious butter. Slowly, the stress of the last few days, the snow, the cold, all melted away.

I was in Iceland to study the food of hard places. I had copious notes from my fieldwork in Newfoundland as a comparison, full of tales of cod tongues, salt pork for Sunday dinner and seal flipper pie. Now here was another island on the ragged northern edge of the world, full of friendly people, tidy settlements and interesting cuisine. Iceland is conveniently located between the December gloom of London, where I had just been, and the December gloom of Vancouver, where I needed to be. On the plane from Heathrow, I'd perched on the edge of my seat, excited to expand my horizons, meet new people and see new things. And, of course, excited to eat. My optimism had dwindled once I'd landed. Twilight gave way to driving snow, and the bus from the airport began to fishtail in the darkness. Out in the night, impossibly neat cottages were barely visible. None of this seemed to concern the jolly older man sitting beside me. He was happy to engage me in a one-sided conversation about the joys and struggles of being an aurora scientist in northern Scotland. He talked the way older men talk, alive with the joy of having an interested audience. At home, he had plenty of the darkness needed for his craft, but it was far too overcast. Instead, he spent time in Siberia and Iceland, supplementing his scientific work by giving aurora tours to wealthy tourists. I looked out the window, skeptical of his chances for success. I couldn't even tell where the sky ended and the forest began. The wind began violently rocking the bus. I could see the driver tense his arms; his knuckles were white under the occasional streetlight. The aurora scientist frowned at the snow. He shrugged.

"Don't worry, it will clear. Behind this storm, it will be clear and still."

"Don't you get cold, watching the aurora all night?"

"Oh, it's a dry cold. You hardly notice it."[1]

"I'm here to study food."

"Oh, that's grand. Such fish and dairy. Be wary of the shark, though."

He shuttered a little and turned to the window, lost in contemplation of the darkness. The bus slid merrily across the road, the driver cursing in a melodic tongue. I burrowed into my coat and hoped that the hotel would have room service and maybe a sauna.

Iceland is awash in interesting food. I talked to restauranteurs in the snow and dark. I visited thermal greenhouses in the snow and dark. I chatted with ice-eyed fisherman in the snow and dark next to an ocean of such a forbidding temperament I couldn't turn my back on it.

I loved it. The noonday sun barely graced the horizon long enough to cast a glow on the mountains across the ice-choked harbor. I enjoyed tasting everything I could get my hands on, prowling the streets like a hungry wraith of midwinter. I ate fish as fresh and delicate as snowflakes. I did end up nibbling the

---

1   The idea of "dry cold" is a lie told by people living in extreme climates to convince ourselves we shouldn't flee to the equator.

fermented shark meat I'd been warned about and regretted it for several hours as the smell and taste hung on me like a pungent ghost. I munched on lichen. I tossed back salads grown with the heat of volcanos and ate bread cooked in the ground. I ate a great quantity of skyr, the yogurt that is really a cheese made from the milk of the Icelandic cattle descended from cows brought from Norway in the tenth century. They are now a distinct product of their harsh home, small in stature and few in number, with only thirty thousand lactating cows working to fill the breakfast bowls of Iceland. They are unusual cows, their coats pied or brindled in six colors, as plush as cats. They are tended on 700 farms that tuck into fertile valleys along the coast, where they eat the local vegetation in small plots of pasture, isolated for a millennium from the rest of cattle kind. The Icelandic cow is different, and its milk — extremely high in protein and low in fat — passes that difference along to the sort of butter one can eat by the spoonful. As my aurora watcher noted, the dairy was sublime. This place and its people have existed for centuries by the graces of fish, cows and sheep.

The world has found Iceland. Tourists flood the streets of Reykjavík. Skyr, so rich and wonderful, is an increasingly prized export in a food-obsessed world. So prized, in fact, that the cows of Iceland cannot possibly keep up with demand. A possible solution would be to crossbreed Icelandic and Norwegian cows to increase production per acre, but in the process the purebred Icelandic cow would likely go extinct from introduced disease and genetic mixing. There is no real way to make the magical cloud of butter brooding on a slab of volcanic rock available to a wider audience without making it into a pale copy of itself. That butter emerged from centuries of harsh landscape and slow cattle-breeding combined with skilled preparation. To lose the butter of Iceland, and the foods like it, would be a great loss.

Many of the unique foods that help to make the world a diverse and interesting place are in danger. The forces of globalization, industrialization and ecological collapse threaten the wealth of culinary products that make our cultures distinct. Some of these foods are becoming rare, some are becoming much more expensive and some face outright extinction. Some have already become extinct.

To understand these threats, imagine a feast. It can be any feast: a Las Vegas buffet, a family holiday dinner, a South Pacific pit BBQ, or an Indonesian rijsttafel, the classic meal of many small dishes, served for special occasions. Imagine a meal with many dishes and more food than can possibly be eaten at once. There are two things in that feast, aside from a great deal of hidden labor. There are dozens, if not hundreds, of species of plants and animals, a sort of culinary menagerie. There is also a huge body of culinary knowledge, the accumulated knowledge of growing, harvesting, processing and preparing foods handed down and improved upon over generations. A feast is a bit like a book, but a tasty book we read through eating. Now imagine that the dishes start to disappear one by one. The raspberries for the waffles, the sage on the Thanksgiving turkey, the poi or the pisang goreng. Gone. Slowly the table becomes less interesting, less captivating, and as each species disappears, the accompanying cultural knowledge vanishes with it.

This is the paradox of the lost feast. Even as we enjoy a time in which food is cheaper, more diverse and more available than ever before, the specter of extinction threatens to radically challenge how we eat. In fact, it is already happening.

I took another slice of bread slathered with that fabulous, perhaps endangered butter. Outside, the snow had stopped, and the sky was deepening into a crisp cobalt glow. The restaurant was called Lava, an aptly named set of rooms nestled beside Iceland's Blue Lagoon hot pools. I was taking some quiet time away from the rush of restaurants, fishing piers and new flavors. I needed a break from the hours of trudging through deep snow, bent into the wind, my skin cracked and my eyelashes frozen. Floating aimlessly in a pool of hot water with a fine restaurant close at hand seemed an excellent alternative for a day. The water is the by-product of a nearby thermoelectric plant, and the locals have cleverly converted it into a world-class spa. There is even a bar right inside the pool, and the Icelanders give out wristbands that track alcohol consumption so that one doesn't overindulge and drown. Lava, where head chef Ingi Fridriksson leads a team dedicated to highlighting Icelandic cuisine, is one of the few fine restaurants in the world where one can wear a bathrobe to the table. And, of course, they have that wondrous bread and butter.

Butter is an old innovation. When one milks a cow, the cream separates to the top as a liquid filled with microscopic globules of butterfat that are protected by a membrane. When we agitate cream, we introduce air to the mix, forming a colloid better known as whipped cream. But as any overenthusiastic cook knows, beating the cream further forms something new: butter. Unbeknownst to most, they have ruptured the membrane that has kept the fat in suspension, releasing it into its new form.

Humans figured this out as early as 6500 BCE, leaving a buttery residue as evidence on ancient pottery. By 2500 BCE, the Sumerians were crafting tablets illustrating the preparation of butter from cow's milk, a durable if heavy instruction manual. Butter spoils quickly in hot climates, forcing the development of other innovations. They were adding salt to their butter to extend its shelf life by Roman times, and in India they discovered that one can remove the solids to create a much more lasting substance, known as ghee. In northern Europe and the United Kingdom, butter was packed into firkins and stored in bogs, where it became rancid but remained edible for a very long time. Occasionally, we still dig up the odd forgotten barrel.

The making of butter is such an important culinary innovation because it takes a product with a very short shelf life, milk, and turns it into a product that lasts longer and is easier to transport. And, of course, we like butter. We like the taste and we like its texture. It's both rich and satisfying, and in the world of cuisine, satisfying matters. We need food to stay alive; we embrace cuisine out of enjoyment.

I was wandering Iceland's midwinter darkness because I'm a professor of culinary geography, a job that combines my love of travel with my love of eating. It isn't all hot pools and butter, though. There are long days of solo travel in difficult conditions, red-eye flights, upset stomachs and lonely nights spent typing up notes in strange hotels. But these inconveniences are outweighed by the time I get to spend with people who are truly passionate about food and cuisine. I talk to farmers as they rave about new crop varieties, and I get to sit down with chefs after their shifts to swap culinary memories and discuss food adventures. I cross paths with writers poking into every single aspect of the food system, and all of these people feed me, and I feed them.

Lately people who love food have been sharing a growing sense of concern. Farmers shaken by floods and droughts talk to me about the changing climate and the challenge posed by increasingly unpredictable weather. Fishers talk of declining stocks and unpredictable prices shaped by international markets. Wild foragers tell me of shrinking habitats and vanishing ecosystems. I'm still enjoying the incredible culinary bounty as people open their kitchens to me, but there is a sense of urgency, the sense that the hour is growing late. Our diverse food systems are increasingly under threat.

Cuisine is a language. Languages have two central properties, and the language of food is no different. Primarily, a language allows us to communicate, permitting us to pass on what we have learned to future generations and to other groups of humans, no matter how remote. Through language, we can trade important messages about food. Where to find it, how to prepare it and where in the forest we might want to be on guard for hungry leopards while we forage. However, each language is also a unique way of looking at the world, a point of view influenced by place and time. Each language contains concepts that do not translate easily, and if a language is lost, those ways of seeing the world are lost too. The French idea of terroir is a good example of this. The term translates very roughly as "the taste of the landscape" and suggests the character of a food is intrinsically local. Terroir is shaped by climate, soil, growing techniques and processing traditions, creating foods linked to a specific land and people. Cuisines have terroir, bringing together ecology and culture to tell a story of what it is to be human. In Canada, for example, we occasionally cook with snow,[2] using the sap of the sugar maples found only in eastern North America. Oaxaca, Mexico, is famous for its seven moles, Singapore for its chicken rice. The Scottish have their magical whiskeys imbued with brooding peatlands, smelling of wind, long train rides, cozy pubs and winter nights spent reading gothic novels. Some foods are so local that they tell the story of a single valley, river or mountain range.

---

2 Prairie muffin recipes and tire d'érable, maple taffy, are the best examples but are certainly not the only way Canadians use snow in cooking.

Our understanding of cuisine has progressed in fits and starts across many cultures at different times, though the modern use of the term is quite new. The word comes to us from the Latin *coquina*, from coquire, "to cook." In the Western world, the idea of cuisine didn't enter popular use until late eighteenth-century France, when it was coined by Jean Anthelme Brillat-Savarin, a lawyer who narrowly survived the intrigues of the French Revolution. He initially caught the attention of the Revolutionary Committee with a spirited defense of capital punishment, but when the revolution turned into the Reign of Terror, he found himself on the wrong side with a price on his head, and he had to flee France. Less enthused with capital punishment when it was so very personal a matter, he found himself at loose ends in New York, where he ate, drank and brooded. He learned to play the violin, eventually performing professionally. In the New World, he pined for the food of his homeland. Under the next regime, he was able to return to France where he eventually became a magistrate. He pulled back from politics with Napoleon's rise. Tired of the cut and thrust of the political arena and motivated by a love of the emerging restaurant scene in Paris, he wrote the first serious Western study of food. His masterwork, *The Physiology of Taste*, was published in 1825, a few years before his death. From him, we get the roots of the modern understanding of cuisine, from its triumphs to its extremes. If you find yourself watching a rerun of the "Battle Fruitcake" episode of *Iron Chef*, you can probably blame Brillat-Savarin.[3] His most famous quote is unfortunately the mistranslation "you are what you eat." What he really said was "dit moi que tu manges, je te direr qui tu es," which translates into "tell me what you eat, I will tell you who you are," a

---

3   Brillat-Savarin is one of the fathers of modern food writing, and he was also fond of mixing unexpected things together.

much deeper statement on how important cuisine is to identity. To Brillat-Savarin, cuisine was more than the sum of its parts. If we lose our cuisine, we lose a part of ourselves.

And oh, such parts. The "words" of the culinary language are ingredients, and the overwhelming bulk of our ingredients break down into species, though multiple ingredients can come from a single biological source. The complexity of each specific dish has developed over time. Our most fleeting and ethereal meal draws on the experience of centuries. There is, however, still a lot to learn. We are clever at exploiting our environment, yet the potential riches of the world's biosphere are vastly greater than what we currently consume. Plants provide the bulk of our calories, and of the roughly 400,000 plant species on earth, some 300,000 are potentially edible. Yet we have domesticated and farmed only a few hundred of these plants, and the vast bulk of our calories come from just three: corn, rice and wheat. This might seem like a shocking lack of imagination, but domesticating a plant takes a lot of work and time. The wild ancestors of many of our most popular food species would be almost unrecognizable to us. Along with our domesticated species, we eat a few thousand wild foods that are harvested regionally, but the vast bulk of edible species are still largely unknown.

Our animal protein choices are equally limited. We have a wide variety of foods available from the 65,000 species or so in the chordates: fish, mammals, amphibians, reptiles and birds. Yet only fifty or so are domesticated and farmed regularly, and the bulk of animal protein comes from chickens, cows, pigs and ducks. But we can eat almost all of the chordates, with a few shockingly poisonous exceptions.[4] In addition, about one-quarter of the 70,000 known

---

4   Consider *Phyllobates terribilis*, the golden poison frog. It's descriptively named; if you see one, don't pick it up.

mushrooms are edible, though many more are either too woody or contain nasty surprises. In the orchard by my house, little patches of destroying angel mushrooms crop up. These look appealing, but cause vomiting, cramps, delirium, convulsions, diarrhea and death. Not an ideal lunch. The possibility of poisoning combined with their rather poor food value might explain why the fungi are unexploited. The same can be said of the invertebrates. We love lobster and toss back a smattering of species such as snails and sea urchins, but we don't even know how many invertebrates there are on earth. We certainly haven't tasted them all.

The idea of culinary extinction had been haunting me for some time. I spent my days thinking about the rich complexity that food brings to our lives and the loss of species used by humans in their food systems that chips away at that richness. A plant here, an animal there. And with them, piece by piece, goes cuisine.

Cuisine is important. And if cuisine is important, culinary ingredients are also important, as are the ecosystems they come from. On my return from Iceland, still thinking of those Icelandic cows, I decided I needed to know more about the set of threats looming over the plants and animals that support our food system. There are already lost foods, and each one has a story to tell.

My idea to study culinary extinctions was just that: an idea — musings at 30,000 feet. For the idea to become an obsession and then a story, I needed to share it with someone also prone to obsessions. I knew just who to talk to. Plan at the ready, I cruised high above Greenland, enjoying my inflight treat of Yule síld.[5] As I dozed against the bulkhead, I was blissfully unaware that in less than twenty-four hours, I would be attacked by birds.

5   Christmas herring. No, really. It's a thing, and it's on Icelandair's Yule menu.

—

I was mugged by a colony of gulls. It was a warm morning, and I was shaking off a restless, jet-lagged night, jotting lazily in my notebook at Granville Island Public Market. I was already exploring how I could expand on my airplane "eureka!" moment. Mapping out a story of the extinction of culinary species in my head was one thing, but getting it onto paper was another matter entirely. Three coffees into my day, I decided it was time for lunch in the market's oceanfront courtyard. I bought a plate of Pad Thai, popped on my headphones, and walked through the door, my focus already distracted by the bridges and towers of the city, the shimmering ocean. The market courtyard is an urban back porch, a hidden oasis. Surely it could give me some inspiration.

The gulls were waiting above the door. I thought I had the courtyard to myself as I juggled my plate of Pad Thai, my laptop, my iPhone and my coffee, and I mentally dismissed the sign on the door warning of aggressive birds. After all, the warning was for tourists. I was a local, an old hand when it came to Granville Island and everything it offers. I was cocky. A half-dozen large and aggressive male glaucous-winged gulls dropped onto my head in a fury of pecking beaks and beating wings. They also managed to deliver some well-placed kicks to my eyes with their rubbery little feet. In seconds my food was on the ground, my coffee was on my shirt, and I was huddling under my laptop, wondering how anything so unpleasant could be accompanied by so much comical squeaking. On the water, a young woman on a paddleboard glided by. Her look of horror suggested that in me she saw some terrible warning, some indication that if she wasn't careful about her life choices she could end up surrounded by a cloud of screaming, sauce-stained gulls.

Stunned, I watched the birds pull apart my lunch and flap away in a satisfied flurry of feathers and screeching. I touched my head and was surprised to find my fingers came away bloody. I knew someone who would want to see this. And it was this same person I wanted to lure into my culinary extinction experiments. It was fate.

"You don't need stitches. Still, impressive."

My old friend was trying very hard to supress a smile. Some small part of him was on the side of the gulls, and I accepted that. He dabbed disinfectant from his field kit onto my scalp.

"This is interesting behavior, you know, quite striking aggression for gulls."

"They mobbed me. They took my Pad Thai. I wanted my Pad Thai."

He made a noncommittal grunt. "They are becoming increasingly well adapted to city life. I need to set up cameras down there, see if I can capture enough aggressive attacks to work into a conference presentation. Hey, can I take a picture of your head?"

For the sake of anonymity, I will call him Geography Dan. He studies, and is obsessed with, the animals that don't need protection from humans. Raccoons. Rats. Demonic gulls. He follows the lives of the animals who live with us, the sort of animals most humans are rather unhappy to encounter. He loves creatures that even a vegan would surreptitiously crush under their non-leather boot. Dan is also an old college friend and a wealth of information on every grifter in the animal world. For there are animals we admire in the wild, animals we keep as pets and animals we use for food. And then, there are the other kind. Dan lives in their world.

Once students together in Toronto, Dan and I now both work and teach on the West Coast. We commiserate about research grants and fieldwork, and he offers a sympathetic ear for my ramblings about food. He does, however, occasionally try to serve me insects. I mentally reminded myself to search my lunch for anything with too many legs. Dan made us a quick meal of reheated borscht with a generous dollop of sour cream and a chiffonade of green onion and leek, served up with a nice crusty sourdough. The soup was rich with cabbage and paprika and freshly chopped dill. Dan's borscht is a medley of *Brassica oleracea* and *Beta vulgaris*, spiced richly with *Anethum graveolens* and *Capsicum annuum* and a handful of other ingredients, a random collection of species brought together over the years by Dan's sprawling family. Dan and I had first met over food, arguing about the merits of cilantro.[6] As Dan poured some wine, I began naming the components of the soup.

"What's on your mind?" Dan asked. "You seem even more food obsessed than usual."

"I've been thinking about species as components of cuisine, and how species extinction has a direct impact on cuisine. Culinary extinction, if you will."

"Hmm. I know you think I never worry about extinction, but those gulls are actually declining in number all around the Pacific Rim. We don't know why. But food species. It seems to me that we have a pretty compelling reason to keep culinary species alive and well. Surely, few of the foods we eat have gone extinct as we value them too highly."

I paused, breathing in the warmth of the soup. "It's not that simple, and culinary extinction isn't all that rare. I've been thinking that if we look at historical culinary extinctions, they could show us how our own food systems are in danger."

---

6   I hated it, while he felt anyone could train themselves to like it. The jury remains out, but a decade later I still think it tastes like soap, thanks to a variant of the olfactory receptor gene *OR6A2* found in 10 percent of the population.

"Still, if we ate seagulls, I think we'd be more careful about their numbers."

"What? Wait, that doesn't . . . Dan, there isn't any seagull in this soup, right?"

"No, not as such. Not yet. I mean no."

"You aren't allowed to serve me seagull."

He paused. "No promises."

From that strange avian attack and our conversation, my idea finally crystalized into a plan of action. I didn't think of gulls as a species that could be threatened as they were all around me, flapping and screeching, stealing my Thai food. Dan didn't think of food species as threatened because we needed and valued them. Few people make the direct link between the natural world and food species, as we keep them in separate boxes in our minds. We all do it. I might scold Dan for not considering food species as vulnerable, but it's true that I still have a hard time imagining his demon gulls (and rats and roaches) as vulnerable to threats such as habitat loss and climate change.

I wanted to understand the connection between the natural world that feeds us and the culinary culture that nurtures us, and what happens to that connection when foods disappear. This is a story about a lost feast of extinct species we once routinely dined upon. An extinct food is more than a lost source of calories; it is a break in the chain. When we lose a food, we lose recipes, preparation and harvest techniques, and economic niches vanish forever. Tackling the scope of this loss drove me to ask what would turn out to be a haunting question: how serious is culinary extinction, and how serious might it become?

I am not the first writer to ponder the question of culinary loss. Imagine Rome, where scholar and civil servant Pliny the Elder wrote his *Naturalis Historia*, much of it in the bath, between 77 and 79 CE. He dictated notes to one servant while another read him passages from his extensive library. As imperial administrator for the Emperor Vespasian, Pliny's days were full. He wrote late into the night and had himself carried from place to place so that he could jot down a few words while commuting, sparing a few moments to berate his nephew Pliny the Younger for not making enough of his time. As Pliny the Elder worked to catalog the trees and plants of the empire, he gave special attention to silphium, one of the most valued herbs of the ancient world. But Pliny, whose gift of description resonates throughout his writing, was reduced to cribbing his description of silphium from the *Historia Plantarum*, written by the Greek philosopher Theophrastus, who had lived four centuries earlier. For Pliny the Elder, despite his wealth and power, likely never tasted silphium, a plant described as so useful that it was considered to be a gift from Apollo himself.

At this point, we need to ask ourselves a question. How did one of the most important trading goods in the Roman world, one of the most valued of foods and medicines, simply disappear? Pliny the Elder asked this question as he bathed and wrote by lamplight. He was the first scholar we know of to question the disappearance of a culinary species. How could something that tasted so good simply be gone?

Extinction is a part of the natural world. For each million species on earth, about one species goes extinct per year. As there are about ten thousand known edible species on earth, in a balanced ecosystem, we would expect one culinary species to go extinct each century. However, they experience a special stressor: predation by humans. Historically, culinary species have suffered an extinction rate roughly five times as high as the background rate.

Each of these lost species can teach us an important lesson about today's global food system. And each also shines light on an ecological vulnerability threatening our planet's plant and animal life. Our ecosystems are not in balance, and the loss of food species is almost certain to grow.

Culinary extinction didn't begin with silphium; it was just the first loss we noticed. Our species came of age in the Paleolithic period, and our story begins there. The Paleolithic is more than an inspiration for a fad diet; it was a period that accounts for 95 percent of human history. The Paleolithic humans were nomadic hunter-gatherers. A deep dive into the true Paleo diet would also be an excellent excuse to spend some time thinking about mammoths, one of my favorite charismatic species. I had found my starting point.

Early modern humans hunted many large animals, known as megafauna, into extinction long before we settled in cities, developed farming or ever mused about opening a restaurant. I'm not going to explore all of these lost beasts; this isn't an exhaustive listing of culinary extinctions but rather an illustrative one. But mammoths are a must. They were a keystone species, a term we use to describe a species that plays an important role in its ecosystem. The loss of the mammoth changed the planet, changed us and provides lessons we can use today.

But before I got to my mammoths, there was something I needed to do first. I needed to go back to the time of Brillat-Savarin and the French Revolution. For alongside restaurants and regicide, the revolution was the crucible for a terrifying and heretical understanding: species die.

Chapter Two

GODS AND MONSTERS

T he dodo shouldn't be a famous bird. Endemic to one small, remote island, likely never plentiful in number, this large flightless relative of the pigeon vanished from the earth a decade before the American Revolution. Yet when I address extinction in my undergraduate classes and ask the students to name the first extinct creature that comes to mind, the dodo is overwhelmingly the first vanished creature they name. This could be because the dodo was so physically striking, or because one makes an appearance in *Alice's Adventures in Wonderland*, but it's more likely that we recall the dodo because it was one of the first creatures whose extinction was actually noticed. Even when Pliny described silphium, he considered it to simply be missing, perhaps to reappear at a later time. For the Western world, understanding extinction required a great leap of understanding that wandered into the territory of heresy.

But first, consider the dodo. Don't get too attached to this large friendly bird with the oversized beak, for it didn't stand a chance. The dodo was such an unusual bird to the European mind that they believed it was mythical for a couple of centuries, a sort of waddling unicorn. The bird, which was very much real, occupied the remote and beautiful island of Mauritius: a lush, well-watered place composed of 2,000 square kilometers of deep forest and volcanic hills. Mauritius is part of the Mascarene Islands, tucked away in the Indian Ocean, east of Madagascar. It boasts several hundred kilometers of white sand beach and the third largest coral reef in the world. However, its remoteness kept it shielded from the arc of history. The island was unpopulated until after classical times. The Greeks might have known it existed, and the Arabians definitely sketched its form onto a few maps. But it wasn't until the Portuguese visited in 1507 that Mauritius became a place known to the wider world.

The remoteness of these islands made them home to some of the world's rarest plants and animals. Evolution goes a little wild on islands. Small animals become large and large animals small, and without predators, birds take to the ground. Mauritius abounded with flightless birds and large reptiles, and the ecosystem remained relatively stable for eons, filled with exotic organisms, each thriving in its own little niche. Five hundred years later, the island is almost unrecognizable. Only 2 percent of the original forest remains, and 100 plant and animal species have gone extinct. To put this in context, that is about the same number lost in all of continental North America in the same time frame, despite North America being 12,000 times bigger. And one of those lost species — just one — is now famous.

Let's go back to those first Portuguese sailors who visited in 1507. They immediately noticed a striking bird that dotted the lowlands of the island. The dodo was previously unknown, the descendant of a type of pigeon that had settled on Mauritius four million years earlier. Without predators, the bird lost the ability to fly, and it began nesting on the ground. The dodo also exhibited the strange property of island gigantism. We tend to imagine the dodo as a medium-sized bird, but it was no such thing. Where most pigeons weigh in at a few pounds, adult dodos clocked in at as much as fifty. It stood nearly three feet tall, and though it is now depicted as rather fat and clumsy, that might reflect the fact that the few images that survive were made from captive birds in Europe and India. It was a striking bird with brownish-gray coloring, yellow feet, a tail tuft and a black, yellow and green beak. It was a bit of a bruiser, the sort of bird one wouldn't want to run into in a dark alley. Its beak could easily crack bone.

Oceanic explorers tended to grab everything they could in their travels, bringing home standard treasure such as gems and gold and also interesting botanical and animal specimens in the hopes some profit might be made in some fashion. A few dodos made it to England and to Europe and a few more to India. The only reason we know what they look like in detail is because these scattered survivors were captured on canvas. These sorts of exotic animals were exhibited for money; the only surviving eyewitness account of a dodo visiting London comes from English writer Sir Hamon L'Estrange, who describes his encounter as follows:

> About 1638, as I walked London streets, I saw the picture of a strange fowle hong out upon a cloth, and myselfe with one or two more then in company went in to see [the bird]. It was kept in a chamber, and was a great fowle somewhat bigger than the largest Turky cock, and so legged and footed, but stouter and thicker and of a more erect shape, colored before like the breast of a yong cock fesan, and on the back of dunn or deare contour. The keeper called it a Dodo.

Back in Mauritius, the dodo was not faring well. Some of the dodos were being eaten, first by the Portuguese sailors and then by the Dutch, who settled the island in 1638 and named the island after Maurice of Orange, the stadtholder of the Dutch Republic. These settlers leave us at least a few accounts of meals built around dodo meat, though opinion is decidedly mixed as to how enjoyable they were to eat. The best accounts predate settlement entirely. One is from 1598, when Admiral Wybrand van Warwijck, who led the first major Dutch expedition, noted that the longer the dodo was cooked, the tougher it became, though the breast meat was pleasant and tender. A more complete account is given by Sir Thomas Herbert in 1634 in his descriptions of travel in the region. He notes the bird is reputed more for wonder than for food, claiming, "To the delicate they are offensive and of no nourishment."

While they may have been eaten reluctantly, it was not human voraciousness alone that doomed the dodo. When humans arrived on Mauritius, they brought their non-human companions with them, both those they chose and those that chose them. The island colony was not a thriving place and never had more than a few dozen residents. In 1710, the Dutch abandoned it completely, leaving behind a different and more lasting sort of invasion — rats, pigs and monkeys. These animals devastated the island's ecology. Dodos nested on the ground, laying one large egg each season. These eggs were easy pickings for the invading species and the last confirmed dodo sighting was in 1662. They were promptly forgotten, along with the flightless red rail, the broad-billed parrot, the Mauritius owl, the Mauritius night heron and all of the other lost flora and fauna of the island. It was as if they had never existed at all.

The rediscovery of the dodo would have to wait until June 1, 1833. That day, the new issue of *The Penny Magazine of the Society for the Diffusion of Useful Knowledge,* an English magazine rather like today's *National Geographic,* presented a vivid description of a lost bird along with a plate image that we all likely can picture, as it is still used today when dodos are mentioned. They claimed the image "represents a bird, of the existence of whose species a little more than two centuries ago there appears to be no doubt, but which is now supposed to be entirely extinct. It must be obvious that such a fact offers some of the most interesting and important considerations."[7]

At the time, the English were struggling with a difficult concept introduced by the French a generation earlier. It was a pious age, and the Bible was very clear that God had in one swoop created the animals with the command to "Let the waters bring forth swarms of living creatures, and let birds fly above the earth across the dome of the sky."[8] If a species could completely disappear, at the hand of man, how could that possibly fit with God's plan?

Before I could dig into my specific culinary extinctions, I needed to explore the idea of extinction itself and I hadn't yet gone back far enough. I needed to go further than the time of the Victorians, or even the age of the dodo. To understand extinction, I needed to look first to the ancient world.

The people of the ancient world lived in a time of gods and monsters. Though they lacked the technology to build railways, corsets, top hats and Dickensian slums, the people of

---

7   In our era of shock journalism, that statement might not seem scandalous, but in the context of Victorian times it might as well have had three exclamation points.

8   Or waddle. The dodo only crossed the dome of the sky if it fell off something tall.

the ancient world had a much better grasp of the vanished and vanishing creatures of the earth than we once believed. In fossils, which they unearthed regularly, the ancient Greeks, Romans and Chinese imagined the remains of a lost world filled with wondrous people and creatures. The three-thousand-year-old book of divination, the *I Ching*, described fossils under the generic term "dragon bones" and noted them as a good omen for the farmer who discovered them, and as they were quite valuable, there was a material benefit to turning them up in a field. As Adrienne Mayor explores in her book *The First Fossil Hunters*, the Greeks and Romans saw in the great bones the remains of a young and vigorous world in which everything was grander. This narrative of a world in decline framed both myth and reality, and if mankind was the diminishing remnant of a time of heroes, the Greeks and Romans were hungry for remnants of that mythic period. Fossils became coveted and valuable, a must-have accessory for the upper classes of ancient times.

Roman villas have a way of reaching across the centuries to evoke real estate envy. Their rooms, often spacious and richly decorated with frescos and mosaics, were arranged around atriums filled with plants. Their furnishings could be lush and comfortable, and they were built in beautiful surroundings to take advantage of cool breezes. They offered a respite from the summer heat of the big cities, an escape from the cut and thrust of urban politics. They were open and airy and often included plumbing and heated floors. Exploring the Roman ruins at Bath, I was struck by the aesthetic beauty of Roman construction and the comfort provided by the saunas and pools. Staring at the steaming water, I was struck by the thought that the magnificent pool was on the very edge of the Roman Empire. I imagined the wonders that existed in Italy itself, picturing a landscape of olive groves, busy kitchens and long dreamy evenings feasting at lantern-lit tables in the orchards. The Romans saw villas as physical expressions of power and wealth and also astute investments because of the food they produced. Romans grew wealthy off the literal fruits of their estates, and after a fine meal and maybe a turn in the steam room, they might take in the wonders of the *Antum Cyclopis*, a space for displaying fossils, for the richest Romans decorated special grottos with ancient bones.

In one of the more detailed descriptions of these spaces, Pliny notes that Marcus Scaurus fitted a sunken garden with pools, statues and the bones of a sea monster. This particular sea monster was thought to plague Ethiopian shipping as punishment for Cassiopeia's vanity, and was thus a particularly valuable specimen. The Romans believed their myths were based on historical fact, and the bones of centaurs and giants were valuable items of trade. The Emperor Augustus kept a vacation house on the island of Capri that featured a particularly vast display of giant bones, and giant tusks were displayed at the Temple of Apollo in Cumae and at the Temple of Athena in Tegea. The Emperor Constantine made a long pilgrimage to view a satyr preserved in salt, and ancient authors repeated even older myths linking fossils to epic stories, a process known as geomythology. Many of these creatures were denounced as fanciful even in the day, and some ancient scholars came very close to understanding extinction centuries before our modern exploration of the concept. The civilizations of Rome and Greece were already having a severe impact on their environment and the species within it. At least a few wondered, as they reclined into the late hours with wine and pastry, what if we are using too much? What if we are overhunting?

And on the fringes, Rome's explorers pushed on, far from the warmth and hospitality of their home city. Deep in the Taklamakan Desert of central Asia, beyond the edge of the classical world, is a fierce wasteland of heat and light. The sands in the north give way to the Tian Shan, or the Mountains of Heaven. To ancient Romans, the region was near mythical, a source of fabulous gemstones and gold. Few who dared venture there returned, as the climate was fierce and the landscape filled with shifting sands and optical illusions. The scholars of the ancient world, however, blamed griffins for their missing explorers. The griffin was classed by the Romans as a real creature of the great desert and a scourge of treasure hunters. It had a sharp beak, a lion's body, and great wings. No Roman had seen a griffin, but a few had seen the creature's bones, and as with the bones of giants and sea monsters, it was considered to be strong proof of the creature's existence. Perhaps, scholars wondered, humans were driving these beasts out to the edges of the world. Pliny had noticed certain birds could no longer be found in settled areas, and that the lions were gone from Greece, the bears from Attica and the ostriches from Arabia. Could something humans were doing be causing these animals to disappear? Lucretius the Epicurean wrote in the first century that "one thing dwindles and another waxes" and that "many species must have died out altogether." He felt everything would have its "day of doom," accepting a concept that was so troubling to the Victorians.

The Greeks and Romans struggled with the question of where species came from, and this colored their understanding of species loss. Let's go back to silphium and to Theophrastus for a moment. He tells a peculiar story about the famous herb. Silphium grew only in a small area of North Africa in what is now Libya, at the site of the Greek city of Cyrene. The scholars of Cyrene claimed that silphium first appeared seven years before the founding of the city in the seventh century BCE. A sudden black rain fell upon the landscape, and silphium emerged where it fell. Descriptions of the region described vast stands of the plant, surrounded by barren desert sand. Such stories were common and challenged the ideas of Lucretius that living things could vanish completely. Most people believed that if a plant or animal did wane, it might suddenly reappear.

Could the reason one only found the bones of griffins, and never griffins themselves, be because humans had killed them or driven them away? This line of reasoning didn't quite take hold, as it went against Aristotle's view that species were immutable (but able to spontaneously regenerate), an idea that would later influence biblical thought. Lucretius aside, most scholars believed species were unchanging, and when eighteenth century botanist Carl Linnaeus composed the first catalog of the earth's species, he didn't include an extinct category of animal. Scholars knew that species could vanish locally, but surely they survived elsewhere, or perhaps they could regenerate, popping back into existence at the will of gods and goddesses or mysterious black rains. Linnaeus simply couldn't believe that humanity could seriously damage creation and argued that "we shall never believe that a species has entirely perished from the earth." The spark of the idea of extinction faded into slumber, much like the protoceretops bones that gave rise to the legendary griffins of Tian Shan.

To solidify our understanding of extinction, we need to meet three unusual men. They liked to solve problems and lived through times of intellectual turbulence. The first, Georges Cuvier, described extinction in the form we understand today. The second, Charles Darwin, fit extinction into a larger understanding of life on earth. The final man, Luis Alvarez, closed the circle on our understanding of extinction. Extinction is evolution's dark mirror, a concept that Darwin understood as necessary but disturbing. For change to happen, there also had to be death.

The story of life is most often written as survival of the fittest, but the overwhelming reality for most species is a quick expiry doled out to evolution's runners-up. Each ecological niche shapes species, favoring random mutations that give certain individuals the slightest of reproductive edges. Over time these mutations gather to the point of divergence, and a new species adapted to ecology, climate and other species thrives. However, adaptation isn't guaranteed, and when climate shifts too rapidly, or an ecological niche is destroyed, or a species is outcompeted, extinction is a grim probability. When the Dutch wandered ashore at Mauritius, the dodo was as good as dead; there was no path for it among the rats and dogs and pigs.

But how did we come to understand extinction, and, more importantly, why does extinction seem to occur at different rates at different times? And why do these linked concepts, evolution and extinction, trouble us so?

Let's begin with the most famous of naturalists, Charles Darwin. Few figures are as polarizing as Darwin, who was on the receiving end of adoration and revulsion in equal measure. There are films about his life, celebrations of his work, detailed bibliographical information about even his most unpromising scientific explorations, including his two moderately unproductive months in Australia and the years he devoted to the study of barnacles. My hometown of Vancouver held an Evolution Festival on the 150th anniversary of the publication of *On the Origin of Species*. Events included lectures, Darwin impersonators, a Darwin versus Galileo debate, a "Darwin and You" discussion series, including "Darwin and your sex life," and even a Darwin birthday cake contest. The winner was a cake the baker described as a "host-dependant replicate." The cake featured chocolate eggs containing instructions for producing the next generation of cakes, adjusted for variability and heritability. So the host, or baker, picked an egg and baked a new slightly different cake. Most scientists don't inspire cake contests. For a naturalist, Darwin is a pretty big deal.

Yes, Darwin was a genius, but he spent twenty years puttering around with chickens while he procrastinated on releasing one of the most important scientific works of all time. He struggled with the enormity of his results and likely suspected not everyone would embrace them. Even today, half of Americans don't believe in evolution, though America is a bit of a global outlier. By contrast an overwhelming majority of people everywhere believe in extinction, even though it is by some measures a more heretical idea. Yet few people know the name of the man who developed our modern understanding of extinction: Georges Cuvier.

Cuvier is a puzzle. Though he is considered the father of paleontology and was famous in his time, the record of his life is scattered and conflicting. Cuvier survived the turbulent politics of his lifetime by ruthlessly curating his own image. Rumors of his life can be found in letters, hinting at his ambitions, his fiery temper and his personal tragedies, but he fostered a public persona of the ultimate scientist, a man who placed knowledge above religion or politics. He was endlessly curious and somewhat of a showman. He came very close to scooping Darwin's discovery by a generation. He had all the pieces he needed to understand evolution, but he couldn't accept that a species could change or, as we think of it now, adapt. In his mind, species were perfectly fitted to their environment, and the slightest adjustment would render their survival impossible. This stubborn belief would end up greatly changing his role in the history of science.

Born Jean Léopold Nicolas Frédéric Cuvier in 1769 in Montbéliard, France, childhood illness confined the young scientist to artistic and intellectual pursuits. He began collecting natural specimens, exhibiting boundless curiosity while taking a methodical approach to his work. As his health improved as a young man, he spent four years at the Caroline Academy in Stuttgart, Germany, where he excelled. On graduation, he was both broke and ambitious, and he moved again to take a job in Normandy as tutor to the son of the Comte d'Héricy. His young charge took only a moderate amount of George's attention, so he used his surplus time to begin began a detailed study of his patron's collection of fossils. Ambition burned in Cuvier, and an idea was forming in his mind. He completed his role as a tutor and set out to Paris with a small bankroll to establish his reputation. Arriving in Paris in the midst of the revolution, he rose rapidly as an academic while also courting influence with the government. His skill as a scientist and as a networker paid off, and he was awarded a post as a university professor at the age of twenty-six. He was deeply interested in politics, but it isn't clear how Cuvier managed to stay free of the troubles of the revolution. Intrigue seemed to wash by him as he rose to increasingly important positions at the National Museum of Natural History in Paris, likely cover, in part, for a certain degree of intelligence gathering for his influential friends.

Cuvier survived the tumult to become a favorite of Napoleon, who made him a chevalier. Yet he again emerged unscathed and somehow found favor with the returning Bourbons, who made him a baron. He became wealthy and amassed one of the largest private libraries in Europe. He was a university chancellor, sat on the Ministry of the Interior, and was appointed president of the Council of State. Through all this, his primary love was his scientific work and he spent his entire life building a lost world.

We know little of Cuvier's private life, aside from the sorrow it held. He married a widow with four children and had four more children with her, but they all died. Brought low by grief, he retreated to the museum, where he immersed himself in his research. His goal, at first, was to complete a definitive collection of the remains of all of earth's species, a sort of museum-bound Noah's Ark. He expanded his museum's fossil collection from a few scattered items to over 10,000 carefully documented pieces and used his influence to encourage government-funded expeditions to the far reaches of the globe. He also encouraged amateur naturalists to send in their specimens. With such excellent materials at hand, he had the luxury of writing from the comfort of his office, completing a work on quadruped fossils in 1812 and a history of fish in 1828 that is considered the foundation of ichthyology. But we don't remember him for the fish. Cuvier made his mark on history with elephants.

Cuvier was a voracious reader who was lucky enough to have access to the greatest books of both the ancient world and his own era. As he read about the gods and monsters of the ancient world, he saw kernels of truth, elements that matched his own experience as an expert of animal anatomy. On April 4, 1796, Cuvier made his first public lecture at the Institute of Science and Arts in Paris, under the title "Mémoires sur les espèces d'*éléphants* vivants et fossiles." It was a bold lecture, particularly as he was only twenty-six and had been in Paris for just a year. However, during that time, he had spent hours studying the elephant bones that were arriving at the museum. With a keen eye for puzzles and an extensive understanding of how animals are put together, he quickly came to two new conclusions. Asian and African elephants are not the same species, and the bones of mysteriously large elephant-like animals, one group from Siberia and one from the Ohio territories of North America, were two more entirely distinct species. He then made a bold leap: he posited that these two species, which he called the mammoth and the mastodon, were no longer to be found on the earth. They were extinct.

Over the years that followed, he described what he called "a world before ours," populated by a growing menagerie of espèces perdues, animals lost to us. To many, this was heretical, to others, a simple impossibility. In 1784, Thomas Jefferson had argued strongly against extinction, writing that "such is the economy of nature, that no instance can be produced of her having permitted any one race of her animals to become extinct; or her having formed any link in her great work so weak as to be broken." As president of the American Philosophical Society, Jefferson represented the norm at the time, and his word was considered to be correct. The world was seen as orderly, static and new, the product of a divine hand. Extinction was unthinkable. Cuvier faced an uphill battle to gain acceptance for his lost world.

Cuvier's advantage over his contemporaries was that he brought together extensive readings of the classics with the most current information pouring in from Napoleon's global adventures. Cuvier had access to classified reports from distant lands and he also had mastodon bones gathered by the Second Baron of Longueil, who had stumbled upon the curious specimens in 1739 while marching down the Ohio River. Cuvier's brilliance was in realizing that what the evidence showed to be true simply must be true. The mammoth was gone. Once he accepted the possibility of extinction, he rapidly populated a past world with espèces perdues. By 1800, he had twenty-three extinct species in his collection, including one he called the ptero-dactyle, or wing fingered beast. In 1812, he published a complete account of his lost species, which now numbered forty-nine, and introduced the concept of extinction into Western thought. But his unwavering belief that species could not change would blind him to evolution and leave him only half-correct on the question that bothered him most: how could entire elements of creation simply disappear?

We know little about Cuvier's dedication to religion, but his opposition to evolution was based on scientific rather than religious grounds. He couldn't imagine how species could change and still be optimal for their ecological niches. In effect, he committed the same mistake that Jefferson made in dismissing extinction. However, we do know Cuvier was quite willing to overturn the medieval concept of a "great chain of being," in which all things in the universe were ranked, from inanimate objects to God, bottom to top, unchanging since the beginning of creation.

His contemporaries could scarcely deny Cuvier's growing mountain of evidence and dipped their toes into the waters of extinction by drawing on the story of Noah from Genesis to demonstrate God's willingness to kill his creations. Cuvier used this story and others like it to a different end: using his vast knowledge of mythology, he reasoned that one potential mechanism of extinction could be the massive floods mentioned in many ancient myths, as well as in the Bible. This viewpoint, known as catastrophism, suggested that extinction happened in bursts. Loss of species could then be divinely corrected by a mechanism proposed by Cuvier and others such as special creation, or the Godly act of repopulating the earth after extinction bursts.

Cuvier's refusal to see evolution in the evidence before him and his insistence on catastrophism to preserve the divine nature of creation left him open to attack. He had a long-standing nemesis in Jean-Baptiste Lamarck, a minor French noble who was both soldier and botanist. Lamarck developed a theory proposing the inheritance of acquired characteristics, a precursor to the theories of Darwin. Lamarck had suffered Cuvier's attacks against evolution for years and, sensing an opening, fought back by dismissing extinction entirely, arguing that Cuvier's lost beasts had simply evolved into other creatures.

A middle theory suggested that extinction did happen, but only gradually and only through existing processes, not through mythical floods. This view, known as uniformism, was championed by Charles Lyell, who also suggested that species might reappear. Lyell's work greatly influenced Charles Darwin, who incorporated extinction into his theory of evolution. Darwin wrote that species disappear gradually, one after another, first from one spot, and then another, and then from the world. He framed extinction as one of the three forces underlying species change, along with competition and environmental change, an inevitability of the survival of the fittest. His view prevailed, and Cuvier's model of catastrophism faded after his death in 1832. But Cuvier was half-right, and catastrophism is critical to the understanding of extinction. This, in turn, is critical to understanding the threat extinction poses to food availability and cuisine.

The final piece, proving that extinction could happen in bursts, would have to wait another hundred years for the arrival of one of the stranger figures of modern science, Luis Alvarez. Driven and curious, he distinguished himself as a particle physicist, eventually earning the Nobel Prize in 1968, for his work on the fundamental building blocks of nature. He rose to prominence in the Second World War and he was one of the only people to fly on both of the atomic bombing missions. His job was to calculate exactly how strong the explosions in Hiroshima and Nagasaki were.

He had the same penchants as Cuvier: charisma, energy and an eye for a good public side project, though he combined this desire with the zeal of a carnival barker. In 1965, he used muon tomography to search for additional chambers in the pyramid of Chephren in Egypt (he found none), completing the work in a marathon session, pausing only for the 1967 Six-Day War. He also devised an experiment using cantaloupe to demonstrate how the Zapruder film of the Kennedy assassination supported the theory of a lone gunman. But his most famous side project was conducted with his son Walter, a geologist, and two nuclear chemists, Frank Asaro and Helen Michel. Together they set out to uncover what killed the dinosaurs, an occurrence we know as the Cretaceous-Paleogene extinction, abbreviated as the K-T event. This would be the missing piece in the story of extinction.

Digging into the earth is, in effect, going back in time. New soil settles onto old soil, deposited by water and wind, and then slowly compresses into rock. Walter Alvarez began his project inadvertently, when he noticed a thin layer of clay on the boundary between the Cretaceous period and the Paleogene, coincidentally an age in which a great deal of the earth's life seemed to vanish very quickly. He noted the layer of clay to his father, who immediately assembled a team to analyze the clay and look for similar layers at other sites. The team found this layer of clay around the globe and discovered that it contained high levels of iridium, rare on earth but common in asteroids. They proposed that a comet or asteroid had impacted the earth on one very bad day sixty-six million years ago, and the resulting chaos led to massive extinction. The team published their findings in June 1980, in a paper titled "Extraterrestrial Cause for the Cretaceous Extinction." The impact of such a large body, estimated by them to have been ten kilometers in diameter, would have been devastating. The force of the explosion was a billion times that of the bomb dropped on Hiroshima. The blast and resulting tsunami directly affected most of North and South America, and the massive superheated dust cloud generated by the impact incinerated many animals where they stood. From this firestorm came enough soot to plunge the earth into the equivalent of nuclear winter. Photosynthesis ground to a halt, and entire ecosystems vanished. Sulfuric acid blasted into the atmosphere lowered temperature and created rain that turned the oceans acidic, and atmospheric temperatures plunged for decades. Roughly three-quarters of the earth's species died. Aside from turtles and crocodiles, no large animals survived. The dinosaurs are the best-known victims, but many other species vanished as well. Entire niches were opened up; the world we know today blossomed as the dust settled.

The world's paleontologists did not respond well to the intrusion of a Nobel Prize–winning physicist into their realm. They denounced the paper, defended uniformism and were critical to the point of rudeness. They refused to publish the team's further work and criticized them in public. But the evidence kept building. The dust was found to contain soot, glass and tiny diamonds, a result of the incredible forces at work. The K-T layer was found at many more sites around the world, strengthening the hypothesis. But the smoking gun, in this case, was the rediscovery of the 180-kilometer wide Chicxulub crater on the ocean floor in the Gulf of Mexico. Oil companies had detected the enormous scar beneath thick sediment, and cores taken from the crater floor revealed the presence of glass consistent with a meteor strike.

The elder Alvarez didn't live to be vindicated, but the K-T impact is now accepted as the official cause of the extinction event that killed the dinosaurs. The event is a clear example of Cuvier's catastrophism.

So extinction can occur in two ways: gradually, as a component of evolution, and suddenly, as a result of some sort of cataclysmic event. This can be a global effect or a local one; the dodo disappeared along with a wave of plants and animals on Mauritius, a local example of a catastrophe. In that case, the "asteroid" was a Dutch colony. Catastrophism matters, for if culinary extinction only happens occasionally, it isn't a matter of high and immediate concern. We can cope with a few culinary losses over time, even if they do limit our menus. But with catastrophic extinction events possible, culinary extinction is a real and present threat to the world's food systems. As Elizabeth Kolbert explores in detail in the *Sixth Extinction*, at least five major extinction events have rocked the earth over the last billion years or so. The most shocking, at the end of the Permian, involved a huge release of carbon dioxide that eliminated as much as 90 percent of the life on earth. More worryingly, she argues, we are now in the midst of a sixth such event, this one driven by human activity.

The story of the Lost Feast is the story of an element of the earth's sixth mass extinction event, an extinction that is unfolding now. This extinction is being called the Holocene event, after the geological epoch in which human civilization arose. Unlike the other great extinctions, this one is ongoing, and we have an active part to play in determining whether this event is a minor one or a major series of losses that mark the geological record for eons to come. The driver of the Holocene extinction is human activity, and the current rate of extinction is estimated to be roughly one hundred times the background rate.

The Holocene extinction began with the loss of the large land animals, the megafauna, and it continues with the loss of species in almost every ecosystem on earth. The food system is linked to the Holocene extinction at almost every step — we've overexploited wild stocks, expanded our farmland and grazing land relentlessly and introduced exotic species wherever we have settled. E.O. Wilson suggests that by 2100, one-half of earth's species will be gone if today's rate of extinction continues. Somewhere between 7 and 10 percent of our era's species have been lost already.

—

Dan invited himself over to show me a video of a rat eating pizza.

Rain lashed the kitchen windows. I'd put together a sauce of shallots fried in butter and white wine, finished with a heavy lash of cream. I tossed the sauce into some fresh pasta and sprinkled the dish with some nice crumbled Stilton, fresh tarragon and chopped hazelnuts. When I served it to Dan, he attacked the pasta while somehow still maintaining a monologue about subway rats. Through the window, I watched the little rivers of water on the street as they traced the courses of long vanished streams. We were watching a looping video of a rat carrying a slice of pizza up some subway stairs.

"I'd like to see a dodo do that. No wonder the rats won. Look at him go," Dan said.

"I will admit that the dodo probably wouldn't have thrived in the New York subway system."

"So, this project. You will link historical extinctions to our current food system?"

"Right," I said, twirling my pasta. "We know extinction happens for reasons — loss of habitat or where an animal was not numerous to begin with."

Dan waved his fork at me. "Sure, or they face a new human technology or are challenged by an invasive species, I know. But where do you start? When are you suggesting that culinary extinction began?"

"I think it really started with the megafauna, back in the Pleistocene. And then once agriculture developed, we see a whole new scale of impact. Suddenly our food systems support larger populations and affect much broader swathes of ecosystem. About 14 percent of the earth's surface is in field crops already, and about another 25 percent is used for forage."

"And then industrial agriculture comes along, I imagine."

"Later. First comes trade. It's regional at first and then global in scope."

"This pasta better not be threatened. I want more."

We all want more.

Humanity's food systems sit within the earth's ecosystems, nestled like an egg in a nest. At first, as hunter-gatherers, we caused minor, but not negligible, disturbances. We developed during the Pleistocene epoch, a period lasting roughly two million years and ending 11,700 years ago, ushering this epoch, the Holocene. Glaciers retreated, the earth became temperate and humans developed agriculture. We cleared forests, we burned grasslands, we diverted rivers and streams. Yet this impact, large as it was, can't compare to the great trading empires that arose, taking humans and their hunger to every corner of the globe. The development of industrial-scale agriculture, particularly after the development of chemical fertilizer and mechanization, raised the bar once again.

And a fifth age of food is nearly upon us, an age of unimaginable technology, in which the egg of human food systems begins to rival its nest in size. Some scientists claim these changes are so profound that we are now entering a new epoch called the Anthropocene, or the age of the human. I will circle back to this idea in detail, but for now, I want to leave the concept just on the horizon. It is enough to say that the future of our food systems and of our cuisines will hinge on how well we cope with reconciling the scale of our activities with the limitations of the planet we call home.

Dan mopped the last of the sauce with his bread. "Dinner. Let's have dinners, as you work. A dinner per concept. We should cook as you do this project. Cook the recipes. I know you, and there are always recipes. And I'm always hungry."

I paused and absently swirled my wine. Dinner sounded nice.

"I'm game, but how do we cook things that are extinct? I'm not doing some weird postmodern thing where we stare silently at empty plates."

Dan became rather animated. "Look at this rat. Look at what he's doing."

"Eating pizza?"

"No! Well, yes, but no! He is improvising. In the wild he would eat seeds and nuts and fruits, but in the subway, in this strange hostile environment, he is eating pizza."

"Everyone eats pizza in New York. I don't see the connection."

"He's improvising. Let's improvise. You put together your material, and then we will cook a meal approximating the extinct foods you're exploring. We can use my kitchen; there's more room."

The offer of Dan's fully tricked-out kitchen sealed the deal. He'd paid some renovator to completely transform a standard kitchen and two adjoining rooms into a Food Network–inspired dream, but he spends most of his time eating pizza in front of his laptop. The lost feast dinners were born. If I was going to be writing about potential mass extinction, the least I could do was to stay well fed.

"So where will we be starting? Some sort of ice age theme?"

"Yes," I said as I cleared the dishes. "And we will work towards the trouble with cows."

Dan froze, the last crust of bread halfway to his mouth. "There is *not*, I repeat, *not* anything wrong with cows. I mean, cheese. Hello? Cheese?"

On the laptop screen, in the background, the rat dragged his slice up a loop of never-ending stairs. It was time to dig into the fall of the megafauna.

Chapter Three

ACROSS THE
SEAS OF GRASS

"Do you think we need another can of gas?"

My friend Shannon was expertly arranging and rearranging tubs full of supplies. Water. First aid kit. Survival kit. Tent and gear. Spare car parts. Bug spray. More bug spray (the woman had traveled with me before). The living room looked as if we were mounting a major expedition, and in a way, we were; 3,000 kilometers north on a research trip to some of Canada's most remote and beautiful landscapes. We would also be traveling back in time, to a world before farming, to the world of grasslands, tundra and, most importantly, megafauna. If I wanted to understand the mammoth and the culinary extinctions that allow the existence of the modern cow, I needed a landscape grand enough to put the cow in perspective. I also had a few standing invitations in the Yukon to sample northern cuisine.

Canada's North isn't forgiving, and this wasn't the sort of trip I would do alone. Fortunately, I had a friend insane enough to drive north with me, a friend who was comfortable in the wilderness and would ensure I didn't end up as a pile of bleached bones on the tundra because I forgot the insect repellent. Lawyer by day, Shannon was a serious wilderness buff. We had two spare tires, road flares, fire starters, emergency blankets. Axes, knives, folding shovels. Jude, Shannon's active little black cat, hopped from container to container, looking concerned.

"Another can of gas," Shannon remarked to herself. "You just never know. And maybe an extra axe. And more snacks."

"Yes. More snacks. I approve of snacks."

I fished Jude out of the supply tub and turned my thoughts to the North. I wanted to see the world before farming. I wanted to lose myself between the sky and the waving seas of grass.

The North is the living shadow of the Paleocene, a world without farms or fences. Driving north took several days of winding highways and sprawling forests. Before each town, I would get rather hopeful about the possibility of lunch, only to encounter an empty crossroads with a few weathered houses and perhaps a gas station. I had hours to ponder strange food trivia. The northernmost Denny's in British Columbia is in Terrace, roughly 300 kilometers north of the Peace Arch at the Canada-U.S. border. I was out of the range of even the possibility of twenty-four-hour pancakes. How odd.

By the time we reached Dawson City, the sun barely bothered to dip behind the horizon. It was July, and midnight was as bright as a lazy summer evening back home. We feasted on sourdough bread spread thick with fireweed jelly, sampled pickled spruce tips and sipped Labrador tea. One morning, a really lovely chef served me a steaming stack of sourdough pancakes studded with wild blueberries. I slept long, ate well, and breathed crystal air. Most days, the horizons were free of human presence and the world boiled with wildlife. Ravens squawked and chortled at us. Black bears gave our car menacing glances, and one evening all of the hair rose on my neck as a grizzly did exactly what it pleased as it passed our picnic site. The sky was the deepest of blues, and the air smelled of herbs, sunlight and ice. I found a really friendly pizza joint in Mayo, Yukon. It had a sign on the wall listing the coldest recorded temperature at that spot as minus eighty degrees Fahrenheit. Outside, the endless summer sun shimmered on the river, a tease.

There were, shall we say, a few insects. Even with the repellent, mosquitos would settle on me like a blood-sucking blanket. They hung over the landscape like buzzing smoke. Shannon, who was quirkily immune to all insect life, would watch in interested horror as my neck swelled rapidly. I tried to be brave.

"Did you know there is a type of mosquito that feeds on tea plants?" I asked.

Shannon, serene in the knowledge that every insect in the North was feeding on me, had bared her arms to the sun. "Let me guess, the tea from those plants is more expensive."

"Yes, it tastes different because the plant has an immune response to the bites. The leaves develop an enzyme."

"You might want to try that. An immune response. Maybe if you drink that tea, they will leave you alone."

I slapped ineffectually at a new wave of mosquitos.

A few days later, after marveling at shivering green lakes, wind-ruffled hillsides and escaping an angry beaver,[9] I found what I was looking for. We rounded a corner as we dropped back into the province of British Columbia and were surrounded by wood bison. They meandered along the road, blocking our path. Shannon and I stared at the massive creatures as they walked to and fro in front of the car. There were dozens of them. They

---

9   Canada's national symbol, these industrious creatures are generally well tempered. Except this one, who used his tail to toss rocks at us.

were beautiful and wild, their great coats full and shining. The males watched us warily, and the females nudged along the calves, who were a much lighter shade of brown. They were surrounded by thick clouds of flies that didn't seem to bother them particularly, though one of the half-inch-long bulldog horseflies found my arm and carried off a large bite of flesh. I watched a few more flies navigate around Shannon to reach my exposed skin. The grand animals shuffled past us, munching on the grass. They probably were no heavier than dairy cows, but they felt bigger. Maybe it was the landscape. Maybe I just felt smaller. A soft brown stream of plush muscle, they stopped us in our tracks, and I had the overwhelming urge to get out of the car and sink my fingers into the thick shoulder fur. They looked like they were wearing the world's most luxurious shawl. I felt for a moment what it was like to stare into the Pleistocene, that golden age where we find the beginning of the anthropological culinary extinction.

The bison are a living reminder of the age when megafauna ruled the planet. Mammals are opportunists, and when the skies cleared and the earth warmed after the Cretaceous extinction sixty-six million years ago, the age of reptiles was over and the age of mammals had begun. It was a lush time. Herbs and grasses carpeted the continents. Mammals diversified across the earth's land masses, and the jungles of the dinosaurs gave way to gentle savannas. Mammals began to grow larger, and as glaciers advanced and retreated in the epoch we call the Pleistocene, gentle and not so gentle monsters ruled the grasslands. This period, roughly two million years long, gave us mammoths, mastodons, dire wolves, saber-toothed cats, giant beavers as large as small cars, American camels and cheetahs, giant flightless birds, deer with antlers ten feet across, aurochs and, of course, wood bison. The vast landscapes were littered with massive animals of two general kinds: herbivores who traveled in herds and carnivores who lived more solitary lives, picking off the weak and old from the protective clusters of plant eaters. For millennia, these species ruled an endless sea of rich scrub.

But then a dying began. In a rapid wave of extinction, the world's megafauna began to vanish. In the last 50,000 years, the world lost half of its large mammals in a burst, beginning in Africa and spreading to Europe, Asia, the Americas and finally to Oceania. In North America, the wave of death peaked around 12,000 years ago, when ninety genera of animals weighing over forty-four pounds went extinct. This included giant sloths, several species of bears, tapirs, the American lion, giant tortoises, sabre-toothed cats, giant llamas and the two largest species of bison. Several musk ox species vanished, along with the giant beavers and giant armadillos. The very landscape changed; megafauna turn plants (or plant-eaters) into energy, and without this constant grazing, forests spread and vegetation shifted. This pattern, this wave, mirrored our expansion as a species. It proceeded at walking speed; and many of these extinctions can be blamed on our appetite.

Imagine the human of the Pleistocene. We call this period of human development the Paleolithic period, and it was a long age of nomadic wandering. Humans began to use tools in the Paleolithic and coalesced into small bands. We gathered plants and berries, fished, scavenged the kills of larger predators and began to hunt animals. As we began to develop art, language and storytelling, our bodies evolved into what we see in the mirror: *Homo sapiens*. We used fire, and we began building boats. By foot and by paddle we spread. About 50,000 years ago, our toolmaking made a leap forward in complexity, including the appearance of projectile weapons such as the spear. This allowed us to hunt animals from a safer distance.[10] The loss of megafauna near the end of the Pleistocene is called the quaternary extinction event, and it closely mirrors the spread of humans during the transition from the Pleistocene to the Holocene epoch. As the earth warmed, humans prospered. The quaternary extinction continued right into modern times, with the extinction of the giant birds of New Zealand shortly after the arrival of the Polynesians. As we moved, we hunted; when one area's large animals became scarce, we moved on.

How do we know these are human influenced extinctions? Before our species appeared, the rate of extinction among large mammals mirrored the background rate. As large land mammal extinction rates rose in region after region following the timeline of human arrival, the large marine mammals and smaller mammals saw little change to their own rate of extinction (small animals gave us too little return on the effort of a complex hunt, and we hadn't yet learned to hunt at sea). Human hunter-gatherers caused what has been called an ecological shock. Larger animals tend to breed more slowly than smaller animals, and the megafauna couldn't reproduce fast enough to offset losses from human hunting. Their greatest asset, their extreme size, protected them from most predators, but made them an easier target for us.

The largest and slowest vanished first. Climate change was likely also a factor, but the overwhelming evidence suggests these were culinary-assisted extinctions. As time passed, we honed our skills, developing better weapons and more skilled use of fire to distract and panic large animals. Wild creatures couldn't

---

10   Comparatively. Standing a few yards back from a beast as big as a small car
     likely felt more comfortable than sneaking right up to it, armed only with
     a stone knife.

evolve fast enough to counter our development. Humans learn, and they pass that knowledge to their young. The outcome of our increasing efficiency in hunting is well illustrated by one of the better-known lost animals, one that Cuvier knew well, and the one that I most want to talk about: the mammoth.

Like the dodo, the mammoth is an extinct species. In popular culture, a mammoth is depicted as a fuzzy elephant with curled tusks who lived among early humans during the last ice age, but the reality is more diverse. There were many mammoth species, from the huge to the tiny, living in the warm climates to the coldest. The term mammoth covers the various species of the genus *Mammuthus*; they are known for their tusks, large prehensile trunks, and, for many of them, woolly hair. Like the bison I admired on the Alaska Highway, the northern mammoths were shaggy beasts, built for cool climates. They appeared roughly five million years ago, and the last mammoths lingered into the age of written record, vanishing for good roughly 3,500 to 5,000 years ago. They are cousins to the two living kinds of elephants and populated all of the continents save for Australia and Antarctica. They vanished first in Africa, then in Europe and China, lasting the longest in North America and on the remote islands of the Arctic. We hunted and ate mammoths. We used their coats for clothing and their bones and tusks for tools and shelter.

We know rather a lot about mammoths, as a great number of well-preserved specimens have been found over the centuries. They were large, some species reaching up to four meters tall and weighing up to ten tons. Most of the species, however, were about the size of elephants. Both sexes had tusks and, judging from cave paintings, they likely lived in matriarchal herds similar to those of elephants. And like elephants, their weakness was their long gestation, which, combined with the large areas of grassland needed to support them, resulted in a low overall population. From their frozen remains, we know that they had huge fat reserves, allowing them to survive harsh conditions for long periods of time. This might explain their survival in the far North long after their southern populations were gone. They vanished from region after region once we walked into town but survived where humans couldn't easily follow.

The mammoth was a shambling department store of fat and protein, wrapped in warm fur and sporting long ivory tusks we could carve into tools, weapons, jewelry and art. Mammoth ivory remains valuable and is excavated on the margins of the permafrost as climate change exposes new sets of remains. Hunter-gatherers subsisted primarily on plants, but the 20 percent or so of their diet that came from animal protein was important. As humans moved north into regions where the plant life was sparse, the percentage of animals consumed in their diet rose. Small bands of humans likely followed the mammoths and other megafauna, killing them as needed. Megafauna provided critical nutrients that allowed humans to have more and healthier children. Their existence was central to human development.

Mammoths grazed on trees, shrubs and grasses. They could also eat moss in lean times and favored the aromatic herbs of the grasslands when times were good. They likely lived about as long as humans if they could avoid disease and injury, elders surviving until their formidable molars wore out. From the habits of elephants, we can reason that mammoths ranged widely to avoid destroying their environment. Until they encountered humans, they proved extremely adaptable. This is one reason why the extinction of the mammoth was primarily a culinary extinction. It was once believed that mammoths vanished because of climate change, but that didn't make a lot of sense given their wide range. As humanity increased its own range, the mammoth disappeared, a strong piece of circumstantial evidence. But we also have found mammoth kill sites, including ones where stone spear points are embedded in the mammoth remains. At one site in Lehringen, Germany, a mammoth was killed 120,000 years ago with a fire-hardened wooden spear. Some of these sites were likely created by our extinct cousins, the Neanderthal. From the many human camps filled with mammoth bones, we can safely assume that the animal was a prized menu item.

We can't entirely know how quickly early humans eliminated mammoths once they entered an area, but we can glean clues from what we know of the mammoth's habits and breeding. Studies of tusk show that when humans entered a herd's territory, sexual maturity of female mammoths began happening earlier, a sign of predation we see today in stressed animal populations. (Climate change, on the other hand, would have had the opposite effect.) In some areas, we have found shelters built with mammoth tusks and bones, suggesting mass killing over a sustained period. Mammoths might seem fierce but were likely easy to sneak up on. A quick blow with a poisoned arrow or spear would do the rest, as they had weak points on their belly and neck. Such a bounty likely spurred the invention of an entirely new technology. As no group of humans could consume so much meat while it was fresh, there would have been a need to preserve some of the kill for a later time. Archeological evidence suggests humans weighted mammoth meat and submerged it in cool ponds, where it would stay somewhat fresh. Later, the earliest food technologies — smoking, drying and salting — emerged to protect similar meaty bounties. From such hunting, we developed the first really critical culinary skill after fire: leftovers.

We also know about mammoths from ancient cave art. Some ancient cave complexes were both shelters and the first places of worship. Rouffignac cave in France, known as the cave of the hundred mammoths, is a good example. To get to the farthest decorated chamber is a forty-five-minute walk underground. Oxygen levels are low and ancient artists would have been working by the flickering light of wicks floating in burning oil. Paintings of mammoths, woolly rhinoceroses, horses, bison and other animals adorn the ceiling. Its location deep underground has protected the cave from light and the elements, giving us a good idea of the look and color of the live animals. Some are depicted at a run, galloping across the walls. The artists engraved lines into the rock and filled areas with pigment. Mammoths dominate the art, suggesting their great importance.

It is hard to say with certainty how we cooked mammoth, but archeologists can give us a rough idea. We had controlled fires a million years ago, though cooking pots didn't develop until 20,000 years ago, and our mammoth snacking days fall somewhat in between. We had sharp stone knives and probably cut meat into chunks or strips to roast over or alongside the fire. The people of the Pacific coast of North America roasted salmon in thin strips by wrapping them around wooden sticks and planks and propping the planks near a fire, a technique that would work for mammoth as well. The fat would run over the meat and could be collected in shells at the bottom of the sticks. It is unlikely our mammoth chefs had much salt, but from dental plaque studies, we know the mammoth hunters ate herbs, and so perhaps they prepared a crushed herbal rub to massage into the meat. Today's barbeque techniques have a very long pedigree.

An early human site in the Ukraine revealed a diet rich in plants and mammoth and signs of frequent cooking. Cooking causes meat to lose calories as the fat melts out, but it is easier to digest, reducing the caloric cost of digestion by as much as 15 percent and giving humans another critical edge. Early humans didn't know that, of course, but they did know that cooked meat tasted better. One reason for this is known as the Maillard reaction, in which sugars and amino acids react to produce compounds that make seared foods tasty. Once early humans got a taste of caramelized mammoth with wild thyme, they were likely hooked.

The last species of the genus was the woolly mammoth, and these animals began to die off as humans followed the retreat of the glaciers. By 10,000 years ago, they were gone from the continents. On the remote Wrangel Island north of Alaska, a site that humans never colonized, the final pygmy mammoths vanished about 1650 BCE. These mammoths were never hunted but encountered a different problem: climate change. As the sea level rose, their habitat shrank until, eventually, the environment couldn't support them.

The loss of the mammoth and similar animals left us with a problem: without megafauna, humans were hungrier and weaker. Our numbers contracted and our territories shrank. We needed a new way of interacting with the environment. Mammoth was off the menu.

"What happened to your neck?"

Dan and I were catching up after my time in the North. I'd managed to snap some impressive "city raven" photos in and around Dawson City. The big scruffy birds just sort of hang around town, like bored teenagers. Dan admired the images and then returned to worrying about my neck. I was still looking a little weathered, sporting a sunburn and an impressive array of swollen bites. That morning, I'd found a small stick tangled in my hair. It would take a few more hot baths and a couple loads of laundry to get me back to urban respectability.

"I contributed to the local ecosystem by donating blood. And flesh."

"So, about our first extinction dinner. I wish we could serve preserved mammoth. Do we know anyone who could get us mammoth? Like at the Explorers Club?"

I sighed. From the gleam in Dan's eyes, I knew that he was taken with the romance of the strange stories of people eating carrion mammoth meat found preserved in the permafrost. Tales have circulated since the first few frozen corpses were found, and one of the grandest of these stories involved the Explorers Club, founded in 1905 by a group of adventurers. On January 13, 1951, as they sat down for their annual dinner in the ballroom of New York's Roosevelt Hotel, to a lavish repast of spider crab, green turtle soup, bison steaks (at the time much more unusual than they are today), cheese straws and, as legend has it, stewed mammoth. This last dish had been widely advertised to club members, and the dinner as a whole began a tradition of serving unusual meals that continues to this day. The story was so established in club lore that the tusk of the mammoth allegedly committed to the stew pot can be found in the club's lush, curio-crammed quarters on East 70th Street, where it hangs over a rather handsome stuffed penguin. Certainly, many club members lived, bragged and died believing they had eaten mammoth meat. Well, no. The club definitely intended to serve mammoth, and they presented the meal as mammoth, but we now know that it was counterfeit.

The mammoth hoax would have been the perfect crime (after all the evidence was consumed at the dinner) except a member of the club, taxidermist Paul Howes, was absent that night and asked if the club might send him his share of the mammoth in a sample jar as a trophy. The dinner committee complied, and the meat was dispatched along with its story of origin. According to the club, the mammoth meat had been

sourced in the Aleutian Islands by Bernard Hubbard, a glaci-
ologist, especially for the club.

Howe never ate his sliver of meat and it ended up in the
Peabody Museum, a curious little institution on the outskirts
of Boston. There it sat, forgotten in a back room. In 2014, Yale
student Matt Davis, who was a member of the club, began to
wonder if the mammoth meal could really have taken place. He
knew ancient meat decays quickly upon exposure to air. One of
his professors had mentioned the museum sample, and Davis
sought the institution's permission to test the meat. This wasn't
easy, as DNA degrades over time, and the meat was stewed,
mixing in with whatever else the chef had fancied. The results,
once they were carefully teased out, bore no mammoth DNA. It
was, rather, green sea turtle. Likely part of the same turtle that
found its way into the soup. Whatever happened to Hubbard's
mammoth, it hadn't made its way to New York.

The Explorers Club was likely inspired to eat mammoth by
a story borne out of one of the first excavations of an intact
mammoth. In Victorian times, there was a frenzy of interest in
mammoths and a rush to get an excellent specimen. When, in 1901,
a hunter and his dog stumbled upon a great gray corpse frozen
into the banks of the Berezovka River in Siberia, the governor of
Yakutsk alerted the St. Petersburg Academy of Sciences. A team
led by entomologist Otto Herz was dispatched immediately to
claim the prize, and paleontologist Eugen Pfizenmayer kept a
careful diary as the expedition moved east. At first, the trip was
idyllic. They traveled by luxury train, bringing along a saloon
car, dining car, church car, piano and bathtub. Otto suspected
the existence of the remains would be a false alarm, and so he
reasoned they might as well at least travel in style. In Irkutsk,
they transferred to steamer, then swapped to horses and then
later to a reindeer team. Leaving luxury behind, they smelled

the mammoth before they saw it, still frozen into the crevice where it had died. A few wild animals (and the dog) had chewed on the head, but otherwise it was perfect. The team built a small cabin around the animal and began frantically working to thaw the ground enough to remove it.

For decades afterward, stories circulated that the expedition had stretched its insufficient supplies by eating the excess flesh of the great beast. Alas, this too was a myth. Pfizenmayer notes in his diary that the meat, when first exposed, was pretty tempting. It was red and healthy-looking, filled with ribbons of fat. Once thawed, however, it turned deathly gray and quickly congealed into a putrid mush that gave off a horrid stench. It was 35,000 years old and was not going to land in any stew pot. Instead, they cut the beast up, stowed it in cowhide and rushed it to Irkutsk and a refrigerator car. Reassembled in St. Petersburg, the beast drew rave reviews, though it retained its horrid smell. The tsarina, stunned by the stench, asked politely if she might tour another part of the museum, preferably one quite far away.

Mammoth flesh. Maybe we don't want to eat it, but it does still exist. These freezer-burnt remains lie in various museums and, with our boundless optimism over the power of technology, an interesting question emerges: could we bring the mammoth back? This idea, which emerged right after the first discoveries of preserved animal remains, was largely science fiction until the rise of bioengineering, but now, the potential to bring back the extinct elicits optimism from people with a mild understanding of the topic as well as scientists with decades of training. It turns out that there are a lot of people out there who dream of living forever in a perfect future full of resurrected mammoths and dodos. In a world where nature is in rapid retreat and countless species face extinction, it is tempting to think this might be possible, but it would be wise to check our optimism slightly.

Consider the mammoth. The use of preserved genetic material has long been discussed as a pathway to restoring vanished animals, a process known as de-extinction. Thanks to advances in genetic technology, this possibility has begun to move out of the realm of science fiction. These revived animals are known as necrofauna, and there are dozens of projects to reverse extinctions around the world, usually through cloning or back breeding. There are three major projects to restore the mammoth alone, one in Japan, one in South Korea and one in the United States. The complete genome of the mammoth has been sequenced and was published in 2015 by Swedish scientists. A Harvard team has inserted some mammoth genes into elephant stem cells. By using elephants as host mothers for mammoth-elephant hybrids, it is possible that we could slowly bring individuals with high percentages of mammoth DNA into the world, though currently our technology is still insufficient. Beth Shapiro's book *How to Clone a Mammoth* outlines the technology in detail, including the difficulty of extracting DNA from frozen remains. (DNA fragments upon death, which created a puzzle for the scientists attempting resurrection.) Inserting crafted sections of DNA into elephant DNA and growing hybrid cells in culture is a laborious process. The issue of an elephant's ability to carry a mammoth to term is also thorny and beyond our current technology; miscarriage is almost certain. Shapiro also asks the critical question, "What would happen if we were successful?" It's a vital question to ask if we want the species to be more than a zoo curiosity. Is there enough room for them in their home ecosystems? Would they outcompete other species? Could they reintegrate into the food chain?

Let's return to my trip north and to one of the few megafauna that is not extinct and can be found in the wild, living a life fairly similar to the one it lived in the Pleistocene: the bison. The two existing species of North American bison didn't go extinct, but they came close. Their collapse ended nomadic living on the American plains and made possible mass colonization and farming. The North American industrial cow would not exist if the buffalo still roamed. I kept thinking about the wood bison. Why were they there, grazing peacefully by the road? Did they spend most of their time standing on the Alaska Highway, or were we just lucky to cross their paths? The herd Shannon and I visited turned out to have a name, the Nordquist herd, and they are a hopeful symbol of the survival of the iconic species. They also represent how difficult it is to maintain endangered megafauna, even in areas of the continent where there is almost no human presence. In the face of the effort to maintain the Nordquist herd, de-extinctionists start to sound a little naïve.

The Nordquist herd contains somewhere between 120–150 individuals, introduced by the Canadian Ministry of the Environment in 1995. Before that, the last wood bison in British Columbia had grazed in the early 1900s, hunted to local extinction. They were generally thought to be extinct after that, but in 1957, a wildlife patrol flight spotted several hundred animals browsing deep in Wood Buffalo National Park, where they had gone unnoticed for decades. This herd provided needed genetic diversity for a herd of plains bison on Elk Island near Edmonton, Alberta, that had been purchased from the United States. Elk Island now hosts both subspecies, and the Nordquist herd was established from these animals as part of a British Columbia strategy to reintroduce the species. The restoration is part of a larger Canadian wood bison recovery strategy, which aims to release free roaming animals throughout their range. They began with forty-nine animals, and the herd has slowly grown from there. It is one of three such herds in British Columbia.

But the wood bison still face real challenges. For starters, they really do like standing on the highway. The forest no longer burns as often or as completely as it once did, so the bison clump together on the one clear spot available: the highway. Ten to fifteen animals a year are killed in car accidents, and the population expansion is limited by the narrow forage band. Expensive habitat enhancement is needed, including the reintroduction of fire into the landscape, which clears the forest and allows forage to grow. This process is underway, and the bison will hopefully spread throughout Muncho Lake Provincial Park, which is 88,000 hectares in size and is surrounded on all sides by wilderness — no roads, no human activity. The area free of roads surrounding the bison would swallow Belgium; Germany would fit into British Columbia three times over. And still, preserving a few herds of bison is difficult and expensive.

The terrible truth is that as long as humans exist in our current and growing number, and as long as farming requires large swathes of land, maintaining existing herds of megafauna is difficult and expensive work. Restoring them is even more difficult, besides being morally debatable and impractical. We can learn a few things from the loss of the megafauna, including the mammoths. Large animals that breed slowly and require huge ranges for survival are fragile and quickly fall prey to human technology and intrusion. Our remaining megafauna, such as bison, moose and elephants will survive only if we don't hunt them and if we give them adequate room. We can't eat wild megafauna widely and expect them to exist, and if we try to farm them, we will find it an inefficient and environmentally intensive experience. This brings me to the one place we can apply our lessons from the quaternary extinction, for in our food system, one surviving example of megafauna remains: the cow.

Section Two

BEEF
OR
CHICKEN?

Chapter Four

THE BEAST IN THE JAKTORÓW FOREST

S cratch scratch scratch.

My hand was cramping. The cow's forehead was covered in short, bristly fur. Her eyes snapped open, and she gently closed her lips around the cuff of my jacket. She let out a small inquisitive moo.

Scratch scratch scratch.

I was at the Abbotsford EcoDairy, learning a little bit more about the lives of cows. These cows were classic black-and-white Holsteins, and they were friendly animals, accustomed to being stroked and prodded by tourists, school children and the likes of me. My new bovine friend finally wandered off to be milked in the robotic milking parlor, a demonstration project of an advanced technology that allows the cows to be milked on their own biological rhythm. Another cow rubbed against a rotating wall-mounted brush, preening herself. I enjoyed watching the animals move, loping gracefully around the room despite their giant bulk. A heavy cow funk wafted through the barn, but it wasn't exactly a bad smell, just a more concentrated version of the earthy animal musk that hung over the entire region most days. Welcome to dairy country.

Cows, friendly or not, are impressive and intimidating animals. A full-grown dairy cow weighs as much as 700 kilograms. When they aren't mooing for head rubs, they're eating. They require about a hectare of land for a sustainable supply of fodder.[11] They eat about 2 percent of their body mass every day, and in warm weather, they drink 120 liters of water a day, more if they are giving milk. They also produce about forty kilograms of manure each day. Cleaning a cow barn isn't a small task.

I approached another cow as she stood placidly chewing away. They are by far the largest of the culinary land animals. And there are a great number of them. Cows for dairy. Cows for meat. Cows for leather. Cows traded, stolen, worshipped. Cows for hamburgers, steaks, beef bourguignon, key wat and beef rendang. Cows for cheese, butter, ghee, kefir, yogurt and ice cream. Our relationship with cows is an old one.

The cow in its current form is a human creation, and there are 1.3 billion of them on the planet at any one time.[12] The cow isn't like other domestic animals. For all intents and purposes, it functions much as the extinct great megafauna did, turning grasslands into calories. The cow breaks the rules we learned from the mammoth. It, too, is large, breeds slowly and requires vast tracts of land to survive. There shouldn't be so many of them. They are out of balance with any wild ecosystem we know. So we maintain high numbers at a great price to our water and

---

11 Depending on latitude. This number is slightly less in the tropics and much higher in Canada's North or in places such as Iceland.

12 This number is an estimate; sources diverge sharply, ranging from one billion to one and a half billion cows. Counting cows is harder than it seems.

land and to the wild spaces that could exist if we weren't so busy covering the planet in cows and their fodder crops. The world's cows require a cumulative pasture larger than the continental United States, and in terms of climate change, recent studies suggest that each cow has a more damaging impact than the average car. While the details of these numbers are a little more complicated than this first glance suggests, raising so many cattle is one of the most damaging activities humans inflict upon the environment. But how did this come to be? How did such a large animal become so important to our food system? The answer lies all the way back at the end of the Pleistocene.

Imagine a nomadic band of Paleolithic humans wandering through the fertile region where the Tigris and Euphrates rivers meet. Megafauna were growing scarce, and so groups begin to linger near fishing grounds and particularly productive patches of wild vegetable crops. They start to improve these crops, clearing weeds, burning forest, irrigating. As the Pleistocene transitioned to the Holocene, Paleolithic humans became Neolithic humans. They became farmers. We call this transition the Neolithic revolution.

The Neolithic revolution contained two parallel paths of innovation. Some humans worked to master plants, and by 10,000 BCE or so, farmers were producing the eight Neolithic founder crops: emmer wheat, einkorn wheat, barley, peas, lentils, bitter vetch, chickpeas and flax. Rice was domesticated separately in China, along with soy. The other path of the Neolithic revolution was the domestication of animals. Pigs were domesticated in Mesopotamia in 13,000 BCE, sheep in 11,000 BCE. These two innovations, farming and herding, utterly changed what it meant to be human, and they provided two ways of survival. These paths, which now seem indistinguishable, have at times been strongly at odds; farmers by their nature need to stay sedentary, while herding cultures roam. This tension is captured well in the story of Cain and Abel in the Book of Genesis. Cain was a farmer, Abel a shepherd, and they each made sacrifices to God. We know what happened next, of course, but the story has older roots. There are earlier Sumerian stories describing conflict between nomadic shepherds and settled farmers, and the story of Cain and Abel also resembles that of Dumuzid and Enkimdu. Nomads need to roam, and farmers need fences. The tension between herder and farmer led to a compromise: mass domestication. Animals that once wandered freely were confined, and they evolved both randomly and through targeted selection to be fatty and docile.

The Neolithic revolution was a gamble. At first, the price of stationary living made farming a risky proposition. Overall health declined to the point where modern anthropologists have wondered why people gave up the hunter-gatherer life in the first place. As a food theorist, I suspect the only reasonable explanation is one of numbers. Our population had risen to the point where we couldn't gather enough food, and we had hunted the great megafauna to extinction. At first, nomadic herding was certainly the healthier option, but the long game was won by farming. The nomadic peoples of the world have been forced into a controlled retreat as farms carpet the globe. Even the great cattle drives of the storied American West were met with hostility from farmers, and many a cowboy encountered fences and loaded shotguns as they brought their cattle to market.

The retreat of the nomad brings me back to the world of the cow. The friendly Holsteins at the EcoDairy may not look it, but they are as much Pleistocene megafauna as the mammoths or the wood bison. At least, their ancestors were. Cows are descended from the wild aurochs of Eurasia and were likely domesticated sometime around 8500 BCE. Aurochs, however, did not survive the Neolithic revolution. Though less well known than the mammoth, the extinction of the aurochs was not just a culinary extinction, it was also the first documented extinction that we observed as it happened (unlike the dodo, which we noticed after the fact). Aurochs were also one of the first animals we tried, and failed, to preserve.

Our relationship with the aurochs is an ancient one. In the Lascaux caves, a complex of tunnels and caverns in the Dordogne region of southwestern France, beautiful Paleolithic paintings detail the aurochs in a number of positions and poses. In the Great Hall of the Bulls, they thunder across the walls. Our ancestors marveled at their speed, their size and their elegance. The aurochs were also plentiful — maybe as plentiful as the bison. They emerged shortly after the Cretaceous extinction event as grasses and herbs replaced the ferns and conifers of the age of the dinosaurs.

To imagine an aurochs, first imagine the meanest bull, then double it in size, give it a lush brown coat and double the length of its horns and give them a reverse curve. Edit out the fatty nature of modern cattle and replace that fat with rippling muscle. Cattle on steroids. Aurochs occupied almost all of Europe and large parts of Asia and North Africa, following the grass as the ice of the Pleistocene advanced and retreated. The Egyptians watched them graze on the marshes of the Nile, and in Mesopotamia, they were hunted from horse-drawn chariots. The Pharaoh Ramses II hunted them in 1170 BCE, a hunt captured in historic documents.

From the aurochs, we created the cow. Before that domestication, there were no cows on the earth. The exact nature of that domestication is lost completely. This is a shame, as the domestication of aurochs must have been challenging. But once completed, the domesticated version began displacing their wild cousins. Humans took over the grasslands for their now domesticated herds and the wild aurochs were doomed by the same forces that doomed the mammoth. They no longer had free access to the huge tracts of land they needed for grazing and they were vulnerable to overhunting given their slow rate of reproduction. They were rare in southern Europe by Roman times. Julius Caesar writes about them but likely never saw them; rather he created his description from the second-hand accounts of his legions. He describes the size of the bulls as equal to an elephant, perhaps an exaggeration but, given their speed and bad temper, they likely seemed very large indeed, particularly if they were running towards the observer. The aurochs was a symbol of Rome's great northern frontier, an impenetrable wilderness that covered 60,000 square kilometers.

The Roman poet Virgil wrote about a small group of aurochs in northern Italy in 30 BCE, and he noted their incredible size and speed as well. He likely saw them in person, one of the last Roman writers to do so. He documented the retreat of wild animals from the Roman world, describing several remnant populations on the fringes of the empire. The aurochs were hard to miss; the males were as much as twice the size of females and were particularly prized in the Roman arenas. They were gone in England by 1300 BCE, by 900 CE in France and in Hungary by 1250 CE or so, where they were hunted only by royalty.

The last stand of the aurochs was in Poland, in the great forest of Jaktorów. In this sea of primordial trees and grasslands, the royal family attempted to preserve the great beasts they saw as their spirit animals. Special "hunters" fed them, counted them and used dogs to keep them within royal lands. A few hundred animals lingered on for centuries, but as humans thrived, the aurochs struggled, poached by hungry locals, hounded by logging and sickened by diseases such as rinderpest, transferred from the ever-growing numbers of their cousin the cow. The royal family passed several edicts to protect the great beasts. They exempted their gamekeepers from taxes and made it a crime punishable by death to poach one of the remaining beasts. Despite their best efforts, there were only four by 1620, and the last aurochs died in the winter of 1627. The forest itself is now gone, long ago turned to farmland and grazing area for the ever-growing plague of cows.

Aurochs may be little known in popular culture, but they left a large hoof print on human history. They are mentioned in the Bible as a symbol of power and strength; the power of God is compared to that of an aurochs. They were worshipped by several early societies, a practice that carried over into the worship of bulls and led to legends such as that of the Minotaur. They were much larger than cows and bad tempered, with horn spreads as much as a meter wide. They are depicted as black or reddish brown in cave paintings, and similar images exist in Egyptian tombs. The last herd in Poland was described as having gray stripes and extremely warm, double-layered fur. An aurochs cloak was an object of great value and status, a special gift bestowed by the Polish royal family on favored friends.

Domesticating such a beast must have been truly daunting. One possible method would have involved fencing in a herd and then killing the meanest animals over many generations, but this must have seemed a desperate and foolish undertaking with little short-term payoff. The first person to imagine the domestication of the aurochs — to imagine that an angry lump of muscle the size of a Volkswagen van could possibly be made docile — is a person I wish I could meet. It likely took generations, but they were domesticated by about 7000 BCE. At first, the cow and the aurochs coexisted, and likely interbred, but the cow's genetics diverged from their wild ancestor, and by the medieval period, cows and aurochs could no longer crossbreed.

We largely forgot the aurochs once they were gone, and it was only in the last century that we realized they were the sole ancestor of the cow. In 1827, aurochs were shown to be a separate species, and in 1927 we proved that all cows descend from them. Recent DNA studies have shown that every cow on earth descended from as few as thirty aurochs, suggesting the cow is possibly the result of a single domestication event. In truth, there might have existed only one human clever and daring enough to contain the great wild cattle. It is strange to think that with one broken fence or one outbreak of illness, one of our most popular domestic food animals might have never existed. The aurochs is a literal ghost, a shadowy minotaur hiding in the maze of DNA within the modern cow. That ghost led to one of the strangest stories in the long history of cattle, a classic tale of two brothers, a monstrous regime and the infamous Nazi cow.

Heinz and Lutz Heck grew up surrounded by animals. Their father, Ludwig, was the head of the Berlin zoo, and he is considered by some to be the finest zoologist of the late nineteenth century. His sons grew up with strange and exotic species as playmates and were enchanted by the beasts of ancient times. They read and reread the adventures of the German warrior Siegfried, the hero of the epic poem *Nibelungenlied*. Their dreams were filled with wisent and aurochs, great wolf and tarpan (a subspecies of the horse). The stories of Siegfried stress the superiority of the German warrior, but in the beginning, the Heck brothers were simply sad that so many wondrous beasts were lost. They were particularly sad about the aurochs, who vanished so tantalizingly close to their own time. The two brothers mourned the aurochs in different ways: Heinz saw the loss of the aurochs as an inevitable result of the expansion of nomadic tribes. Lutz, however, saw the loss as an example of a primeval Germany, a lost mythic past free of weakness and impurity.

Both brothers became obsessed with a strange idea: could one pull an aurochs out of the cow? Could breeding work both ways? Other zoologists had attempted to recreate the aurochs by leaving cows alone in the wild. These attempts tended to create more willful cows, but they didn't magically double in size and grow reddish brown coats, and they had a bad habit of dying in cold weather. Something more was needed, some trick to pull the aurochs back into the world.

The brothers both followed their father into the family business. Lutz was director of the Berlin Zoological Garden, and Heinz became the director of the Hellabrunn Zoo in Munich. They could now attempt in practice what they had mused about in theory. They believed that by "back breeding," or breeding for older traits, the cow could be reverse engineered into an aurochs. They decided to work separately to increase their chances at success and both wandered Europe looking for the biggest, meanest cows they could find. After each cross, the brothers compared their animals to notes from paintings, literature and cave art. They ruthlessly culled their herd, and while Heinz preferred the fighting cattle of Spain and Lutz the highland cattle of Scotland with their formidable shaggy coats and terrifying horns, they occasionally traded cattle, as if they were perfecting a bovine sports team. Twelve years later, they were closing in on something they felt was about right.

The two brothers' fates diverged as German politics became more complicated. Heinz was suspected of holding communist views, and he had once been married to a Jewish woman. When Hitler took power, Heinz was sent to Dachau. Lutz, however, found Nazism appealing. He had never forgotten Siegfried and never abandoned his visions of the great blond hunter chasing giant beasts in the forest. He joined the National Socialist Party and the SS as well. With Lutz rising through the ranks, Heinz was released and permitted to resume his research, but he never enjoyed the favor of the party. Lutz, on the other hand, made a powerful friend who was also a great fan of Siegfried — Hermann Göring. The commander of the Luftwaffe was also the Reich's Jägermeister, or master of the hunt, and Lutz passed time riding with Göring and even gave him lion cubs from the zoo to chase in the woods. In turn, Göring made Lutz Heck head of Germany's Nature Protection Authority. Göring loved the idea of hunting aurochs, and soon Lutz moved his best animals to the Reichsmarschall's personal hunting reserve.

Together Göring and Lutz Heck developed a grander and more dangerous scheme. In 1930, Göring had visited Poland and hunted in the Białowieża forest on the eastern edge of the country; its 1,500 square kilometers was home to wolves, moose and the last of the wisent. Göring saw it as a surviving fragment of the heroic primeval landscapes he longed for and planned to claim it as his own. This was thwarted by the Molotov-Ribbentrop Pact, which gave the forest to the Soviets. However, when the Nazis then declared war on Russia, Białowieża fell into Göring's hands. Göring and Heck were free to remake Białowieża according to their own horrible values and visions of pure wilderness. Thirty-four villages were burned, and thousands of people were displaced or killed as Lutz Heck populated the landscape with "German" plants and animals, including his "aurochs." Nazi high command rode into the forest on horseback, hunting with hand spears, drunk and high on stimulants, acting out the heroic ancient poems.

The war turned. The Soviets reclaimed the forest as the Nazis retreated, and Lutz's reverse engineered beasts vanished into the Red Army's chow tents. When Berlin fell, the starving citizens seized Lutz's other animals, and he found himself accused of war crimes, including the pillage of the Warsaw Zoo. However, no direct links existed between Lutz Heck and the much greater crimes of the regime, and he was cleared of his charges. Meanwhile, Heinz's herd survived, and today there are several thousand Heck cattle scattered around the world. Are they aurochs? Well, no. Now that we can compare the genes of the aurochs and Heck cattle, we know that any similarities were superficial.[13]

I pondered the fate of the aurochs as I prowled the halls of Hampton Court, the grand palace of King Henry VIII. I was there to study the new kitchen garden and tour the massive kitchens in an attempt to better understand the rise of the modern cow. Lost in my thoughts, I was badly startled by one of the staff. The man was in period dress. He smiled wildly.

"This," the kitchen master said with a strange helping of menace, "is the best possible stove."

I'd been cornered by the equivalent of a medieval kitchen salesman. He sported an honest to goodness maniacal grin, and I did what any good researcher would do: I smiled, nodded and backed away slowly. I briefly jostled a display of brussels sprouts, but I kept edging backwards. I'm uneasy around historical recreationists at the best of times, and he was wearing a particularly disturbing codpiece. I cast a longing glance at the great fireplace, where row after row of chickens turned on spits. The historical recreationist was having none of it.

"The Romans developed these stoves. The heat is even. This was a revolution in Britain. I want to build one in the backyard. Spit roasting is very overrated in comparison to a simple stew, baked in a pie, with a bit of gravy. I don't understand why everyone is so fascinated by those spinning chickens."

---

13 With advances in genetic engineering, the back breeding of the aurochs is much more likely. There are currently three such projects underway.

The fire in the bottom of the Roman stove glowed orange with heat. He was making gravy in a three-legged frying pan, the sort the colonial Americans called a spider. His gravy was bubbling in a jaunty fashion. I backed a little farther away, still smiling. My stove man stoked the small fire lovingly. It was, I admit, a pretty efficient way to cook. The pie maker in the corner shook his head and rolled his eyes. I was clearly intruding on a long-running argument.

"Don't listen. Roast meat is the best meat." The pie maker had leapt into the fray.

I saw my opportunity for escape and stepped towards the rotating chickens. I agreed with the pie maker; they did look rather amazing. Entire cows once roasted in these fireplaces. And for centuries, the real prize, the real feast, was a roasted aurochs. After their extinction, roasting a whole cow was as good as it got. I leaned in and smelled the aroma. The Roman stove was certainly efficient, but spit roasting an entire cow? That was grand enough for a king.

England is an important place in the history of the cow. Until rather recently, killing and eating a cow was a rare affair. They were too valuable for other uses: butter, milk, cheese or muscle power. The Romans called the meat "bubula" and considered it a rare luxury. Their empire ran on animal power; they couldn't spare cattle for the barbeque. If a cow was slaughtered, it was a ritual, in part because there were few good ways to preserve the meat, and so a large gathering would fall upon it. There are thus few remaining records of Roman beef eating, though *Apicius*,[14]

---

14 *Apicius* the book is thought to have been written by Marcus Gavius Apicius, a Roman gourmand who lived in the time of Christ. However, we can't be sure the book was written by the man, and we aren't even sure the man really existed. For the purpose of this text, I assume the authorship to be correct.

the central surviving text of Roman cooking, describes a dish of beef steak with fried leeks. A modern restaurant might serve the same today. The eating of beef was popularized by the Germans and the Vikings and perfected by the British. The Vikings, in particular, would spurn fish, which they had in great quantity, in order to dig into a rich beef stew. In harsh climates, Vikings lived with their cows in the same structure. They'd take those cows across oceans and struggle to provide them fodder in the winter months. A Viking's wealth was in the number of their cows, and so they did everything possible to increase their number. Cows even journeyed to North America with the Vikings, as outlined in the sagas.

I took a break for lunch and enjoyed one of the many pies on offer along with some mushy peas and crusty bread. The cavernous kitchens of the palace were advanced for their time. During King Henry's reign, most people in England were still cooking over an open fire in the middle of the floor. The palace kitchens are a study in hot and cold, and cows are at the center of them. There are cheese rooms and butteries, butcheries and the great fireplaces. And of course, the pies, which contained stews cooked in great cauldrons. As Henry built his palace, England was in the process of reshaping its landscapes with hedgerows and clover fields, all in the name of perfecting cattle raising. Near his palace, farmers tinkered with both cows and fodder, and it was in England that cows were first bred separately for either dairy or meat production. The breeding of cattle became a gentleman's pastime, and the Yeoman Warders of the Tower of London, once paid partly with a daily supply of beef, became known as Beefeaters. The British, with their spits and ovens, also give us the Sunday roast.[15]

---

15   Which is now almost always baked. But we still call it a roast.

—

Beef is the third most popular meat globally and accounts for about 25 percent of meat production worldwide. Since they were first domesticated, cows have held a special place in our hearts and diets. Many of our early gods were bovine. In the Norse creation myth, Ymir is nourished by the milk of a cow named Audumla, and in Egypt, Hathor was the great bovine mother who gave birth to the sun. On Crete, young men leapt over bulls to prove their bravery, representing the story of the Minotaur, half-human, half-bull, who dwelled beneath the palace of Knossos and devoured human sacrifices. In the Bible, in the Book of Numbers, the God El who frees the Jews from Egypt is described as having the horns of an aurochs.[16]

We loved and worshipped our cows; we cleared land with axes to encourage forage and began cutting hay to support larger populations of cows over the winter. Very few Paleolithic humans could digest lactose, a natural sugar that makes up 2 to 8 percent of milk solids. Over time, more of us developed the ability to digest this sugar, and those who did left ten times as many descendants, spreading the ability around the globe. The cow was multipurpose. It could be used for muscle power and provided leather, meat and milk. By the Enlightenment era it was being raised for specific uses, and by the Victorian era dairy breeds and meat breeds were firmly established.

Columbus brought cows on his second bloody voyage to Hispaniola, and Ponce de León brought them to Florida, but it was in the American West that cows would come to dominate

---

16 The Christian god is linked to the aurochs and the cow in several contradictory stories. The Exodus parable of the golden calf suggests a shift from cattle worship to a more anthropomorphic God.

the landscape once ruled by bison. From this period came the iconic cowboy and the invention of the barbed wire that brought cattle raising from a pastoral world to an agricultural one. The rise of the railway, refrigeration, and Chicago's packing companies turned the cow into a cog in an industrial machine, putting beef on every American plate. By 1900, 80 percent of U.S. beef passed through Chicago's maze of railways and factories. What was once the food of feasts became an everyday luxury, and corn-fed cows raised on an industrial scale came to dominate American cuisine. It is really in America that the craze for cow found its stride. Though consumption of red meat is stagnant, Americans still eat on average sixty kilograms per year. Sixty percent of it is beef and 39 percent pork. In America, the cow is king.

Why? Initially, pork was the most popular meat in America, as pigs were easily raised in the forests of the new colonies where they fed on nuts, acorns and tubers. They were finished with the new North American grain — corn — and were penned in the winter months. Cows were reserved, as they had so often been, for plowing and milking. Lamb might have caught on, but the Southern cotton industry, fueled by slave labor, left little room for wool to compete as a textile. But as settlers moved into the Great Plains, they found the perfect landscape for cows. Raising pigs became more difficult as the forests vanished, and cattle ranchers worked with the government and the railroad companies to perfect the cattle industry on an industrial scale. Chicago rose as the world's greatest bovine slaughter site, and rail cars brought cows in to be fattened in feedlots, slaughtered and then sent out on the new refrigerated cars as finished meat. By the 1880s, beef was a cheap source of protein. Grass-fed on the plains that once teemed with buffalo and the people who hunted them, fed with cheap corn in feedlots, the nation's tables groaned with steaks and roasts.

Postwar America was the perfect setting for the next advance in beef's conquering of the American diet. When wartime rationing ended, a newly prosperous and increasingly suburban nation raised a simple beef preparation, the hamburger, to iconic status. The hamburger is an interesting food; the idea of a minced patty of odds and ends of beef likely does trace back to the city of Hamburg, and was a popular, if expensive, menu item as early as the mid-nineteenth century. But served between two slices of bread? That innovation must be American. A number of competing claims suggest the hamburger as we know it was developed in the early twentieth century in the town of New Haven, Connecticut. Though the true origin is lost, the burger took off in a big way in the 1950s. Beef fat acts as a glue in ground meat, and so beef burgers hold together on the grill, a popular postwar tool of the new suburban backyards. Burgers could be made quickly and eaten with friends in casual back-yard meals or even in the car. Cattle were maturing faster and beef was getting cheaper at the same time that salaries were rising. There are many books about the hamburger; it remains a national iconic American food.[17] On average, Americans eat three burgers a week.

The extinction of vast categories of megafauna suggests why cows stand alone in terms of resource intensity and environmental impact. They are just so big. Our cows require an astounding amount of land for grazing and, if they are to survive and grow fat to suit the taste of today's consumer, they also require a large slice of our crops. Of the 14 percent of the earth's land surface used for crop farming, roughly half of the calories we grow are actually eaten by people; 36 percent of the remaining calories are eaten by

---

17 Apple pie might be an American standard, but don't look for it in the South. That's pecan and key lime territory.

animals, with the last portion used for ethanol. In the meat-loving United States, only 27 percent of crops are eaten directly by people. Of course, we do eat the meat, dairy and eggs that are produced, but it takes one hundred calories of grain to produce twelve calories of chicken; the same grain produces only three calories worth of beef. Cows can, and do, also graze, but their range diet today is heavily supplemented with corn and grain. These industrial cows consume 30 percent of the American corn crop, and corn remains one of the country's most heavily subsidized crops, ensuring beef and dairy remains cheap. Along with sheep and goats, they occupy a full quarter of the earth's land surface. As I will discuss in the next chapter, some of this land, such as the scrub of Iceland that yields the world's supply of skyr, cannot really be used for much else. But in other parts of the world, rainforests are still being cleared to ensure the world's hamburger supply remains cheap and plentiful. Two-thirds of land cleared in the Amazon rainforest is used to graze cattle.

Cows, particularly those raised in compact agricultural environments and fed on grain, pack an unusually high greenhouse gas punch. Exact figures are contested, but the Food and Agriculture Organization estimates the impact of all livestock, including birds, is about 14 percent of our total emissions globally. In the case of the beef and dairy industry, methane production is of particular concern. Cows smell like cows for a reason; their four stomachs ferment greens anaerobically to release energy. Greenhouse gasses are a natural waste product of the process and leak from both ends of the cow, accounting for a jaw-dropping one-quarter of the total human-caused methane production. Methane is thirty-five times more powerful as a greenhouse gas than carbon dioxide, so those cow emissions matter. However, the amount of methane produced varies greatly, depending on breed and on what feed the cow is eating. We can drop this dangerous number both through decreasing the number of cows and changing how they are raised. Eating less beef and dairy, at least less industrially produced beef and dairy, is an effective way to lower our environmental footprint.

Beef is also often accused of being a water-intensive food and, depending on what the cows are eating, this can be true. However, numbers quoted in the media claiming a couple of steaks takes a thousand liters of water to produce are misleading. These numbers refer to the water needed to grow the feed for the cattle, that may, of course, be grass-fed or fed grains grown without irrigation.

Cattle may also crowd out the reintroduction of incompatible prairie species such as antelope and bison. And the American prairie of the imagination, filled with endless flower-filled seas of grass six feet high, is as much a ghost as the mammoth. This land is often overgrazed and the biodiversity of the landscape plummets as a result.

The modern cow is a miracle of mechanization. On one hand, the cow of today looks nothing like the cows of King Henry's time or even like the cows of our great-grandparents. They are larger, live shorter lives, and produce more meat and dairy than cows of old, often at the expense of flavor. On the other hand, there are still exceptions in odd corners of the world where cows have been bred with terroir in mind, cows that fit within their landscape. There are the pampered cows of Japan that yield beef worth several thousand dollars a kilo, depending on the cut. There are the Icelandic cows that produced the lovely knot of butter I enjoyed by the volcanic pool. There are the hardy cows of highland Scotland and the herd of cattle in Northumberland on Chillingham estate that has been isolated and feral for hundreds of years. But these herds are exceptions. For the most part, the life of the modern cow, and particularly of dairy cows, is nasty, short and resource intensive.

The space and feed requirements of industrial livestock is such a pressing factor in the sixth extinction that in 2017 over 15,000 scientists called for a drastic reduction in the consumption of meat. What can we do? The obvious solution is to raise fewer of them and feed them on natural pasture whenever possible. However, this would require a radical rethinking of the North American diet, and many people simply aren't willing to give up their steak. What's worse, they don't want to pay more for it. Still, we can exploit a few interesting tricks to dramatically lower our need for beef. For in North America, at least, the average diner seldom orders a Porterhouse or a prime rib roast. A full 71 percent of all beef consumed in restaurants in North America is in the form of the hamburger. And the future of the hamburger might well soon undergo a revolution as radical as the one that occurred when our ancestors first closed fence rails around the aurochs.

Chapter Five

BURGER 2.0

"Please let me cook an entire beef shoulder," Dan said, leaning forward. I swear his eyes were starting to tear up.

"No. We're doing my thing."

"Oh, come on! What about a spit-roasted baron of beef? I have a spit roaster. How many of your friends have a spit roaster? Only me!"

I sighed. Dan is stubbornly carnivorous. I felt a little guilty; the extinction dinners were mostly his idea and, for the first one, I wanted him to eat hamburgers. Hamburgers containing exactly zero cow.

"Jerky? Pemmican? Beef tongue? You wrote a book about tongue — come on, throw me a bone here. Wait! Bones?"

"No. I have a plan."

I wanted to imagine what life might be like in a world with radically fewer cows and, given the ubiquity of the hamburger, it seemed like a logical place to start. The idea of a hamburger without the cow is rapidly becoming a reality, with a few breakthrough products ready to eat. I realized that I needed some extra help with my burger exploration, as Dan was showing strong pro-beef tendencies, and I wasn't a big consumer of hamburgers. I don't avoid them per se, I just tend to order other things. I see them as a bit boring, the fallback option on any menu. Canadian burgers are particularly uninspiring because of a quirk of Canadian law. In Canada, a burger must be cooked to seventy-one degrees Celsius, which is most decidedly well done. As Gilbert Noussitou, Chair of Culinary Arts at Camosun College once lamented, this basically turns a hamburger into shoe leather. In my opinion, Canadians turn their burgers into hockey pucks in a misguided quest for safety. Why would I order something that, by law, must be ruined to be served?

Dan was perfect for the beef-tasting mission. He grinds his own hamburger and knows of secret back rooms in restaurants where medium-rare burgers are served through hidden wall panels. He would judge how well the post-beef burgers held up. But I needed to balance his tastes with their opposite. I needed a vegan. Katya, an old friend from a scholarly club, fit the bill. She is well-read, adventurous, knowledgeable about politics and doesn't eat animal products. Together, a carnivore, an agnostic omnivore and a vegan, we would plan a few burger adventures to see if any of the current alternative burger offerings could possibly displace the cow.

First, the veggie burger. I will admit to holding some prejudice against veggie burgers. As a graduate student in an environmental studies program in the 1990s, I ate many a dry, flavorless, rubbery patty that claimed to be a cousin of the burger. It usually came perched on a bun made of an alternate grain, such as spelt or hemp, often as dry as the patty it held. Now, it's the twenty-first century. Science has managed to put all of the world's knowledge into my phone, so maybe it's also found a way to force some flavor into a veggie burger. I arranged a shopping trip with Katya and told Dan to start making salads.

Veggie burgers are everywhere these days, made out of just about anything one can imagine, from tofu and seitan to nuts and oats. Yet the veggie burger is a recent invention that owes its existence to a man named Gregory Sams, who developed it in London in 1982. Sams, who became vegetarian at a young age, opened SEED, one of the first vegetarian restaurants in the United Kingdom. It served staples such as rice and seaweed with flatbread and was frequented by many famous regulars, including John Lennon. Sams was always trying to make up new and interesting things for his customers; his first attempt at a meatless patty was made with seitan and tamari, mixed with oats and beans. It was, I imagine, a little rubbery. He kept tinkering though, and eventually marketed his burgers in grocery stores. His biggest obstacle? He had never actually eaten a beef burger, so he was creating a simulacrum of a food he had never tasted. Despite this, his idea caught on, and imitators sprouted up around the world, bringing their own versions to the table.

Today, there are a wide range of burger patties available that are vegetarian and vegan. They couldn't all be terrible, I thought. Katya and I popped by Whole Foods where she made a pitch for her favorite, a yam burger.

"This one is good. It has a nice flavor, the texture is good, and it isn't full of soy. I think it is about the best one of the standard veggie burgers available."

While we shopped, Dan was doing everything he could to make the best of a bad situation. He was frying up onions, warming some excellent buns and slicing locally made pickles. Some edgily named microbrew was chilling in the fridge. He heated some oil and made some of his excellent rough-cut french fries. We walked in as he was plating up a commanding display of condiments. We unpacked our burgers and handed the patties off to our chef. He gingerly lowered them into a preheated pan and waited. Ever the scientist, he jotted some notes into a spiral notepad as the burgers began to steam.

"These certainly don't cook like a burger. There isn't any fat. They don't sizzle. They smell like yams," Dan noted.

He had a point. The disks hissing in the pan both looked and smelled of vegetables. We plated them up, took the whole meal out onto Dan's patio and dug in.

"See?" Katya said as she chewed a big mouthful of burger. "They're great."

Katya, it should be noted, has not eaten a beef burger in years.

Dan was less impressed. He chewed slowly, as if something unpleasant was happening.

"No. The flavor is okay, but it's completely unlike a burger. I mean, the shape is right, but the texture, the flavor, it's all very vegetable. Not bad. But definitely vegetable."

I had to agree, at least in terms of how closely the yam burgers mimicked beef. While it was a lovely meal, I couldn't see the yam burger taking the place of beef on the barbeque.[18] As we cleaned up, Dan was still grumbling, and I realized we would have to up our game. We agreed to try again later in the week.

"I cannot believe we're in the meat section!"

Katya and I were digging around the freezer section of the one grocer we found in Vancouver with advanced veggie burger options. So advanced, in fact, that it is sold in the meat section,

---

18   In fact, if one put it on the barbeque, it would catch fire, which is definitely a flaw.

next to the cow burgers. It was time to try the Beyond Burger, a next generation meat replacement from Beyond Meat, a company founded in 2009 by Ethan Brown and funded by such unlikely partners as Tyson Foods (one of the largest chicken producers in the world), Bill Gates and the Humane Society. Ethan Brown had founded Beyond Meat to produce substitutes that meat eaters might actually want, reducing the environmental impacts of the meat industry. Ethan grew up in farm country and understands animal agriculture intimately, yet he worries about the growing demand for meat around the world. His first products rolled out in 2012, including faux chicken strips that have fooled food critics in blind taste tests, and his products are now widely available in the United States.[19]

The burger, released in 2016, is a success. The market for meat substitutes is growing at a rate of 7 percent annually, and that rate is increasing in many places. The Beyond Burger took ten years to develop and carefully balances pea protein with a laundry list of plant-based ingredients that give it flavor and color, including inactive yeasts that pack a very strong umami flavor. Other highlights are beet extract, which gives the patties a very "meaty" red color and coconut oil to provide fat. A cow-based burger is 20 percent fat, the great majority of which is saturated. This is both one of the critical reasons burgers are so delicious and a central reason why they are so unhealthy. The Beyond Burger has a similar ratio, though it uses vegetable fats. The beets and yeast give the burger a meaty overtone that isn't masked by the pea protein. Or, at least, that is what we were told.

---

19   Canadians enjoy far less selection in their retail landscape than Americans. Katya and I spent half a morning chasing rumors of Beyond Burgers in Vancouver before finally locating some.

Frozen patties in hand, we headed over to Dan's, where, per my instructions, he was making exactly the same accompaniments as before.

"Well, those look different, at least," he mumbled as we dropped the thawed burgers into the oiled pan. "And they smell less like vegetables."

It was true. The Beyond Burgers looked quite a bit like cow-based burgers as we placed them into the pan. The coconut fat began to liquefy, spreading out in little rivulets.

Dan sniffed at the pan.

"Ok, I can suspend my disbelief as long as I imagine these burgers are from cows who were eating coconuts on their farm. Tropical cows, maybe?" Dan said.

There was a touch of coconut in the air, but also something more, well . . . meaty. The edges began to char a little, much as beef does. Following the advice of bloggers, I set aside the officially mandated Canadian caution and I aimed to cook the burgers only to medium-rare. As we nestled them into buns, even Dan seemed excited. I took a tentative bite. It tasted and smelled like beef. Unnervingly so. Pleased, I took another bite.

"Ok, I like that. It's a lot more like eating a burger than eating a yam patty. There is a definite meat overtone in there," I said.

"It doesn't quite look like beef," said Dan, "and it doesn't quite taste like beef, but this is a step in the right direction. The fat doesn't exactly work like the fat in beef, but I'd definitely eat this. Maybe not if a big juicy sirloin burger was sitting next to it, but I'd eat it."

With the carnivore almost satisfied, I turned to the vegan. Katya looked a little disturbed.

"Okay, the first bite started out fine," Katya said, eyeing the burger with suspicion. "But the more I chew it, the meaty taste becomes kind of overwhelming. It's just too close, too . . . I mean, it isn't bad, but I find it a bit disturbing. I think I'll stick with the yams."

We finished up our burgers and relaxed on the patio. The Beyond Beef burger had raised the bar on our search for the best beef substitute. If Dan could enjoy a burger made with vegetables, then perhaps there really was a way to lower consumption of actual beef and to reduce beef's environmental hoof print in the process.

There is another step in the evolution of burgers, and it begins with one of the very first food innovations: fermentation. Technically, fermentation is the anaerobic breakdown of a substance by bacteria or yeast, creating both effervescence and heat. Yeast is like a factory that converts sugar into alcohols and starches. Thousands of years after we first noticed that fruits and grains left on their own could magically turn into something otherworldly, yeast remains one of the most important elements of the food system. Simple fermentation creates both alcohol and bread, forming the basis of a solid picnic. Lactic acid fermentation, in which glucose is converted into lactic acid, can create a whole different range of wondrous substances. Pickles, cheeses, yogurt and skyr. Yeast might be a single-celled organism from the fungus family, but it is pretty much the best addition to the kitchen since fire.

The current breakthrough step in burger technology involves taking that single-celled factory and recoding the yeast's DNA to produce something other than alcohol or lactic acid. This might sound like science fiction, but the reality is that it has already been done. And this technology forms one arm of a new way of farming: cellular agriculture.

A few years ago, I traveled to San Francisco to attend the

first conference on cellular agriculture to better understand how the future of food production might involve fewer fields and more labs. I'll be honest, I was mostly chasing down the story of growing meat in vats, as the media was still abuzz about scientist Mark Post of Maastricht University and his public demonstration of the first "cultured meat" burger in 2013. Post's research group creates meat without animals by gathering fast-growing bovine cells, bathing them in a medium of nutrients and then attaching them to a scaffold of some sort, ideally one that is edible. That first lab-grown burger cost over a third of a million dollars to produce, but the cost has now fallen to around fifteen dollars per burger patty, prompting writer Matt Simon to proclaim, in an article of the same name, that lab-grown meat is coming whether we like it or not.

Talk of lab-grown burgers dominates the media's discussion of cellular agriculture, and those in the meat and dairy industries who are not backing these new technologies financially are lobbying governments for controls on who, exactly, can call their products "meat" or "milk" or "cheese." Now, I agree with Mr. Simon that cultured meat is coming, and I see rearguard actions by conventional producers to curtail such production as Luddite, but I think that the focus on growing meat in labs is missing an even more disruptive innovation coming out of cellular agriculture: yeast.

That first conference of cellular agriculture, "New Harvest 2016," was a who's who of food system disruption. San Francisco Bay shimmered below the presidio, and the air smelled heavily of eucalyptus trees. The packed conference was a wonderland of lab magic. There was Gelzen, a company making vegan gelatin out of mastodon DNA (their demonstration was a bowl of mastodon gummy bears, but they weren't giving them away, unfortunately). Spiber was showing off its spider-silk jacket, produced in a collaboration with North Face, a clothing company. The jacket was both silky and tough and shone in a suitably futuristic manner. There was leather made in vitro by Modern Meadow, and Perfect Day's cowless milk technology.[20] And, yes, there were sessions on the cellular agricultural creation of meat, including updates from Mark Post.

The conference was organized by New Harvest, a research institute and lobby group founded "to build and establish the field of cellular agriculture" with a vision to create "a strong foundation of accessible, public, fundamental cellular agriculture research, upon which we can build a post-animal bio-economy, where we harvest animal products from cell cultures, not animals, to feed a growing global population sustainably and affordably." They fund research, conduct public outreach and support start-up companies. But can a handful of technology companies really challenge a food system based on the domestication and keeping of animals? Maybe not entirely, but the negative environmental impact of cows and other domestic animals ensures that the production of meat at a rate sufficient to feed the entire world at the level of consumption enjoyed by North Americans is impossible. Something needs to change, and the least efficient part of the animal food system is often the animal itself.

So what is cellular agriculture? Most applications fall into one of two groups. The first, the production of agricultural products from cell cultures, involves the construction of organic molecules such as proteins and fats, like the burger turned out by Mark Post's lab group. The second is the genetic alteration of yeast and bacteria, a strange combination of biohacking and

---

20 I'm skeptical about the time it will take until I will be able to dine on cultured meat, but milk produced without the cow might beat this book to press.

fermentation. Vat burgers get the lion's share of media attention, but early applications based on much simpler compounds have been around for quite a while.

Insulin, for example, was first used as a treatment for diabetes in 1922 by Frederick Banting, Charles Best and James Collip, who collected insulin from pig pancreases. This method had drawbacks; it was expensive, difficult to standardize and could create pork allergies in the long run. In 1978, a team of researchers inserted the gene for insulin creation into bacteria, using yeast as tiny living chemical factories. It worked, and almost all insulin is now made in this way. The pioneers of this work, Boyer and Cohen, are considered to be the founders of genetic engineering, and their development has saved countless lives.

Within the food chain, another little-known product of cellular agriculture can be found in the field of cheesemaking: rennet. This odd set of enzymes is found in the stomach lining of ruminants, and when mixed with milk, they catalyze the curdling of the casein protein within, yielding the curds that become cheese.[21] Extraction of rennet for cheesemaking was a slow and difficult process, and by the 1970s, the world's continually growing appetite for cheese outstripped rennet production. But in the 1980s, scientists figured out how to genetically alter bacteria and yeast to produce rennet through fermentation. Rennet produced this way is not technically classed as a genetically modified food, because it is a by-product of the fermentation process. Artificial rennet was the first time enzymes were produced in this manner and then allowed in the food production chain by the U.S. Food

---

21   One of the theories of how cheese was discovered involves an early human storing fresh milk in a bag made of a cow's stomach. Our protagonist then went on a horse ride, agitating the bag. When they stopped to rest, their milk had solidified into a tasty treat. We will never know for sure, but it's a charming story.

and Drug Administration. About 90 percent of all cheese made in the United States and the United Kingdom now uses artificial rennet. These cheeses are considered kosher, halal and vegetarian, since the cheese produced no longer uses animal enzymes.

This brings us to milk, which is made of fats, minerals and two proteins — casein and whey. It's possible to genetically alter yeast to produce these proteins, and of course fats can be sourced elsewhere, like the coconut fat in our Beyond Burgers. Perfect Day Foods is working quickly to mass produce such a milk in a lab, with a focus on initially using it to replace milk and milk solids in processed foods. However, lab milk could also be made into butter and cheese. The impact could be huge. World dairy demand is growing by nearly 5 percent a year, with a total production of 240 billion liters annually. Yet the dairy industry is a difficult one, as expenses for feed and care of the cows often eclipse the profit to be made from the milk. In addition, the demand for veal is dropping, leaving dairy producers without a market for the young cows created during milk production. As a result, small dairy producers around the world are struggling. Industrial-scale farms have moved in with a more cost-effective but destructive model — raising more cows in regions with lax environmental standards and cheap labor. Dairy is an industry ripe for disruption, and its future might look more like a lab than a barn.

The technologies on display at New Harvest 2016 entranced me. An alternative pathway for creating milk could, for example, help Canadians improve nutritional outcomes in the far North where cows can't easily be raised. However, I also felt the tiniest bit threatened. This was an entirely new way of thinking about food, with profound implications for production chains and also for the rural landscape. One of my main areas of study is farmland protection. Would we need as much farmland in the future? Would we even need many farmers?

And what of Dan and Katya's reactions to the Beyond Burger? Burgers taste the way they do because they contain myoglobin, which contains heme, a substance in blood that gives meat a strong umami flavor. Beyond Meat focuses on recreating this with beets and yeast, and it was enough to intrigue Dan and disquiet our vegan. Food expert Mark Bittman couldn't tell the difference between Beyond Meat's chicken wrap and one made from an actual chicken. Could the plant-based alternatives eclipse the need for cultured meat entirely? Even in the realm of milk, many people are quite happy with plant substitutes, and fermented cashew cheeses are evolving rapidly. No, these products aren't likely to be the same as a wheel of fresh Humboldt Fog cheese, but could they get close enough for most purposes?

Cellular agriculture continues to evolve. The Impossible Burger burst onto the food scene in 2016, the brainchild of Stanford biochemistry professor Patrick Brown. Dr. Brown began development of a new burger in 2009, in an effort to counter what he felt was the world's most pressing environmental problem: industrial animal agriculture. This led to the founding of his company Impossible Foods in 2011, and in July 2016, they launched their "meat analogue," the Impossible Burger, marketed as a "carnivore's dream." Dr. Brown realized the key to shifting away from a meat-heavy diet would be to understand why meat tastes like meat.

The Impossible Burger has strong environmental credentials, using 95 percent less land, 74 percent less water, and emitting 87 percent less greenhouse gas. It is a little leaner than a beef burger, with no cholesterol and fewer calories. In many ways, it is similar to the Beyond Burger, save for one important addition. The Impossible Burger contains that critical ingredient, heme. They use leghemoglobin, which is a vegetable version of the substance found in animal muscle, and they make their leghemoglobin using cellular fermentation. In other words, they have taken yeast and genetically altered it to produce a flavoring agent that achieves a meaty taste. They claim that the addition of heme makes the Impossible Burger sizzle, smell, bleed and taste like meat. The Impossible Burger is now available at a wide range of restaurants in the United States, ranging from some of the fanciest dining rooms in the country to a selection of White Castle restaurants.

There is a lot of hype about heme. An iron-containing molecule that occurs naturally in animals, it allows blood to carry oxygen. As noted, in animal muscle it is carried in a protein called myoglobin. But yeast, recall, can create proteins such as rennet, insulin or, in this case, leghemoglobin, which is similar to a protein found in legume roots. Impossible Foods generates the compound using genetically altered yeast. The FDA approved the Impossible Burger and its heme in 2018. Would the Impossible Burger best the Beyond Burger in our kitchen arena? Unfortunately, "impossible" also stands for "impossible to find in Canada," so we had to postpone our sampling, but we agreed we were all game to try this next step on the burger frontier as soon as we could get our hands on some.

We won't have to wait long. The plant-based substitute market will continue to grow on the strength of health benefits and improved environmental impact. The Beyond Meat burger represents a definite leap forward as a veggie burger, but it isn't a game-changer for the average meat eater. Cultured meat will arrive eventually, though likely later than its proponents suggest. Once cultured meat and dairy is cheaper than conventional sources, it will replace animal products in processed foods, fast-food restaurants, and institutional settings. This is a huge market; McDonalds uses one billion pounds of beef each year in its American restaurants alone.

High-end meat and dairy won't disappear. Gourmets such as Dan will seek these products out even if cellular replacements are available. This isn't entirely a bad thing; in Nicolette Niman's book *Defending Beef*, she points out that grass-fed cattle often use land that cannot be cultivated, though agricultural grazing also disturbs natural grassland ecosystems. I don't see Dan giving up his grass-fed porterhouses any time in the future, but that isn't really the point, even if we ignore the impact of grazing. High-end meat and dairy make up less than 10 percent of the market, so even a partial conversion to cultured beef and cellular agriculture could radically remake the food system, and, as we will explore later, the face of the planet. In a way, the rise of cultured meat simply reflects the hegemony of meat itself. That hegemony isn't going to vanish overnight, but that doesn't mean it won't transform. That transformation could radically lower the impact cows have upon the environment while also decreasing animal suffering by ending industrial-scale animal production. We aren't saints, but cultured meat will win out for the simple reason that it will be cheaper someday.

There are a couple of elephants in the room, however. Firstly, the rise of cellular agriculture could be hindered by the lingering disquiet around GMO technologies. The question of GMO safety invokes great angst, but the reality is that we are already eating GMO soy and corn with no obvious negative effects. In addition, GMO-assisted products such as insulin and vaccines have been used successfully for decades. Still, when the issue of food safety arises, we all tend to be a little more conservative. Discomfort with GMOs ranges from mild to extreme moral opposition, though I can't help but note that we already change the genes of plants and animals — just in a slower way — through selection and crossbreeding. The cow itself is a genetically modified organism, carefully bred for temperament and milk or meat output. Still, the requirement that we reduce our farming footprint might force us to become even more comfortable with genetic engineering.

The second elephant is the production of sufficient "feed-stock." The fermentation processes used to create new molecules consume sugar as an input, and much of the industrial-scale production of sugar has a large impact on sensitive tropical environments. However, we already produce a large sugar surplus. We could shift sugar use to cellular agriculture and trim our addiction to cheap sugary snacks. There is another danger, too. The production of cellular agricultural products could shift our impact from cool, grazing climates to tropical ecosystems that are already suffering environmental degradation. One possible solution is to utilize waste products from existing food production chains as feedstock for cellular agriculture. If we can harness our leftovers to produce burgers and other animal products, cellular agriculture could prove to be an endgame of the Neolithic revolution, the next step in an arc from hunting megafauna to domestication to breeding for desired traits to crop specialization to industrial agriculture to bioreactors.

As I reflected upon the Impossible Burger, I couldn't help but feel my journey had taken me full circle to the Pleistocene. It won't happen overnight, but I can imagine a future where the cow looks more like the megafauna of the Pleistocene, cropping the herbs and grasses carpeting farms that once grew feed for industrial beef and dairy production. Though moral arguments and ethical decisions such as those that shape Katya's vegan diet will be a strong selling feature for cellular agriculture and its related technologies, their dominance of the food system will occur because they will be cheaper, they will be easy to manipulate to improve our health outcomes and because they will allow for almost infinite variety. We need only a few cells to create meat products in the lab; why not finally have that mammoth stew?

It's too early to say whether cultured meat and cellular agriculture will look like microbrewing or market gardening, where small local producers craft careful products, or whether large companies will control massive flows of synthesized meat. Likely there will be a balance between the two, particularly as the economics of cellular agriculture becomes more competitive. The ultimate implications of farming in a lab will depend on larger social, economic, environmental and political forces rather than upon any intrinsic qualities of the products themselves. Will cellular agriculture write the butcher's requiem? It is too early to tell just yet.

Chapter Six

THE LIVING WIND

One spring morning a few years ago, I met a crow. I was on my porch sipping coffee and nibbling a croissant when he arrived, a blur of shadow, to land in a tumble on the deck. He looked ruffled, feathers askew, a small wound on his back. We looked at each other, unsure how to proceed. Eventually he perched warily on a planter box.

I didn't quite know what to do with my visitor. East Vancouver is alive with crows, specifically the northwestern crow *Corvus caurinus*. They roost inland and fly out to feed at the city's beaches, eating fish, shellfish and crabs. Dan took me along one summer to film them dropping clams onto a seaside tennis court; the hard surface popped open the clamshells, and the hovering crow would dip down to grab the meat. Every dawn and dusk they commuted between roost and beach, a river of velvet wings draped across the sky in the thousands. The neighborhood honors them in murals, in art, in media. One, Canuck the Crow, became locally famous when he removed a knife from a crime scene and flew off with it. Dan has filmed crows tearing up lawns to get at the chafer beetle grubs below and documented them dive-bombing unsuspecting pedestrians who wandered too close to their sturdy nests during hatching season. The crows are there, part of our landscape, pecking through garbage, perching on wires. And now one was on my porch, gingerly grooming his feathers. I took him some crumbs of food and a little water, then settled in next to him with a good book. I was worried he would attract the neighbor's cat. He had a way of twitching his wings, as if to shrug in a noncommittal manner. By the end of the morning, I was calling him Mr. Flap.

My visitor healed quickly from whatever terror had so ruffled his shimmering feathers, leaving no sign of a scar on his back. But he kept coming for breakfast. We developed a little ritual; I would put out a bowl of dry cat food, he'd settle at arms-length, and we would watch the day unfold. And then one day I slept in, only to be awoken by Mr. Flap, perched on my window ledge, food bowl in his beak. He was rapping the bowl against the glass impatiently. Apparently, I had a standing coffee date with a corvid. From then on, I made sure I appeared for morning coffee in a timely fashion, and I began changing my dietary preferences away from anything that involved birds. Now that I had an avian friend, eating his fellows seemed like bad manners.

I was thinking about Mr. Flap one afternoon as Dan and I chatted about pigeons. Crows might be part of my urban landscape, but for most urban folks, the feral rock pigeon, *Columba livia domestica,* is the bird they are most likely to notice. We practically trip over them. They are one of Dan's favorite species that has adapted to life with humans, and around one hundred million of them flit about our cities worldwide. The grandest human building is just a convenient nesting cliff to a pigeon, and they peck daintily on the buffet of garbage we leave scattered along our streets. They are friendly, and around the world, urban dwellers have raised them on rooftops or fed them in parks.

And, yet, the pigeon is a living reminder of the world's most perplexing extinction. For the rock pigeon is not native to North America. Our skies were once owned by a much grander bird — a larger, faster bird — the most plentiful bird, we believe, to have ever lived on the earth. That bird is the passenger pigeon, and we know more about its extinction than almost any other vanished animal. We even know the exact date of the last passenger pigeon's death: September 1, 1914. Her name was Martha. Her story, and the story of her species, highlights the transformation of humanity from an age of small-scale agriculture to an age of industrial farming.

My study of passenger pigeons began where the species ended: Ohio. I was enjoying a sunny morning in Cleveland, taking in the local culinary scene before attending a conference on the resurgence of local food initiatives in the American Midwest. I was watching a small flight of pigeons wander around the square, their heads bobbing, pausing to peck at a scattering of crumbs. Cleveland's Market Square Park was quiet and sun dappled, and I was peacefully sipping coffee while contemplating the shoppers entering the West Side Market. The air smelled faintly of food, a mix of apples, salted meat and freshly baked bread. Cleveland was being good to me that morning. The city's light rail system was clean and efficient, the bridges over the Cuyahoga River were, as advertised, grand, and I had a historic market hall to explore and new regional foods to try. I was cheerful. I smiled at the birds, who paid me no mind at all.

Cleveland doesn't get a lot of culinary love, and that is a shame. I conducted a reverent blitz of the region's foods, beginning at the West Side Market. Pizza bagels were possibly invented here, and the ones in the market hall were loaded with spicy tomato sauce and bubbling cheese, still steaming and dripping from the oven. Generations have washed these hearty breads down with chilled buttermilk, thick, sour and dusted with nutmeg. I was surprised by how refreshing it was. The pizza bagels were so good, I ate two of them, though I saved room for lunch, as I had to track down the iconic Polish Boy, a thick, spicy sausage sandwich topped with fries and coleslaw. I was sweating a little by the time I settled back into the square, and there was definitely no room for a coconut bar — a cube shaped white cake covered in chocolate frosting and rolled in coconut — a local sweet that is similar to Britain and Australia's Lamington cake.

Full of the fruits of my research, I returned to the square. With no further food to distract me, I began to wonder why exactly feral pigeons thrive so well amid humans, yet the much more numerous *Ectopistes migratorius*, the passenger pigeon, did not. The existence of the *Columba livia domestica* bobbing about at my feet is a complicating factor in understanding the extinction of their wild cousins. Contemporary observers of the passenger pigeon experienced awe at their numbers, and for decades after the last flocks perished, writers suggested the birds were in South America, hiding at the poles or even roosting on the moon. And no wonder. Passenger pigeons were so plentiful that their presence dominated the landscape. A description from the 1840s, reprinted in *Cleveland: The Making of a City*, is typical of the times: "For days at a time, Cleveland skies were darkened as millions of passenger pigeons soared overhead. The roar of their wings 'sounded at the distance of miles like the heavy surges of Erie beating an iron-bound coast.'" One shot could bring down several birds, which were sold for a penny apiece at the market square where I now sat. I decided that to understand the passenger pigeon I needed to understand how, exactly, they had been killed.[22]

Passenger pigeons did several things extremely well. They formed migrating flocks, they flew very fast and they roosted in huge colonies within the dense forests of eastern North America. These traits were wondrously effective at protecting them from predators, until they encountered humans armed with the weapons of an industrial society. Humans attacked them on two fronts: they were vulnerable to habitat loss because they needed so much territory for forage, and their roosting behavior made them vulnerable. With weaponry they were trivially easy to hunt.

Their extinction wasn't inevitable, however. The birds coexisted with Indigenous Peoples for thousands of years, and as the incoming settler population grew, passenger pigeons managed to survive in an uneasy balance for several centuries, a time marked by forest loss for settlements and farmland and a rising human predation. But once professional hunters could learn of major roosts instantly via telegraph and then, thanks to the railroads, descend in droves on the defenseless birds, numbers plunged.

These two technologies, the telegraph and the railroad, are key parts of the evolution of the modern food system. Before this, wild foods could play a major yet still sustainable part in humanity's food system. After, however, no land animal or plant could be expected to survive our ability to harvest it, and wild foods faded from our daily diets.

When Europeans first encountered the passenger pigeon, the birds, as individuals, seemed familiar. They were large, and naturalist John James Audubon depicts them as rather pretty.

---

22 The terrible details of the destruction of the passenger pigeon made for the most disturbing research of this entire project. Approach the suggested readings for this chapter with caution.

They were about a pound in weight, fifteen to eighteen inches in length, and the males sported patches of copper, blue, gray and purple. The females were more subdued in their coloring but shared the gentle calling patterns of the males. They built loose nests out of sticks and defended their chicks with vigor if provoked. The passenger pigeon, however, had one very distinctive feature not found in their old world counterparts: they flocked in numbers beyond belief.

The centennial of the passenger pigeon's extinction in 2014 sparked renewed interest in this lost species. In naturalist Joel Greenberg's book *A Feathered River Across the Sky*, he argues their flocking behavior sets them apart from any other bird that has ever lived. They were described as living wind, as clouds, as great forces that would block the sun for hours or days. There were as many as five billion birds, as much as 40 percent of the total bird population of North America. They were migratory, traveling in arcs from the shores of Hudson Bay to the American South, each cycle taking several years to complete. They would roost for months at a time and then take to the skies, flying at speeds of up to 60 miles an hour. Their scientific name, *Ectopistes migratorius*, means migrating wanderer in Latin, and for good reason: the continent's forests were vast, but no one area could support that many birds for more than a season. Alexander Wilson, the father of American ornithology, studied the birds in Kentucky in 1810 and described them as a "living darkness, a loud rushing wind similar to a tornado." His fellow ornithologist John Audubon described a three-day dusk as the birds passed overhead along the Ohio River in 1813. He wrote, "The air was literally filled with pigeons; the light of noonday was obscured as by an eclipse . . . the continuous buzz of wings had a tendency to lull my senses to repose."

They were also imposing on the ground. Passenger pigeons were creatures of the air, but they had to roost for four to five weeks to raise their young. In the trees, the birds and their eggs were vulnerable to predators, and they compensated by gathering in the tens or hundreds of thousands or more. They liked areas of low, wet woods that offered both water and some protection from their predators. These roosts varied from a mere ten acres in size to one roost that was estimated to cover over a thousand square kilometers. Most covered several kilometers of forest at least.

The pigeon embodied density. They built hundreds of nests per tree and gathered in such numbers that they formed piles of birds. Writers from the time describe birds sitting on the heads of other birds; they crushed and shattered mature trees and left dung nearly a foot deep beneath the roost. In extreme cases, roosts contained tens of millions of birds. This behavior makes sense when individual predators, relatively small in number, are picking off only one or two birds for an easy lunch. Humans, however, didn't stop with one or two. We turned these great flocks into cheap food available at the newly built public markets in the great cities of the North American East. American ornithologist Alexander Wilson wrote in his masterwork *The Natural History of the Birds of the United States* that passenger pigeon was served at every roadside tavern, and that "wagon loads of them are poured into market . . . pigeons become the order of the day at dinner, breakfast and supper, until the very name becomes sickening." The bird was brought to extinction as it was served up in dozens of common recipes.

Passenger pigeons were eaten by a wide array of animals, and their eggs and squabs were even more tempting targets. To survive, passenger pigeons had to keep themselves and their eggs safe from skunks, foxes, lynx and raccoons on the ground, and then falcons, owls, vultures and hawks in the sky. Flocking protects a species from animal predators but puts them in great peril in the face of human predation. A young man in San Antonio, for example, was reported to have killed and gathered over 400 birds by hitting them with a small stick. A casual toss of a net could gather a few meals' worth of birds. For the hungry settlers of North America, the passenger pigeon was the first fast food.

Passenger pigeons were important to the Indigenous groups of North America. They played a critical role in the culture of the Iroquois Confederacy, a political union of five (and later six) groups including the Seneca and the Mohawk, two Indigenous Peoples who controlled large territories in the heartland of the pigeon's migratory route along the Great Lakes. They hunted the adults only, in order to maintain pigeon stocks, and they dried the birds, boiled them and roasted them. As the pigeons only appeared in any one place on a four- to eight-year cycle, these "pigeon years" took on particular political importance, and groups would gather at the roosts to renew alliances, trade and plan marriages. Pigeons appeared in the spring in the Iroquois Confederacy and were eaten after maple sugaring but before the planting of crops. The birds were also fermented to create pigeon grease that was then mixed with grains to form a pemmican similar to that made on the plains.

The first European to describe eating passenger pigeon was Samuel de Champlain, who in 1605 noted in his journal that there were countless numbers of pigeons along the coast of Maine. Champlain's colony of Port-Royal in Acadia (present-day Nova Scotia) was the first European colony in that region of North America, and only the plentiful foods of the surrounding water and land kept this French outpost alive. At first Champlain and his officers scorned local foods as inferior to the foods of France, but as the winter of 1606 ravaged the colony and supplies ran short, he was forced to encourage his men to embrace fishing and hunting, and passenger pigeons were a popular evening meal. Champlain created North America's first gastronomy club, the "Order of Good Cheer," to boost morale; he had the colony's tiny elite take turns hunting and fishing and then preparing classical French recipes with the resulting bounty.

Chaplain and his men were the first, but certainly not the last, early Europeans in North America to rely on such an easy food source; the flights of pigeons that circled eastern North America are described in many early settlement accounts as life-saving. In 1769, the arrival of pigeons saved thousands in the American colonies from starvation as crop failures ravaged the countryside. As Jennifer Price describes in her book *Flight Maps*, the passenger pigeon's numbers were at least partly responsible for the American conceit that this new continent was inexhaustible. She suggests that "the wild pigeons fueled the widely shared conviction that Americans could never deplete their resources . . . that logic may [now] be hard to grasp, colonists perhaps would have had to summon even greater imaginative powers to envision the comparatively empty, devastated landscapes that have become so familiar to us." Settlers from Europe were for the first time free to go out and hunt without regard to the restrictions imposed by local landowners. People were so excited by the arrival of one of the great pigeon flocks that they would abandon their work to pepper the sky with shot. In 1727, Québec City passed a law against shooting within the city's walls, but the laws were almost impossible to enforce. As late as 1821, the police force of Toronto made mass arrests before giving up and joining the hunt themselves. It wasn't easy to resist an event that amounted to free food falling from the sky.

The hunting of early colonists was likely not a huge factor in the extinction of the species. Though the pigeon's encounters with human settlement often ended on the dinner table, hunts were local, limited and offset somewhat by the spreading bounty of America's farmlands. The farmers of the seventeenth and eighteenth centuries describe their own losing battle with passenger pigeons. The destruction went both ways at first. A little digging exposes stories of feathered devastation of wheat, corn and rye harvests, and heavy predation of fruit and seed crops. In Canada, bishops would routinely excommunicate the passenger pigeon flocks for damaging crops, and in the Great Lakes states, farmers would feed them poisoned grain, though this was a dangerous practice that endangered the human population as well. Other farmers fed them alcohol-soaked grain and then gathered the drunken birds for the stew pot. The great flocks were compared to biblical plagues of locusts. The impact of the pigeon in North America influenced the development of agriculture in the region; Daniel Van Brunt developed the first North American underground seeder, a device to thrust seeds deeply into the plowed soil, in 1860. One of the reasons driving the invention was the need to thwart the pigeon's hunger. The bird's impact on farmland would have helped to mask any concern about falling numbers; farmers spared a "pigeon year" that devastated their crops were unlikely to complain.

The arrival of the pigeon flocks wasn't all bad; the birds left chaos behind them after laying waste to entire forests, but they also left the promise of agricultural wealth. Their dung was sometimes a foot thick on the ground in a pigeon roost, and if the roost was burned, cleared and planted, the fertilized soil ensured the lucky farmer a bumper harvest. This was another stress on the passenger pigeon, as some of their best nesting sites were converted to farms after the birds moved on.

Local farmers also organized hunting parties to take as many birds as possible. Entire communities joined in these group hunts, and entire flocks were destroyed while they roosted. This killed not only the existing birds but the next generation of birds as well. The impact on agriculture is the only explanation for the scale of these community killings; the hunting often went far beyond the practical, and after a few minutes of hunting, a community would have more pigeons than they could possibly use. Thousands of dead pigeons were fed to pigs or plowed into fields as fertilizer. And even amid this level of local extermination, the species maintained its great numbers. What the passenger pigeon would not be able to survive were the changes brewing in the way humans procured and transported food. And the passenger pigeon had a terrible weakness: it was tasty.

As I drove around Cleveland, it was hard not to notice the empty lots and ruined buildings. Cleveland's population has fallen to about 40 percent of its peak in 1950, due to the decline in industry that gives this region its nickname: the rust belt. But one hundred years earlier, in the mid-1800s, Cleveland was leaping from success to success, and its market square hummed with the pigeon trade. Brought in by the barrel on rail cars, the pigeons were a cheap and plentiful protein for one of the United States' largest and fastest growing cities. The current West Side Market was built on this wave of prosperity. Often mistaken for a train station, the building is a beautiful example of Beaux-Arts architecture, crafted to reflect the Greek ratio of the golden mean. But first and foremost, the market is a piece of food system technology.

Understanding the impact of public markets such as the one I was visiting sheds light on the fate of the pigeon. On two sides, the market is flanked by an L-shaped vegetable arcade, an open-air structure that allows vendors to take advantage of naturally cool lake air to better preserve their produce. Built in 1912, of granite and glazed brick, the market boasts a Catalan-vaulted brick ceiling held up by five great arches and a clearstory that floods the vast space with natural light. A separate room for the sale of fish contained the odor of seafood, and an elegant clock tower is visible throughout the local neighborhood.

The West Side Market is equally impressive behind the scenes, highlighting the best of the era's technology. The loading dock is long enough to accommodate several vehicles at once, and the freight elevators are large enough to hold multiple sides of beef. The basement is a warren of cold storage that had enough capacity that it was able to rent out its extra cold storage to residents before home refrigeration was common. When the market first opened, it contained fifty-six meat stalls, eighteen butter and egg stalls, nine fish stalls and the vegetable and flower market.

Without refrigeration, most families would need to go to market almost every day, picking up perishables to go with the staples they had at home. A brace of pigeons, reasonably priced, would have been a common meal throughout the nineteenth century. Early industrial markets like this one expanded the sale of wild game to a new and terrible scale.

Our knowledge of the nineteenth century's golden age of markets on the East Coast is largely due to the writing of Colonel Thomas F. De Voe, who lovingly recorded the daily rhythms of life in the markets of New York. Born in 1811 in Lower Yonkers, De Voe traveled to New York as a boy and apprenticed as a butcher in Washington market in Manhattan. The work suited him, and after an early and successful career in the military, he opened his own stand in the new Jefferson Market in the West Village, where he worked for forty years. De Voe's knowledge of meat and game was encyclopedic, and he rose to be a leader of the market community.

De Voe's best-known work is the 1897 *Market Assistant*. I'm lucky enough to have a copy of the original printing, signed in

De Voe's clear hand in brown butcher's ink. The book outlines every single product sold at his markets, with lively details as to how to choose and prepare each item. He was particularly proud of the selection of birds, claiming that the "variety, quantity and quality of wild-fowl and birds, called game . . . received in the public markets, especially of the city of New York, is not surpassed in any other city in the world." He describes a scene befitting a zoo with edible exhibits. Wild birds sold at the markets included swans, two dozen types of duck, wild turkeys, partridges, grouse, pheasants, quails, snipe, plovers, gulls, sandpipers, larks, cranes and, of course, the passenger pigeon. De Voe gives particular attention to the passenger pigeon, as it was the premier culinary bird of his time. He notes that "numerous birds are found in our markets, alive and dead, very plenty, and generally cheap in the latter part of September and October" and that "Great numbers are taken alive with nets, cooped up for several weeks, and fed with grain until fat, then brought to our markets as the prices advance." De Voe describes how most birds were taken in the West, and sent by rail, suggesting a species already in decline in the East.

And from De Voe, we get one of the very few discussions of how the birds actually tasted. He describes "wild squabs, when fat and fresh, are very delicate eating; the cooped bird is also good, the flesh being rather dry; but a poor wild-pigeon is very indifferent eating, even if well and properly cooked." The dry quality of adult passenger pigeon appears again and again in recipes, and many counteract this deficiency with stewing or copious amounts of sauce or gravy.

De Voe conveys the incredible abundance of the pigeon when he describes a professional pigeon hunter at work. The hunter would set out a tamed pigeon tied to a chair or stool. He would then cover the nearby ground with rye and wait for the pigeon's unsuspecting fellows to arrive. The hunter would then cast a net over the whole flock. This is the origin of the term "stool pigeon." In 1858, De Voe observed 650 pigeons taken in a single throw of a net. However, he also suggests that pigeons were no longer present in the great numbers seen in his early years. He describes a depression in general food prices in Boston in 1771, when fifty thousand pigeons were sold in a single day, and notes such events no longer occurred as pigeons no longer arrived in such numbers.

The markets De Voe described in his writing were supplied by dealers who themselves sourced their products from rural farmers and adventurers. The food chain stretched from the cream of America's urban society to hunters working in remote and little-explored regions. The professional pigeon hunters of the mid-nineteenth century were never plentiful; a few thousand followed the flocks, and maybe only a few hundred practiced the trade full time. They lived a life that reads like a stereotype of the American frontier, traveling thousands of miles in pursuit of the flocks. They lived in barns, tents or out in the open, and they sold their bounty to middlemen dealers, like the Allen brothers of Michigan, a pair who came to riches on the backs of the passenger pigeon. The notes of the Allen brothers reveal a species in trouble: as the years passed, they noted the flocks became fewer and farther from the great cities. But no matter how remote the remaining flocks, the railways relentlessly crept towards them. The colonists harvested the flocks of pigeons as they passed through, but the hunters were different; they actively pursued the birds. Records are scant but suggest shipments in the hundreds of thousands from individual nest sites, and many birds were killed that later were wasted thanks to long trips to rail lines and a lack of ice. Live birds were particularly valued in the markets, and as the birds retreated, they commanded ever higher premiums. In the boom years of the pigeon trade, farmers would make occasional sales to the wholesalers if they were lucky enough to have a flock in their region. Times were difficult on the eastern farms and the pigeons represented free money on the wing. Feathers from the birds were made into bedding, and fat from the birds was made into soap. The pigeon's body fed the increasingly efficient machinery of the newly industrialized food system.

At the height of the passenger pigeon harvest, when the birds were both plentiful and cheap, they were popular from the farm table to the railway dining car to the most elegant restaurants of America. But at a certain point in the decline of their numbers, the few remaining flocks commanded a price out of the average worker's reach. Still, America's upper class continued to have a taste for the doomed bird. The preparation of the passenger pigeon reached its apex in the finest kitchen of the time, that of the legendary restaurant Delmonico's.

Delmonico's catered to the most refined class of New Yorker. Opened in 1827, it was the first restaurant in the New World to command high praise from Europeans. It found a ready audience. At the time, Americans of all classes ate most of their meals at home, or at inns and hotels where meals of varying quality were brought to table at set times of day. Businessmen took lunch at public eating houses that were little more than pubs with a sideboard. Sensing the potential for a profitable business, Swiss brothers Peter and John Delmonico opened their first restaurant at 23 William Street in New York, bringing America its first taste of European culinary art. They were so successful that they sent for their nephew Lorenzo, who would become responsible for the restaurant's menu and wine cellar. Under his supervision, Delmonico's would serve some of the fanciest preparations of the passenger pigeon ever offered to diners.

The Delmonico family was wildly successful, moving their restaurant several times to grander quarters, and opening what became known as "the castle" at South William and Beaver streets in 1837. The entrance pillars were imported from the ruins of Pompeii, a fitting tribute to a temple of bacchanal excess. They still stand, guarding the sharp corner.

Lorenzo Delmonico was outgoing and generous, and he knew everyone who passed through his doors. He understood that his family's wealth and power rested on the food they served, and he was determined to ensure that only the best would grace his tables. He personally did the shopping for the restaurant. He would rise at four in the morning and after some strong black coffee and perhaps a handmade cigar, he would visit the Washington and Fulton markets and pick the best products for his diners, including the plumpest passenger pigeons.

Lorenzo gave exceptional attention to his food, and another pillar of his success was his chef: Charles Ranhofer. Lorenzo remarked that at his first interview with Charles, the chef made it clear he was doing the Delmonico family a great favor by agreeing to work for them. He was right, for he was one of only a handful of truly great chefs of his generation. He had become the private chef of the Belgian Comte d'Alsace at the age of sixteen, and in 1856, he had moved to New York to cook for the Russian consul where he was a favorite of diplomats. He cooked at Delmonico's from 1862 to 1896, after he took some time in 1860 to return to France, where he staged grand balls for the Emperor Napoleon III at the Tuileries Palace. Together, Delmonico's and Ranhofer would make New York society the most exquisitely fed in the New World.

We know a lot about Ranhofer as he wrote one of the great culinary tomes of the nineteenth century. His masterwork, *The Epicurean*, contains the best surviving collection of recipes for preparing passenger pigeons for fine dining. Ranhofer slow-cooked the birds with cabbage and turnips. He prepared them with sweetbreads, ham and mushrooms in a velouté sauce and then served them on fried artichoke bottoms. When in a simpler mood, he would pan fry the birds with bacon and then serve them over rice. For an elaborate meal, he would stage dozens of them stuffed with ham and truffles on a gold or crystal stand, decorated with rare fruits. His Huntress Style pigeon presented the birds breaded with crumbs and parmesan and served with truffles and mushrooms. Monarch Style involved braising the birds with pork, mirepoix and cock's comb (for the chef short on cock's comb, he provides a method of crafting imitation ones) surrounded with crayfish and foie gras in a Southern style of spicing. For those looking for lighter fare, he prepared pigeons potted with bacon and pilot cracker (also known as hardtack), stuffed them with eggs and pork and presented these on a bed of turnips and peas, or simply stuffed the breasts with a force-meat of crayfish. On grand occasions, his pigeon with olive dish required building a small tower of ingredients in order to use the pigeon as a meaty centerpiece. But one of his best-known recipes was actually the simplest: passenger pigeon cooked in pork fat and served on a bed of peas.

Ranhofer also bowed to tradition and made pies; his Pigeon Tarte à la Britannia involved using three pigeons, salt, pepper and cayenne. He filled a pie dish with bacon, onion and sautéed pigeons, along with some hard-boiled eggs, and would add gravy, cover it with a top crust of pastry and bake. The convention of the time among the average cook was to leave the pigeon's feet sticking up out of the pie (to indicate what was inside, I suppose), but Ranhofer dismissed this as unbefitting polite company.

—

I spend a lot of time imagining what the foods of history might have tasted like, and Ranhofer is key to understanding the flavor of the passenger pigeon. As the recipes aren't crafted to have another taste dominate the flavor of the bird, we can assume that the pigeons weren't overly gamey by the standards of the time. Elsewhere, they have been described as light and flavorful, and this claim is borne out of Ranhofer's preparations. However, they were also dry and the butcher DeVoe's observation is supported by Ranhofer's recipes. Almost every recipe involves larding with fat, usually pork fat, and many involve sauces that would help balance the dryness of the meat. Ranhofer's tricks and tribulations will be familiar to anyone who has struggled to produce a juicy game dish for the table.

At a banquet for Charles Dickens in May of 1868, Ranhofer served pigeons with peas, pigeons with mushrooms and truffled pigeon patties. The dinner, with over thirty-five dishes (not counting desserts), lasted for eight hours. Passenger pigeon was a popular dish at such events, but it was also served every day at Delmonico's. But even as plate after plate poured from Ranhofer's kitchen, the seemingly endless supply of wild birds was in fact rapidly dwindling.

The farmers noticed the decline first, even as Delmonico's patrons were still feasting on pigeons slathered in truffles. Pigeon years, and the nice bump of extra income they provided, had vanished into history. Professional pigeon hunters, now working on the far fringes of the pigeon's range, began to realize the end of their industry was upon them. By the 1880s most of the pigeon hunters had retired, with too few pigeons remaining to support their business. It is strange to think that a few hundred men might have delivered the final blow to a species that once numbered in the billions, but the evidence supports the theory that organized hunting for market consumption was the killing blow for the species. The final collapse was fast once the great nesting sites were destroyed. As game dealer Edward Martin claimed in the early 1880s, it was "as if the earth had swallowed them." By 1893, they had disappeared from Fulton Market and from the elegant plates of Manhattan's elite.

By the mid-1890s, passenger pigeons were extinct in the wild, and a surprised public began developing theories as to how such a common bird could have been eliminated. Farmers overwhelmingly expected that the wandering birds would one day come back. People spoke of pigeon pie fondly, yet the skies stayed empty. As Aldo Leopold noted in *A Sand County Almanac*, "Trees still live who in their youth, were shaken by a living wind. But a decade hence only the oldest oaks will remember, and at long last only the hills will know." The last known wild bird, named Buttons, was killed in 1900, leaving only three small captive flocks, which dwindled to two, and then to the solitary one at the Cincinnati Zoo.

The pigeons ended in Ohio, with Martha. The Cincinnati Zoo is the second-oldest zoo in the United States, and passenger pigeons were an early addition to the collection. They were kept in a wooden cage, and the twenty or so birds became quite tame. Martha likely hatched near the dawn of the twentieth century, one of the last passenger pigeons to come into the world. The flock, mostly consisting of elderly birds, did not thrive, and one by one the birds died, leaving a lone pair, George and Martha, named for the first president and first lady of the United States. George died in 1910, leaving Martha as the lone representative of her species. She died of extreme old age on September 1, 1914.

A century after the death of Martha in Cincinnati, the passenger pigeon still inspires awe. Martha is more than a footnote; she stands as the ultimate "last thing," a symbol of everything lost in the rise of industrial society. Though Martha deserves her fame, the fact that we fixate on her highlights humanity's inability to grasp ecosystems and species as a whole. We understand Martha's death, yet we don't understand that the passenger pigeon as a species was not the sum of its individuals. Passenger pigeons existed as flocks, and they could not survive outside of flocks. Martha was a living ghost. Faced with a predator they couldn't best by numbers alone, the passenger pigeon fell.

People killed the birds because they were hungry. People killed them because they interfered with farming. They were killed as a quick source of cash to support struggling farms and, once industrial hunting emerged, they were killed to provide a cheap source of food. They were killed to please Lorenzo Delmonico's glittering customers. They were also hunted for sport, but that is a small part of the story. The last birds vanished quickly, but this is understandable given they were a species that depended on their great numbers to survive predation. The ecosystems of North America felt their loss, as is inevitable when a keystone species falls. We suspect squirrel and mice populations flourished, and raptor populations fell. Deer populations rose. A few tree species became rarer as their seeds were no longer spread by pigeon. A silence came to the skies.

Back in Vancouver, Mr. Flap continued to join me for breakfast for several years. He would nab croissant pieces from my hand if I offered them as he chuckled and clucked. One day, he showed up with a small shy friend, a little black crow I began to call Midnight.[23] The two crows would eventually tire of me and join their fellows in the skies about town, only to reappear

---

23 As I am no bird expert, I'm not sure Mr. Flap was in fact a "Mister," though he was somewhat larger and more social than his friend.

after a day or two. Eventually I had to move away, and I'm told they moved on as well. I still look for him sometimes, particularly at breakfast. Like Martha, he lingers in my mind, a patch of shadow and feathers in the wind.

Chapter Seven

ENGASTRATION

"Dan! Over here! I just saw one of your rats."

Dan shushed me and peered into the gloom. "Look closer, I can see three. And the sun's starting to heat things up. Come back at night if you want to see them at their best."

"No, thank you," I said, backing away onto the cracked sidewalk.

I stared into the cool leafy shadow of the blackberry thicket. Dan and I had hiked to one of his field sites, a vacant lot covered in high blackberry canes. Around us, industrial buildings hunkered amid railway tracks and piles of rubble. It wasn't a fun place, but the berry canes did give off a pleasantly green smell. Beneath them, the ground was bare save for a scattering of trash and cobble-sized rocks. There were hundreds of holes hiding in the darkness, and the longer I looked the more rats I saw. Just snatches: a set of eyes, a flash of gray. Dan was half-submerged among the razor-sharp thorns, adjusting a camera. He backed out slowly, blinking in the rising sun.

"Is there anything living on this lot that isn't a blackberry cane or a rat?"

"Not much. The blackberries are *Rubus fruticosus*, and the plants cover disturbed ground completely when they can. They're an invasive from the mountains of eastern Europe, where plants have to be tough to survive long cold winters and hot summers, though the rest of the continent does have native blackberries. Our urban areas are ideal for these blackberry canes, even with poor soils."

He wasn't kidding. They can crack concrete and grow over six inches a day in the summer. The rats like such thickets because the foliage keeps them cool and hidden, safe from predators. Rats also love the berries, of course. They produce up to twenty thousand pounds per acre. If the thorns weren't so nasty, it would be the perfect food plant.

Dan winced as he plucked several curved thorns from his arm.

"So, they haven't always been here?" I asked. "I'm surprised. I always thought they were just part of the ecosystem."

Dan stood up and gave me a thoughtful look. "Well, they are now. Just like the rats are and you and I are, for what it's worth. Ecosystems change. What isn't normal is the gap. The empty lot. In a complete ecosystem, the berries and rats would find balance. It's what isn't here that's unusual. So many gaps, so many empty biological niches. To understand this and why the thicket is a simple place with only a few species instead of beautifully complex like an ancient ecosystem, you need to know what's missing. That's hard."

The sun came out, and bees appeared from what seemed like nowhere to flit from blossom to blossom. We walked on in silence. Dan was correct, the trick was seeing the lack of things within our altered ecosystems. The vanished megafauna, the tiny remnant populations of bison, the empty skies once filled with pigeons. As humans, we tend to think of individuals, but ecosystems are about groups. And some keystone species support entire ecosystems. The passenger pigeon was a keystone.

I was thinking about ghosts a lot as I moved further into my exploration of vanished food species. Great swaths of the planet are now shadow ecosystems, stripped of the wondrous diversity that once flourished there. Some scientists are now arguing that the human footprint upon the world is so great that we have to rethink our understanding of how planetary mechanisms work. Some go further, arguing that we have, in effect, entered a new geological epoch in which the actions of humans are the dominant driver of planetary level change. They call this new epoch the Anthropocene.

Geological time is a bit confusing when we are discussing human history, as we have existed for such a tiny sliver of time in comparison to the earth itself. All of human history fits into what is called the Quaternary Period, a span that began roughly three million years ago. This period is divided, as I mentioned earlier, into two epochs: the Pleistocene and the Holocene. Humans hunted and gathered in the Pleistocene, then began to farm and raise animals in the Holocene. The Anthropocene would be a third epoch of this period. The name is a combination of the Greek words for human, and for new. It is an emerging idea, and while not exactly controversial, it is still under debate.

Defining a new geological epoch isn't simple and it isn't automatic. Currently, the Anthropocene remains a proposed epoch, though in 2016 a working group did recommend that the term be formally accepted, an act that requires the approval of the International Commission on Stratigraphy (the analysis of the order and position of geographic strata) and the International Union of Geological Sciences.[24] The

---

24 Well, someone has to keep track of five billion years of history. I can't even keep my laptop files in order.

term was first used by the Soviets and was popularized much later by atmospheric chemist Paul Crutzen with regard to our influence on the planet's atmosphere. Crutzen argued that our ability to change the actual composition of our atmosphere was both new and profound. It affected every living thing. Since that time, the term has gained widespread traction and spawned several conferences and an academic journal. Exactly when this proposed new epoch began is still a topic of some debate. Some argue that the industrial revolution marks the beginning of our ability to influence the atmosphere, and others trace it back to the beginning of agriculture. However, the most common date proposed is that of the first atomic bomb test in Trinity, New Mexico, in 1945.

The Anthropocene is of interest to our discussion as it also coincides with the sixth extinction we talked about earlier. Our extinction rate is currently somewhere in the range of one hundred times the background rate, but as Dan pointed out, we are also seeing a radical simplification of the earth's ecosystems. This is an age of retreat, an age of less than. If we imagine that all of the earth's biomass was gathered together and weighed,[25] we would find that we have roughly 50 percent less biomass now than before humans dominated the planet's ecosystems. It is impossible to know exactly how much has been lost, but the trend is clear and it is worrying. The extinction rate began rising in about the year 1500, but it is really only in the twentieth century that biomass numbers began to drop sharply. A 2015 study suggests that we have already lost some 7 percent of the species on earth and that humans should be considered a globally present super-predator, consuming

---

25 A messy thought experiment, I know. A surprisingly large part of the pile would be earthworms and krill.

biomass as we spread and increase in numbers. And like the blackberry thicket, once we arrive, we tend to stay, shaping the ecosystems around us.

Evidence for a new epoch is gathering on a number of fronts. In terms of biogeography, we move species around the globe, such as Dan's blackberries. Those species will appear suddenly in future fossil records, puzzling future paleobotanists, if they or their field of study still exist. Future climatologists will be able to chart the rise of carbon dioxide in the atmosphere from roughly 280 parts per million to over 400 parts per million, along with other related changes.

We've also changed the earth's surface, cutting canals and rerouting rivers. We've removed forests and created products that don't decay. These technofossils will remain for millions of years, hiding in rock formations long after everything else we've built has crumbled to dust. And, of course, our atomic testing has created radionuclides that did not exist on earth before 1945. Between the Victorian era and the present, we have created a new planet, the unintentional effect of millions of intentional acts.

If we accept the existence of the Anthropocene, how can we then map the concept onto our food systems? Let's recap. In the Pleistocene, humans were hunters and gatherers, natural predators, and fairly efficient. In the Holocene, we began to farm and to domesticate animals. These actions led slowly but steadily to human-altered landscapes, change we can illustrate by returning to pigeons. Pigeon domestication occurred near the confluence of the Tigris and Euphrates rivers, an area of lush plains and marshes that held some of humanity's first major settlements. Mesopotamian cuneiform tablets from five thousand years ago mention rock doves, though no record survives as to whether people laughed at the first innovator who built an artificial structure to encourage nesting. The birds would have been familiar; prehistoric rock doves lived alongside humans near cliffs and caves. They were easily netted, and Egyptian tombs have been found containing the remains of pigeon-based meals packed away for the dead to enjoy in the afterlife.

The Romans had a great fondness for pigeons and bred different varieties for the carrying of messages (they are very skilled at returning to their home nest) and as an offering to the goddess Venus. The Mosaic of the Doves in Hadrian's Villa depicts pigeons in a shrine and in an aviary, highlighting their dual role. Once pigeons roosted, early keepers would feed the birds and occasionally harvest a few of them (or a few eggs). The caloric content was likely low, leading to squab long being known as a food for the rich. The ancients enjoyed their pigeons, however, and built lavish structures to house them. Some of these could hold thousands of birds. They were fed sparingly and flew off to forage elsewhere.

Each couple produced about ten squab a year, a small addition to the diverse food systems of early human settlements. Their success as an invasive feral bird stems from the same properties that made them easy to domesticate; they easily find their own nesting sites and feed themselves on the rich leavings of an urban population. (As an aside, their young are peculiar in that they don't leave the nest for several months after hatching, an unusually extended fledging period. This is the reason urbanites very rarely, if ever, see a juvenile pigeon.)

Aviaries were important for two reasons. Once humans settled permanently and stopped following food sources with the seasons, they had to ensure food was available at all points of the year. Food storage became paramount, and indeed much of a harvest period would be spent drying, smoking, salting and storing as much food as possible. Live pigeons, however, had the lovely property of staying fresh all on their own, and unlike many other birds, they didn't migrate. The aviaries and dovecotes of great houses, along with fish ponds, bee hives, rabbit hutches and deer parks, stood as year-round sources of fresh food. However, the pigeons played a second and even more critical role: they produced fertilizer. We might not like the deposits pigeons leave in abandoned buildings and back alleys, but for an agricultural society without chemical fertilizers, the pigeon was a miracle bird. Farming before chemical fertilizers was a constant battle with soil exhaustion, and farmers struggled with rotating crops, leaving fields fallow and plowing in anything handy to boost crop production. Pigeon guano is ten times more potent than the dung of land animals because of its high nitrogen content, so the dovecote was a gold mine, or more strictly a potassium, nitrogen and phosphorus mine. In Iran, where the eating of pigeon flesh was forbidden, flocks were set up solely for their value as a source of fertilizer for nitrogen-hungry melon crops. Even today, squab farmers make a lucrative second income selling pigeon guano to organic vegetable farmers. Europeans loved the crop boost that pigeon droppings provided, but the supply was strictly limited. So Europe's farmers were forced into experimenting with different treatments of dung and ash, aging and fermenting different dung blends with exotic additions such as bone and live shellfish to try to enrich their soil. The continent was struggling to produce enough food to keep up with population growth — could other sources of guano be found?

In the Western Hemisphere, an answer waited. The farmers of South America had long known about the sea-bird covered islands of the western Pacific and the large guano deposits of bats, sea birds and cave birds, hundreds of feet thick in places. The precontact empires of South America traveled to those distant islands and brought guano back to the mainland to fertilize their elaborate terrace farms, ensuring a steady supply of critical crops such as corn, chocolate and chili. Guano was so important that the Incan Empire punished the disturbance of guano birds with death. The discovery of these islands of high-quality bird droppings by European explorers came just at the right moment.

Enter Alexander von Humboldt, a young aristocrat hungry for adventure and opportunity. Born into a wealthy Prussian household, he spent his inheritance on a five-year expedition that would bring huge areas of South America to the attention of Europe for the first time. A man of incredible energy, he voyaged up the Orinoco River in what is now Venezuela and Columbia, discovering its connection to the Amazon. There he became the first European to see an electric eel, an experience that almost cost him his life.[26] In Ecuador, his party climbed within a thousand feet of the summit of Chimborazo, setting a world record by reaching 19,200 feet above sea level. Von Humboldt charted ocean currents, measured magnetic fields, documented plants and animals. And in Peru, where he also observed the transit of Mercury across the face of the sun, he studied the properties of guano. His writing would inspire a gold rush of guano mining around the world. Soon, large shipments of guano were pouring into Europe from Peru, the Caribbean, the Central Pacific and islands off the coasts of Africa,[27] allowing for an unprecedented increase in food production. Over one hundred thousand indentured Chinese laborers worked the mines, leaving a lasting imprint on the culture and population of South America. Inevitably, these guano mines, deposited over

---

26 He let it shock him to prove it was actually "electric." It was.

27 These islands belonged to someone else, but that didn't dissuade the Europeans. The environmental and social effects of guano mining can still be seen today.

thousands of years, were exhausted. As the Holocene unfolded, humanity had domesticated a useful species, harnessed a product of that species and then explored the globe for better sources of that resource, a pretty typical Holocentric approach to a problem. But ultimately, as our numbers grew, we needed a better source of soil nutrients.

The defining moment in the agricultural transition to the Anthropocene in my view occurred over a few frantic years in Germany, in the opening decade of the twentieth century. Guano was such an excellent fertilizer because it contained nitrogen, phosphorus and potassium in forms that plants could easily utilize. We can mine phosphorus and potassium easily enough, but nitrogen in a form useful to plants is hard to come by. Frustratingly, the atmosphere is 80 percent nitrogen atoms, tightly bonded into pairs. It is a bit like the plant equivalent of dying of thirst on an iceberg.

Wresting nitrogen from the atmosphere in quantity was finally tackled by a team of scientists led by Fritz Haber, a chemist trained at a technical school where he learned how to solve problems in an industrial setting. Before turning his mind to the conversion of atmospheric nitrogen to ammonia (a form that can be used by plants), he worked on practical and non-spectacular problems such as preventing the corrosion of gas and water mains. In theory, the problem of ammonia production was rather simple, and Haber easily sketched out an ideal process in which nitrogen and hydrogen were mixed in the presence of metal catalysts under extreme temperature and pressure.

This process was theoretically easy, but finding a good source of hydrogen and picking the right catalyst were challenging problems, as were creating the high temperatures and pressures needed. The technical issues facing Haber's theory were addressed by Robert Le Rossignol, and the entire process was scaled by a young engineer named Carl Bosch. The team's process was largely perfected by 1913, and we often call their method of producing bioavailable nitrogen the Haber-Bosch process. Bosch himself gave credit to the dozens of scientists who worked in teams to perfect the process, one of the first instances of a large group of scientists and engineers collaborating in a formal team to solve a major industrial problem. Haber and Bosch won a Nobel Prize for their efforts.[28]

Today, over 400 million tons of ammonia fertilizer is produced each year, using 5 percent of our natural gas production as a feedstock. It is responsible for multiplying agricultural production by a factor of four and is estimated to provide roughly half of the earth's calories. Field crops now cover about 14 percent of the earth's land surface, and it is unlikely we could find enough land to grow the same amount of food without nitrogen/phosphorus/potassium (NPK) fertilizer. Critics argue against the use of chemical fertilizers, claiming they are artificial and deplete the soil's ecosystem. There is some truth to this, but they will be needed for some time to come if the world is to be fed. The combination of intensive agriculture and advances in genetics and cellular agriculture is creating a farming system that looks more like a science lab than our idea of an old-fashioned farm, but it is an approach that might meet our near-future food needs until global populations plateau and the widespread degradation of farmland can be tackled.

Farming in the Anthropocene will look different than it did during the previous ten thousand years. But what of extinction in the Anthropocene? Are we doomed to lose thousands upon

---

28 One of the first uses of Haber-Bosch ammonia was in the creation of explosives for World War I, giving Germany an initial advantage.

thousands of species in a sixth mass extinction? Let's return to the loss of the passenger pigeon from the wild, which did, arguably, have one positive impact: it effectively ended the sense that the American continent was an inexhaustible frontier and spurred interest in the conservation movement. One of the people deeply affected by the fate of the passenger pigeon was Arlie Schorger, a research chemist turned naturalist who wrote the first book about the extinction of a species, *The Passenger Pigeon: Its Natural History and Extinction*, in 1955. Schorger collected first-hand accounts of the pigeons, laying the groundwork for an under-standing of what was basically a continent-sized forensics puzzle. As a professor and board member of the Audubon Society, he fought to ensure such an event could not happen again.

But a lesser-known, curious book might turn out to be even more valuable: Paul Hahn's *Where Is That Vanished Bird?*, which notes the location of surviving passenger pigeon specimens as of 1963. Hahn was a Toronto musician, piano dealer and bird expert who had his own collection of sixty-eight passenger pigeon specimens. The remains of Hahn's birds and others like them contain something that nineteenth century scientists couldn't imagine: a way to bring the passenger pigeon back.

There is, believe it or not, a lab dedicated to bringing passenger pigeons back to the skies. As with the mammoth and aurochs, scientists are actively working to revive the passenger pigeon, and a full-scale effort to restore the species through genetic engineering is being underwritten by the Long Now Foundation, a California think tank dedicated to long-term planning. The Long Now Foundation is an eclectic organization. They are developing a clock that will last ten thousand years, are working to preserve the world's endangered languages and, of course, are working to restore extinct species. As foundations go, they are one of my favorites, in part because they operate a bar called the Interval, which encourages the discussion of the long-term future of humanity over strong drink.

I caught up with Ben Novak, the lead researcher for the Long Now Foundation's passenger pigeon project, by phone. Effusive and deeply knowledgeable, Ben helped me understand a critical element of the passenger pigeon's extinction — how the loss of the bird impacted the larger ecosystem. Ben's interest in the passenger pigeon began at a young age, and when a position at Long Now came along, it was, in his words, a dream job. It is certainly not an easy job, however; there are many steps between DNA and living birds. Passenger pigeons went extinct recently enough that viable DNA can be extracted from the many remaining specimens (including poor Martha), and a close relative, the band-tailed pigeon, is still very much alive. By sequencing both the passenger pigeon and the band-tailed pigeon, then noting the points of difference, Novak believes it will be possible to reverse engineer passenger pigeons by recreating mutations in band-tailed pigeons to make a series of jumps towards living passenger pigeon DNA. At the end of 2017, the project was on track, and Novak is optimistic that passenger pigeons can be created and reintroduced into the wild. He hopes to have birds carrying the first traits by 2022, though, as with much in science, that will depend on funding. One of the difficulties is that Ben and his group don't want to just create a few individuals; they want to reintroduce flocks to the wild.

An individual pigeon would be a wonder of science, but it is a flock that has implications for ecosystem restoration. Ben's passion lies in the interaction of the passenger pigeons with the forests of North America. He believes the loss of the bird severely damaged forest health, as the massive roosts once provided an upheaval in the forest on par with wildfire. When we repress fire, clearings disappear and dead material gathers on the forest floor, smothering new growth. Likewise without the pigeon, the forest stagnates and dies. I pressed him for details.

"Look, the passenger pigeon was the engineer of that ecosystem. They created massive, recurring disturbances, allowing for new growth. The only thing comparable is fire, and we've controlled that as well. Without the pigeons, the ecosystem has become much less hospitable. It isn't the same forest."

Ben also stresses that the guano played a critical role in creating hotspots of biodiversity. As farmers discovered, areas of pigeon disturbance were incredibly lush. Once the pigeons moved on, the devastated pockets of forest would explode with life. Pigeons, Ben stressed, were a keystone species. Given his passion for the interplay between forest and bird, I saw a chance to clear up one other element of that relationship. I asked him if deforestation played a major role in the extinction. Could I clear humanity of a culinary crime?

"No, we hunted them to death. We've modeled the decline, and it's clear that deforestation was never severe enough to account for the losses. They couldn't survive the level of human predation, and the extinction only seems sudden. In reality, the numbers likely fell fairly steadily, but that is hard to tell when the local sky is dark with birds."

Humans and our appetites most definitely eliminated the passenger pigeon, from the traveling hunters to the urbanites paying pennies per pigeon at the market to the gilded customers of Lorenzo Delmonico. Ben explained that because pigeons flocked in such numbers, we would not have noticed the loss immediately. In addition, many captured birds left behind the other member of the breeding pair that would not mate again. This affected birth rates and patterns, with the result that the surviving flock would be composed of older and older birds. Though the damaged colonies would still seem to contain a great number of birds, the average age of the colony would increase each year. Collapse would later seem quite sudden, as the older, surviving birds would begin to die with no offspring to replace them.

Ben is optimistic that passenger pigeons can return to North American skies and stresses the potential benefits of restoration: healthy forests and beautiful flocks of birds. Not everyone shares his enthusiasm. The project has been criticized as a waste of scarce funds that could be put to use protecting existing species, and it has also been called out as ethically dangerous. Would extinction carry the same conceptual bite if there was the possibility, no matter how difficult, of its reversal? Ben feels such views expose a fundamental difference of opinion; critics believe in an unspoiled nature that sits apart from humanity. The idea of de-extinction, on the other hand, stresses the relation between humans and the ecosystem. This is clear in Ben's parting thought: "I grew up in a hunting community. To me, the ultimate success of the project would be in the establishment of a population capable of sustaining a limited harvest. Likely not in my lifetime, but beyond, why not?"

A revenant passenger pigeon is an addition to the burger grown in a vat. Will passenger pigeons grace twenty-second century dinner tables? If Ben has his way, the iconic vanished birds might be back on the menu. I'd like to share his optimism, though I'd be content to watch the birds in the air while munching on a salad.

In the meantime, we can learn a few things from the fate of the passenger pigeon. Like the megafauna, they required large intact ecosystems, but they had three additional vulnerabilities. Firstly, they congregated in huge numbers, making them extremely easy to kill. Secondly, they migrated, making it more difficult to regulate their harvest. Finally, they did not take to domestication. These vulnerabilities guaranteed the passenger pigeon could play no part in the modern food system.

—

If the Anthropocene has an avian poster child, it is *Gallus gallus domesticus*. There are nineteen billion chickens on the planet at any one time. Most of them are not very happy. We consume them in an orgy of eating that requires 140 million chickens per day globally. That is roughly fifty billion birds a year, twenty times the number of ducks eaten, which is the only other avian food source that is even comparable.[29] We also eat eighty billion of their eggs each year. No other species of egg comes anywhere close.[30] We eat most chicken in processed forms. Deep fried wings, pale flavorless breasts, nuggets made from the bits and pieces. We have made the chicken into the sort of bird we wish nature would provide — docile, meaty and fast growing. Chickens don't flock naturally, but it doesn't matter; we can confine them into forced flocks of whatever size suits us. The chicken, however, was a fairly minor part of the food system even as recently as a century ago. How did a modest jungle bird conquer North American menus?

The chicken has a long history. We've raised chickens in small numbers for at least seven thousand years and perhaps as much as ten thousand years. Chickens are friendly birds and easy to manage. They have inspired art, science, cuisine and even religion. Darwin studied chickens in the long years during which he procrastinated about writing *On the Origin of Species*, and he correctly identified them as descended from the red jungle fowl *Gallus gallus*, a ground-dwelling bird from India and the Philippines that

---

29 To be fair, a portion of that number are egg layers, but their meat still finds its way into our food system in highly processed form, including as the ubiquitous nugget.

30 In case you are wondering, the egg really did come first. Reptiles lay eggs, and they predate chickens by millions of years.

browses for insects, seeds and fruit, and flaps up into trees to sleep at night. The Chinese were keeping chickens by 5000 BCE, and by 300 BCE, the Egyptians were keeping chickens as well, decorating their temples with images of eggs. They also developed the technology to hatch batches of eggs by adjusting temperature and humidity in specially built chambers, turning each egg five times a day. The Egyptians carefully guarded this technology and were the first society to produce chicken in quantity.

Chickens were a delicacy to the Romans, who developed both the omelette and the idea of stuffing birds with various fillings before roasting them. They began feeding the birds specifically to fatten them, even experimenting with plying them with wine to improve their flavor. *Apicius* contains an entire chapter on chicken, along with chapters for ostrich, pigeon and peacock. What stands out is the attention to flavor in the recipes; the dishes are liberally braced with silphium, lovage, pepper, coriander, figs, olives and mustard, among other flavorings. Perhaps even in Roman times, chicken was seen as a pretty "tame" meat.

Chicken fell out of favor as the ancient technologies of mass breeding were lost, though they were kept in the medieval period for their eggs. And this is the minor role they played right into the twentieth century, pecking about farmyards, providing a small stream of eggs and the odd pot of soup or Sunday dinner.

I've always liked chickens, which might explain my squeamishness when it comes to eating their dismembered parts. They are smart and docile, and they eat harmful insects. I decided to pay a visit to some chickens to better understand what has made them so successful. Why did the rise of the modern food system purge the passenger pigeon and increase the chicken population so sharply?

I began by visiting some lucky chickens. A friend keeps a small flock on a nearby farm, and in no time, I was eye to beak with these beautiful and affectionate birds. Close up they are reptilian; the movement of the raptors in the *Jurassic Park* films was modeled on that of chickens. I found their activity and their gentle noises calming. After ten minutes, I was surrounded by plump, healthy and curious birds.

"Go ahead, pick her up," my friend said, indicating the bird who was sitting at my feet. "If you have them from a young age, they are really good pets. Just scratch her sides a little."

The chicken roosted on my leg, clucking happily. They are gregarious birds. But these were, of course, pampered chickens that were unlikely to ever visit a stew pot.

The reality of industrial chicken-kind is very different. I managed to join a group of journalists on a tour of a local egg farm, a mammoth operation producing one hundred thousand eggs a day for the nearby city of Vancouver. Before entering, we had to suit up in protective clothing, protecting not ourselves, but the tens of thousands of chickens inside. In 2004, avian flu devastated this region, leading to the death of nineteen million birds through culling and losses. This particular producer is determined not to let such a thing happen again. I would not be picking these chickens up. Inside, the air was warm, with only a hint of bird smell. Everything was white, clean, calm and unexpectedly quiet. All around me, off into the distance, stretched cages of chickens stacked five high in pyramids. Six chickens inhabited every cage, yet it was silent, save for the gentle sound of eggs moving on tracks, eggs rolling down ramps, a white river of eggs pouring out of the building into the inspection hall next door. If I closed my eyes, there was no hint of the thousands of avian minds in the room. At some point, someone in the party snapped a flash photo on a cell phone, and things immediately changed. There was an eruption of panicked clucking.

The farmer looked pained. As the clucking quieted, he whispered, "Don't do that. They don't like bright light."

We moved on, touring the sorting rooms and the washing rooms and the giant hall where the farmer mixes his own feed. The key to the operation is efficiency; feed goes in, eggs come out. As the eggs roll down the tracks, it is easy to forget there are birds there at all. I left with a few cartons of eggs and a general understanding that we use the chicken in such a way because we can, and the passenger pigeon is in part gone because it couldn't survive in a cage. And I couldn't really see the egg farmer as evil or abusive. He kept his birds and barns clean and healthy and gave the customer what they wanted: eggs so cheap they were practically free.

The driving force behind the food system is a factor that hasn't changed over the centuries: cost. Cheap food is the bedrock of modern society. We are used to spending a small fraction of our income on food — roughly 10 percent on average in the United States. In the second half of the nineteenth century, that figure was over 50 percent. Our great-grandparents would marvel at our bounty, but to us it is both normal and expected. The promise of cheap food sustained American expansionism. For a time, the overharvesting of wild foods such as the passenger pigeon was able to support the hungry urban masses. The continent was rich. But one by one, the wild food stocks were exhausted. Oysters, once a staple food of the rich and poor alike, vanished from the waters near New York. Sturgeon stocks collapsed under pressure from hungry workers seeking hearty steaks of fish and elite diners washing caviar down with champagne. Wetlands were drained; rivers were dammed. Wild things became scarce. Domestic animals had to fill the void. Industrial chicken production relies on wholesale markets and easy transport, but it also requires so much more. The modern chicken is the product of breeders, refrigeration technology, feed companies and pharmaceutical companies. We ate passenger pigeons because they could be had free or for pennies, and we eat chickens because we have developed a system designed to place them on our table for as little money as possible.

The real breakthrough in chicken production occurred in the 1920s, with the development of breeds specifically meant for broiling. Large and fatty, these birds didn't dry out in the oven. Farms began to raise chickens in rural areas for shipment to the big cities of the East Coast. Mrs. Wilmer Steele of Delaware is often cited as the developer of the modern broiler chicken industry, and by 1926, she was raising ten thousand birds at a time, a massive increase over the small flocks of a few dozen birds kept for egg money of the past. One of the key developments was the discovery of synthetic vitamin D, which allowed chickens to be kept inside without a need for sunshine. As this system grew, it became more specialized. Feed production and hatching businesses opened, as did processing centers.

Today, large companies keep farmers on contract, providing the feed, the birds and even equipment. It is a difficult industry with vanishingly small profit margins, but it has radically decreased the price of both chicken and egg. In a few short centuries, we've moved from billions of wild pigeons blotting out the sun to billions of chickens in cages that never see the sun. This system continues to grow as chicken production moves into new regions, but I don't know that we are learning the right lesson. As questions and concerns about factory farming grow — such as the cruelty of overcrowding — and farmers struggle with challenging economics, we can at least look to free-range birds as a better option, even if they do cost more. They even have a little more flavor. But if vat-grown chicken joins the burger in being cheaper than industrially produced chicken, that vat-grown chicken will fill our plates riding the same trend: lower cost. No matter the epoch, when it comes to food, cost wins.

It was time for another extinction dinner, and this time Dan was firmly in charge. Sixteen people were coming, and his kitchen was a riot of preparation. He was busily poaching quail eggs for tiny appetizer versions of eggs Benedict, and he was fretting about having enough food for such a large group of guests.

"Seriously, do we need two? I know it's probably too late, and I have a ton of prep to do, but is one enough?" Dan asked. He was making turducken, a kitchen ordeal that would make chef Ranhofer proud. Organized chaos spilled across the tables and counters and the heat from the ovens radiated through the room.

"One's enough, it's huge. It's frighteningly huge. Is that really one turkey?"

"It was a big turkey. Now help me lift this into the oven."

I grabbed one end of the roasting pan and struggled to keep it level as we maneuvered it into the oven.

"And now we wait."

Turducken is a culinary spectacle consisting of a deboned chicken stuffed into a deboned duck, and then the combination is stuffed into a deboned turkey. It is a nested set of animals tightly packed to create an imposing knot of meat. Turducken is a contemporary spin on an old technique much adored by great chefs through the ages called engastration: the placing of one animal inside the gastric passage of another. It is an almost comical amount of work. Outside of North America, the dish is known as a three-bird roast, but turducken is the regional name for the outlandish creation from the American South. As the dish sizzled in the oven in Dan's grand kitchen, it was clear we wouldn't go hungry. It looked like an oversized football of meat.

With the nested birds safely in the oven, Dan began putting together a complicated turducken rub to go with his intricate turducken baste. The man, still smarting from all of the veggie burgers, was intent on providing all of us with the ultimate bird experience. I was almost surprised and frankly a bit relieved he hadn't found a way to put the whole thing into some larger bird, like an ostrich.

The turducken was popularized by Cajun chef Paul Prudhomme in the late 1980s and follows a long tradition of surprising dinner guests by placing animals inside other animals. Prudhomme claims to have invented the dish, though there is no way to know for sure. However, earlier examples of the technique abound: early gourmet Grimod de La Reynière described, in his 1807 serial culinary text *L'Almanach des gourmands*, a bustard[31] stuffed with a turkey, a goose, a pheasant, a chicken, a duck, a guinea fowl, a partridge, a quail and a few other small birds as well.[32] The first Duke of Talleyrand, a French diplomat and amateur gourmand, was known for putting a quail into a chicken along with an ample handful of truffles. He then slid the nested birds into a turkey, which was still somewhat of a New World novelty in Europe. And such dishes were not only found in Europe; the Inuit of Greenland prepare a dish called kiviak that features a seal stuffed with several hundred birds, which is then fermented for up to eighteen months.

I needed a counterpoint to Dan's turducken and its lavish and loud celebration of bird consumption. In the end I decided to draw on Canadian history and focused on a dish that once required passenger pigeon, the tourtière of Quebec and Acadia. Now based on ground meats (usually pork), the tourtière is popular in Quebec at Christmas and New Year but is available year-round as a ready-made meal. This classic dish, however,

---

31 A grasslands bird found in dryland areas of Europe. They weigh about 20 kilograms.

32 He was disinherited by his father at one point for throwing overly lavish dinner parties.

cannot be made as it once was, for in its original form it was made with passenger pigeons, which were known in Quebec as tourte. The dish is so steeped in history that it is still spiced with cinnamon and cloves, drawing on medieval traditions. I substituted ground pork for the traditional pigeon and was liberal with my medieval spicing. The kitchen filled with a wonderful smell of mulled wine, dancing around the much stronger aroma of Dan's mystery rub wafting from the main oven. We made a few simple salads, plated his cute little eggs Benedict and greeted our guests as they wandered in from the rain.

Anticipation ran high. We nibbled at appetizers and chatted, sneaking glances at the oven. Dan kept everyone's glasses topped and stole away occasionally, meat thermometer in hand. When the beast was finally done, we lifted the turducken onto Dan's biggest maple chopping block and lugged the whole thing to the center of the table. His eyes filled with a twinkle of satisfaction, Dan carved. The turducken was as luxurious as butter. We folded it around the stuffing, paired it with vegetables and lathered it in gravy. Conversation became hushed. This was serious work.

As the evening wore on and the wine flowed, people asked for seconds and thirds and, somehow, the turducken still lorded over the center of the table. The duck fat made the dish work, as it melted and permeated the other two birds. It paired up nicely with the tourtière, but it was a reminder of how heavy meat is. Just because one *can* put one type of meat inside another type of meat, doesn't mean that one *should*. I staggered home through the drizzle, sweating steadily and swearing to stick to a plant-based diet. And with that, it was also time to shift my culinary investigations in an herbaceous direction, towards the world of lost fruits and vegetables.

Section Three

THE
BURNING
LIBRARY

Chapter Eight

THE PEAR KING

The day my appendix burst began with the promise of cranberry tarts. It was mid-September and the farmers were flooding the first of the cranberry bogs to float the ripe berries that they would then skim off of the surface of the water. I was excited to watch, take photos and enjoy some clean air accompanied by local fresh baked goods. My home region, the Lower Mainland of British Columbia, is a leader in global cranberry production, pumping out seventy-five million pounds of the fruit each year. That harvest is about 12 percent of the North American total, enough to accompany a lot of turkey dinners. Thanksgiving and Christmas aside, we don't eat that many cranberries, though the market for the dried fruit is expanding. Most of the harvest goes for juice. The crop has very specific growing requirements, and the harvest is now automated, but cranberry bogs are pretty places filled with springy soils, the smell of herbs and the buzz of bees. I was putting together some course notes on cranberries, and I wanted to get some photos in each of the seasons.

I was excited at the thought of being on a farm, but I'd slept poorly the previous night. My stomach was upset, the odd twinge of pain tickling at my brain. But no matter, a little fresh air was all that I needed. And then, just as my hand closed around my phone as I was walking to the door, a tight stab of pain shot through my abdomen and I sank to the floor.

"Tart," I croaked helplessly. Doubled up, I hit redial, hoping the last person I'd called lived nearby. It was Shannon, who was just finishing a fencing lesson down the street. She drove over, bundled me into the car and noted with little complaint that she'd taken me to the hospital the year before when I'd had an allergic reaction. Perhaps we could think of a better fall ritual?

I remember little about the day. My appendix ruptured a few hours after I staggered through the emergency room doors, fortunately after they had filled me with antibiotics. Doctors removed the tattered remains of the organ, and I spent a few days poking listlessly at hospital food. Once released, and in need of a quiet place to recover, I retreated to the family farm. I was forbidden to travel, forbidden to work. I was grounded.

Watery light spilled onto the bed. I could hear my mother puttering away at small tasks in another room of the cluttered old house I had grown up in. My father, after standing in the doorway with a familiar worried look (I had been a sickly child), wandered outside to the orchard. The smell of burning wood wafted through the air. I was swollen and tired, and at the slightest exertion, my blood pressure would spike. No cranberries, no thinking about extinction, no tart. At least I had the internet.

A familiar voice drifted into my ears. The cat stirred lazily on her patch of blanket and yawned at Dan as he fumbled his way into the room with a large basket of fruit.

"That was a bit more of a drive than I had expected. Certainly quaint out this way. Very quaint, hopefully restful."

"I know you don't like leaving the city."

"I like my nature feral. Is it possible to find a cappuccino out here?"

"The café by the general store does a good one, but it's a bit of a drive."

"No matter. Ted put you together a fruit basket. He was really concerned — I think he might be a bit sweet on you. You look, um, maybe better?"

"Ah, Ted's infamous baskets," I said, straightening up.

Ted is a botanist who specializes in timber trees, but he was developing a Food Network–inspired sideline in exotic fruit baskets. I surveyed this latest effort: a few nice-looking Ambrosia apples, a branch of misshapen witch grapes, a handful of fuzzy rambutans, sumo oranges, a papaya, and a bunch of . . . well . . .

"What are these?" I asked, gingerly holding a cluster of spiky, oblong fruits. They were brown and leathery, about the size of a plum and smelled strongly of lychee and blue cheese. Dan fumbled up a small card from the basket which served the same purpose as the guide to a proper chocolate assortment. There were sketches and descriptions of each fruit.

"Snake fruit. Which makes sense, because the skin really is kind of like a snake's. Should we try them?"

"They're food, right? Not garnish?"

Dan shrugged, and we slowly peeled away the reptilian coating to reveal a translucent jelly-like fruit shaped like a clove of garlic. They tasted of guava and pear, maybe with a touch of lychee, and they were extremely juicy. The pit was very large, and the meat of the fruit pulled away easily. My mouth filled with a lingering astringency. A tiny hint of the smell of onions hung in the room.

"I think I need something a little more on the tame side. What else should I eat?" I spun the basket around and found a few perfectly ripe Bartlett pears hiding on the other side. The Bartlett is one of the most popular pears in the world, valued for its buttery flesh and uniform size. Outside my window, my father's ripe Bartletts hung on bent limbs, as they did on countless trees around the world. I took a large bite and felt a sense of familiar satisfaction.

Happily munching, I googled the snake fruit. Also known as the salak, it is the fruit of a palm tree native to Indonesia. The salak and the pear. One exotic, one familiar. The pear, I decided then and there, would be my next focus, for it is an excellent lens for understanding the transition from a regional food system to an industrial one and what we have lost along the way. We have a wider range of culinary species available to us at all times of the year than ever before, yet variety within food species is dropping rapidly. There were once thousands of pear varieties, but now only a dozen or so are common. In an age where snake fruit can land on my bedside table, where have all the pears of the past gone?

I grew dozy in the sunshine. Dan paced the room, anxious to get outside to look for rats and such.

"There's a skunk in the ravine if you know where to look. And my parents will feed you if you like."

His eyes brightened. "I like skunks. Maybe it has a den. And I could use a little lunch."

We are almost entirely dependent on plants. Plants bathe in the sun, capturing energy they then pass up the food chain to our tables. Many of the plants we rely upon emerged at the end of the Cretaceous period, after mass extinction cleared away the great ferns and made space for grasslands and angiosperms, the flowering plants and trees that quickly dominated the ravaged planet. Broadleaf forests flourished, their boughs heavy with a riot of fruit in every shape and size.

Fruit defines us. Our vision sharpened to spot the colors of ripe fruit, our hands became dextrous to pick them and our bodies adjusted to the quick energy rush of sugar. We became generalists in our eating patterns. No single plant has all of the amino acids we need, so we learned to graze on a wide variety of fruits, roots, stems and leaves. Nature became our buffet. Roughly two million years ago, our ancestor *Homo erectus* discovered fire, allowing us to unlock the energy in roots, tubers and rhizomes and also allowing us to cheat some of the chemical defenses of the plants around us. Heat can break down poisons and toxins, leading to fewer upset stomachs. We even learned to like some of these defense mechanisms, seeking out spicy and unusual plants as well as those that alter consciousness. We are creatures of the Paleolithic, our diet today still echoing the megafauna and wealth of fruits and vegetables that surrounded our ancestors.

Much as domestication has defined our relationship with megafauna, agriculture defines our relationship with plants. Farming was the keystone of the Neolithic revolution, emerging around ten thousand years ago in the Fertile Crescent, the Mesopotamian lowlands and China's Yangtze Valley. Other societies, including the Pacific Islanders and the peoples of Central America, developed their own agricultural technologies a few millennia later.

Globally, our agricultural techniques vary, but ultimately, farming is about disturbing an ecosystem and managing the result. This began gradually — first, we simply removed plants we didn't want from patches of useful foraging species, encouraging managed stands of useful wild plants. We learned to clear areas with fire to encourage the valuable species that appear in the aftermath of a natural disturbance, often burning areas on a regular schedule. We then graduated to moving plants from place to place and shaking seed heads over disturbed ground to propagate new patches. Eventually, we began keeping seeds from the best plants and sowing them anew, sometimes carrying the seeds long distances.

As seed savers, we could accelerate the natural process of evolution. We chose the seeds of some individual plants over others, keeping the best tasting and the most vigorous. We carried water to our favorite plants, and then as the centuries passed, we began irrigating by channeling natural water sources into our fields. We domesticated animals to use for labor, and we learned to control pests by excluding them, trapping them and repelling them. As we farmed, we noticed our labors exhausted the soil, and so we began leaving fields to "rest" for a year, and we started adding manure as fertilizer even though we didn't understand exactly what we were doing. We discovered that some cover crops[33] improved soil health and that special substances, such as lime, enhanced certain crops. We advanced our experiments with genetics and isolated desired plants and encouraged them to crossbreed with each other to enhance the traits we liked. Eventually, we developed, as mentioned earlier, the ability to synthesize fertilizers, and we developed chemicals to kill weeds and pests. We planted vast monocultures to maximize the yield of individual species. Now, thousands of years later, we have learned to grow plants and animals indoors, and we can tailor species at the genetic level.

---

33 Cover crops are non-food crops planted in fallow fields to protect soil from erosion and improve soil health. We now know many of them naturally fix nitrogen into the soil.

I've spent a lifetime studying agriculture, but this paragraph sums up ten thousand years of our most important activity. The rest is nuance. It's still all about managing a patch of disturbed ground.

We chose our plants carefully, as they represent both a huge investment in time and effort and a significant risk, given that a failed harvest can lead to starvation and death. Plants that have been domesticated multiple times have fruits and seeds that are easily stored or leaves that can be harvested over a long season. Recall that we eat only a tiny fraction of the 300,000 or so plants available. Domesticating a plant is difficult. Before modern technologies, centuries went into taking a single plant and making it palatable. Wild carrots were tough and bitter. Melons were mostly seeds and empty space. Pears were sandy and tough. We worked carefully to choose only the plants that best thrived in the local micro-climate, and we kept the best seeds of each generation, as well as chance mutations that offered desirable features. The act of domesticating a few hundred plants over thousands of years was extremely hard work.

The revolution that took us from pigeon hunters to industrial chicken producers also overturned millennia of agricultural practice. The biggest disruption came with the development of chemical fertilizers, but equally important were massive improvements in transportation, irrigation, refrigeration and mechanization. Before global transport, fruits and vegetables were seasonal. We stretched the availability of fresh fruits and vegetables through encouraging varietals that ripened at different times as well as with greenhouses and other forms of sheltering, and we developed elaborate preservation methods for each crop. We salted; we dried; we canned; we root cellared. Every region produced as much variety as possible to ensure supply.

The rise of global transport has created a sort of endless summer. With imports available to us all year long, we have concentrated locally on growing those crops that are the most productive and well-suited for travel. We produce some for ourselves but most for economic gain through export. This has been, in some ways, a good thing, as global hunger has decreased and food costs have plummeted. But the unintended consequence of this shift was a massive burst of culinary extinction.

To understand exactly what we have lost in our quest for efficient and uniform agricultural production, we need to review some terminology. Plant species are subdivided in a few different ways, but for our purposes, a species is the basic unit of biological classification and can be defined as the largest group of organisms in which two individuals can produce fertile offspring. However, when it comes to crop species, we need to make finer distinctions. After all, cabbage, broccoli, cauliflower, brussels sprouts and collards are all the same species, *Brassica oleracea*. In botany, we divide species by varieties, a formal definition that often gets confused with other agricultural terms. Varieties are distinct in appearance but will hybridize freely with each other. To add to the confusion, the term *variety* also has legal standing in the world of plant law, aimed at giving a kind of copyright protection to plant breeders and their specific product.

The correct term for culinary varieties is cultivar, a class of a plant selected for desirable characteristics that can be maintained during propagation. It is the most basic classification for crops and should be used instead of variety. The very word implies human agency; cultivars have been cultivated to better suit human needs over centuries of manipulation and selection. A cultivar must be distinct, uniform and stable, and their continued existence requires human interference.

The name of the cultivar is often appended to the species name, and many of our agricultural crops carry such triple monikers. For example, broccoli is classified in the *italica* cultivar group of the species *Brassica oleracea*. The pear I plucked from Ted's basket is known as *Pyrus communis* 'Williams' (the Bartlett was originally known as the Williams pear, but more on that later). The idea of the cultivar stretches back to the fourth century BCE and the Greek philosopher Theophrastus, the father of botany. He recognized that as humans selected the best plants from each generation, discrete categories of organisms were created. The actual word as we use it now was coined at Cornell University by horticulturalist Liberty Hyde Bailey in 1923. He found the use of the word *variety* sloppy, and he wanted something more precise. Cultivar is a portmanteau of "cultivated" and "variety," and it is the building block of agriculture. When you put a plant in your mouth and it didn't come directly from the wild, you are eating a cultivar.

A further distinction helps us understand a fundamental difference between small-scale local production and the larger global agricultural system. Cultivars come in two broad categories: the landrace and the hybrid.

A landrace is a domesticated traditional cultivar of a species of plant developed over time through adaptation to the local natural and cultural agricultural environment while isolated from other populations of the species. The Icelandic cattle from the first chapter are a landrace, though, as they are animals instead of plants, we call them a breed rather than a cultivar. Landraces have broad genetic variety among individuals, yet they are distinctive and identifiable and have adapted over time to regional climate, disease and pests. They are, by definition, tied to a specific geographical area and thus they underpin many culinary traditions.

By contrast, a hybrid is the result of the deliberate combining of qualities of different cultivars or even species in order to bring out desired genetic effects. *Lactuca sativa capitata*, commonly known as iceberg lettuce, is such a cultivar. It was bred over several decades, beginning in the 1890s, to maximize crunch and plant density. This was a concerted effort, but as with human children, hybrids can exhibit characteristics that are not dominant in the parents. Some of our best cultivar varieties were accidental mutations, such as barley with six rows of seed instead of two.

Hybridity between populations has greatly increased as we actively work to create new hybrids with desirable features. But this can backfire. Pollen can travel between farms, and these fertile hybrids can overwhelm nearby local parent species, causing them, specifically landraces, to go extinct. Our reliance on hybridization has thinned genetic diversity, as hybrids tend to vary little in genetic makeup.

A few particularly prolific hybrids have come to dominate in almost every crop category and, as a result, countless cultivars, particularly landraces, have vanished. Essentially what we have done is this: we have developed very productive hybrid cultivars that flourish across a broad region. We then export that crop cultivar to the world, using our efficient transportation system. Those cultivars are fertile and spread, overwhelming the local landraces. The creation of those landraces was a process that took two thousand years of hard work to complete, but it's taken our industrial agricultural practices only a century or so to destroy them. Think of a great library of flavors. For the last century we have been recklessly burning all of the books.

I won't sugarcoat this. When it comes to fruits and vegetables, we have access to only a fraction of the diversity that existed a century ago. We've lost between 90 and 95 percent of named vegetable cultivars and 80 to 90 percent of fruit cultivars. This destruction greatly limits what we find on our table. If we compare the list of modern cultivars to the 1903 USDA master list of available seeds, we have lost 97 percent of the list cultivars of asparagus, all cultivars of broccoli available at the time, 93 percent of the listed carrots, nine out of ten corn cultivars, 95 percent of cucumbers and onions and radish cultivars. It is true we likely don't really need 463 different radishes, but some of the lost ones were likely interesting, and at the time they were valued. Five hundred varieties of lettuce shrank to thirty-six, and while tomatoes did somewhat better as so many people grow them in the home garden, they still declined by 80 percent. We went from 500 varieties of cabbage to twenty-eight, and 86 percent of apple cultivars vanished, as did 87 percent of pears. Compared to a century ago, our kitchen garden looks very bare.

Losses in other regions of the world are somewhat less pronounced but equally disturbing. Italy once boasted eight thousand distinct cultivars of fruit species and now has only two thousand, and 1,500 of those face extinction. In Britain, there are still 200 cultivars of gooseberries, but during the gooseberry craze of the early nineteenth century, which saw clubs of well-dressed members of the aristocracy gather to trade cuttings and discuss new flavors, there were over 700 in shades of yellow, white, blue, black, striped and the more familiar green and red.[34]

Given these losses and given how much we value diversity in our food, we have to wonder what could possibly have caused us to throw away so many cultivars. This loss can be placed largely at the feet of the shift from local seasonal production

---

34 I like to picture lords in top hats with small silver spades lovingly inspecting their newest find, even though I can't recall the last time I actually ate a gooseberry.

to a global food system. For almost all of human history, we grew landraces suitable to our regions. Because plants fruit or mature at set times of year, we also had to maintain a wide set of landraces with different maturation times. Every microclimate needed slightly different cultivars, tuned to provide a harvest over the widest period of time possible. In the case of the pear, local cultivars fruited from the earliest summer to midwinter. We ate seasonally but stretched seasons with cultivars and with clever means of preservation. We had good reason to shift away from using such a system exclusively, but we need to acknowledge what has been lost.

Pears are my favorite fruit. I like the first pears of the season. I like pear crisp with sugar oat topping. I like the tiny Seckel pears that sometimes appear in the market, I like the perfection of a pear at its prime and I love the clever things we do with pears to store them through the year. I make pear jelly each year, and sometimes bottle pear halves in their juice to warm up with a little cream on cold winter nights. One winter in New York, I treated myself to the pears glacé at Russ & Daughters, one of the last great appetizer shops of the Lower East Side. They are best known for their lox, but I adored their fruit preserved through boiling in sugar solution, a method invented in Arabia in the fourteenth century. I ate the sticky sweet fruit with a little ice cream.

Fruit is our first forbidden love, and it is designed to beguile. The future of any fruiting species depends upon desire. Fruiting trees are sexual beings, a fact that caused a scandal when it first became widely known. The Bible took a chaste view of plant life, being clear on "like begetting like" and, as the apostle Paul says in Galatians 6:7, "Whatsoever a man soweth, that shall he also reap."

However, as most gardeners know, this isn't true. I suppose Paul never encountered a mystery squash sprouting in his compost heap. Fruit starts as a flower, and these flowers come in both male and female versions. Carl Linnaeus described flowers as numerous women in bed with the same man, a view that was received about as well as one might expect by polite society. Equally unpopular with the Church, German botanist Rudolf Camerarius published the luridly titled *Letter on Plant Sex* in 1694, describing his experiments with the sex life of grain. Augustinian friar Gregor Mendel came to similar conclusions in the 1850s as he experimented with peas in a walled garden. He mapped out exactly how offspring expressed their parents' traits, discovering dominant and recessive genes. Fruit is, in effect, a plant egg, ready to hatch into something new. And whenever one of the eighty thousand or so edible fruiting species produces offspring, we can get something very close to the parent plant, or mutation or hybridization might produce a surprise. Humans have sometimes watched this process from the sidelines and others have actively helped it along. An old Welsh proverb sums up the sexual magic of fruit nicely; a seed hidden in the heart of an apple is an orchard invisible.

Consider the pear. *Pyrus communis* is one of the oldest temperate fruits, its origin found at the eastern end of the trading routes between Asia and Europe. Recall for a moment the shifting sands on the fringes of the Roman Empire. The Tian Shan mountains, source of griffin lore, are the likely source of the pear as well. The mountains boasted plentiful water and a staggering abundance of wild fruit and are the source of many of our great temperate fruits, including pears, apples, peaches and quince, as well as the drupe fruit *Prunus dulcis*, whose seeds we know as almonds. The Tian Shan mountain range is the source of so many of our food species that the region is a strong candidate for the location origin of the story of the Garden of Eden.

The thick forests and plentiful waters must have seemed other-worldly to early travelers. The exotic fruits fell to the ground in drifts, each tree slightly different. Apples the size of grapefruits; apples with red flesh; apples the size of walnuts. And pears, of course. Travelers, always on the lookout for something of value, gathered the best fruit for their horses and for themselves. In the case of the pear, the fruit moved east and west to China and Europe, respectively. The fruits of the Tian Shan dominate our grocery stores thousands of years later, simply because the ancestors of these fruits were well located.

The pear was valued even in ancient times for its flavor and texture, and it was domesticated in both Europe and China. Today the pear is the fifth-largest fruit crop, thanks in part to those early travelers. There are twenty-three known wild species of pear in two broad categories: the elongated pear of Europe and the round crisp pear of Asia. They are part of the Rosaceae or rose family, which contains thousands of species, including the temperate pome fruits[35] that require warm sunny summers and cold winters to induce a winter dormancy and then spring budding and flowering. Pear flowers do not smell like roses, but if one inhales the perfume of an apple blossom, the family link is clear. Pears are one of the hardier pome fruits, standing up well to disease and poor conditions. These tall oblong trees are found in both hemispheres in areas with temperate climate and are thriving far from the mountains of the Tian Shan.

Early humans gathered fruit where they could find it, but as we settled down in fixed locations, we began to purposely plant and improve fruits. Early fruits we cultivated included the mango and the sweetsop, but we quickly diversified to grow other juicy sweet fruits like the pear and the apple, starchy fruits like

---

35 Any fleshy fruit in the Rosaceae family that contains a core and seeds.

the banana and oily fruits like the avocado and the coconut. By the Paleolithic period, the pear was already radiating away from its mountain home, where it grew wild on sunny rocky slopes. Humans literally carried pears around the world. Scrubby trees sprouted from discarded cores on the edges of early Neolithic fields, and some pear species are still very close to their wild ancestors, such as the European snow pear, which is a key fruit for perry,[36] providing a central element of bitter flavor from its gritty fruit. The *Pyrus communis*, or common European pear, was first domesticated about 2500 years ago, joining a collection of early fruits such as olives, dates, pomegranates and grapes. However, wild pears have been found in Neolithic compost heaps and written records mention pears as early as 2000 BCE. Mass plantings of pears existed in what is now Iran. On the other side of Eurasia, the Asian pear with its crisp flesh and round shape developed from early stock that traveled the trade routes of the Silk Road, along with grapes, sesame, peas, onions, coriander and cucumber, and was flourishing in the Yangtze Valley by 1000 BCE. Asian pears and European pears can still crossbreed; the result is the Chinese fragrant pear, which is a small, oblong fruit with the heavy perfume of its Chinese parent.

The pear as we know it in Europe today began to emerge in Greece, where it was a dominant fruit. Southern Greece was once called Apia, or pear land, and the fruit was treated as a noble food. Early Greek orchardists laboriously multiplied their stock by digging up root sprouts or bending limbs into the ground to propagate new trees. Homer called pears a gift from the gods, and the Greeks embraced this gift, making the first attempts at breeding the fruit for improved quality. The Greek scholar

---

36 Pear cider. Basically, if humans can ferment something into alcohol, they do and always have.

Theophrastus wrote about pears in 320 BCE, suggesting that the different types of pears should have their own names and that the cultivated pears were exhibiting different traits from wild ones. He named three cultivars, beginning a long tradition of ordering pears by traits such as color, season and flavor.

By 400 BCE, the techniques of grafting to produce clones emerged, a technology perfected in Rome and still used today. Grafting involving cutting a sprig from one tree, and splicing it into another so that the living cambium layers touch. The wound heals, and the new sprig grows. These techniques were needed, as every seed in every pear creates a unique tree; if one finds a pear tree of excellent quality, the only way to continue the mutation beyond the fifty-year lifespan of the original tree is to create an exact copy.[37] Historian and politician Cato the Elder, who lived in 200 BCE, described the propagation, grafting, pruning and caring for the trees, and cataloged six cultivars of pear. A few centuries later, Roman orchardists were cultivating at least forty cultivars. And their product was increasingly in high demand.

The Romans adored pears. Pears of the time weren't like the pears of today; they were firmer and slightly sandy in texture. The Romans worked around this by cooking them for long periods of time in wine and in honey, a method that remains enchanting today. The wealthy elite ate the best pears, and the rest of the harvest was dried. The poor even ground them into a powder and mixed them with flour. The pears of Rome were smaller and tougher than today's varieties, but they were still popular enough to travel to every corner of the empire. Their pleasing shape appears in mosaics and other surviving Roman

---

37 For some crops, this is carried to the extreme. Almost all commercial bananas are from identical clones of one plant. So if you feel déjà vu while eating your lunch, you have good reason.

art, and they grew in the gardens of grand villas, often lining decorative waterways. Throughout the ancient world, fruit trees were highly valued, and several societies had strict prohibitions against destroying them, even in a time of war. The Babylonian *Code of Hammurabi*, for example, prescribed a fine of a half mina of silver for the destruction of an orchard tree, which is about nine troy ounces of metal.[38] Orchards were considered to be special places, and it is no wonder that the word paradise comes from the old Persian "Pairi-deaza," a term for a walled enclosure of fruit trees.

Pears are a complicated fruit. For centuries, we have complained about their frustratingly small window of ripeness; enjoying them requires a certain amount of skill and guesswork. On the tree, they rot from the inside out, and so one must pick them slightly green. To pick a pear, you have to gently lift it, and if the stem snaps free, it is ready to come inside. Not ready to eat, mind you, but to come inside. The pears then ripen slowly, though the process is faster if they are stacked gently with their fellows (they give off ethylene gas, which speeds the ripening of fruit). And, after what seems to be an eternity, their hard flesh turns to butter, their fragrance fills the room and they become, in my opinion, perfection. A day later, they are compost. This magic, this fleeting moment, made pears a noble fruit, a rare treat worth praise that still echoes through the ages.

The Romans continued the long process of improving the pear while enjoying them at every opportunity. Their *conviviums* highlighted locally grown foods, and pears played a starring role. In Pompeii, a mosaic features a pear tree in fruit, and pear orchards grew within the walls, not far from the pomarius, or fruit market. By Pliny's time in the first century, some thirty-five

---

38 About $320 American dollars at the time of writing.

cultivars were in common production, including ones named for color (the Purpurea) or aroma (the Myrappia) and some for their season (barley pears, for example, ripen at the same time as barley). Romans also began making perry in volume, as well as pear vinegar. They prized the honey taken from bees located in pear orchards for its hint of fruit flavor.[39] They also carried pear seedlings to the frontier, where they would take root and outlast the empire that adored them.

The pear emerged from the decline of the Roman Empire as the queen of European fruits. Joan Morgan, author of *The Book of Pears*, calls them the most exciting of tree fruits because of their creamy flesh and complicated aromatics, and these are traits that really came into their own during the Renaissance. Medieval pears were mostly tough winter varieties that built on Roman rootstock and were best eaten after they were baked in the coals of the kitchen fire. But pears thrived in cool regions such as Britain and France, where they were improved further through crossbreeding with related wild European species. France and Belgium developed some of the world's best-known pears, including Bosc and Anjou, still available today, a testament to the skill of their breeders.

As pear breeding increased in popularity, an obsession developed with one texture in particular: that of butter. Most pears remained sandy in texture, and breeders began working to produce a pear one could spread with a knife.

The number of pear cultivars exploded, with new buttery fleshed fruit dominating firmer cultivars, shifting pears to an eating fruit from a cooking fruit. By the seventeenth century, there were three clear categories of pear: those for cooking (sandy and crisp), those for making perry (bitter and astringent) and

---

39 Roman doctors also prescribed pears as a cure for diarrhea.

those for eating fresh (soft and fragrant). Among the rich and powerful, pears for the table became a bit of an obsession, and then a mania. Great orchards were laid out at castles and monasteries alike. In Italy, a new course was added to the midday meal that paired fruit and cheese, creating a showcase for the pear that remains enjoyable today. The science of pears advanced as well; Valeris Cordus, a German botanist, set out a formal system for distinguishing pears by shape, color and other characteristics, and he began a long tradition of sketching fruit for reference. He categorized fifty or so cultivars, but this collection was about to get much larger. In France, in one of the most lavish courts of all time, a fruit-crazed king had a mission: to eat a fresh pear every day of the year.

Louis XIV, the Bourbon Sun King, was a proponent of the divine right of rulers, the architect of a unified centralized France and a total freak for pears. As an absolute monarch, he believed it was not unreasonable to demand a perfectly ripe pear in any season. Fortunately, his master gardener Jean-Baptiste de La Quintinie was probably the only man in France more deeply obsessed with pears than the king. At Versailles, de La Quintinie created a twenty-five-acre fruit garden to feed the palace, a task requiring the draining of a swamp and the carting of excellent soil from the Satory hills. Pears dominated the grand square of this Potager du roi, and de La Quintinie used stone walls to create microclimates to stretch the seasons. He assembled an unprecedented 500 cultivars of pear but reluctantly conceded that only about thirty had the buttery quality loved by the king and court and prized by breeders. He worked to improve this velvet quality, and his trees inspired a frenzy not unlike the tulip mania in the Netherlands. The king likely never did get a perfect pear every day, but he loved the orchard so much that de La Quintinie taught him pruning techniques, and visitors were occasionally shocked and terrified to find the King of France busily trimming a pear tree. For his part, de La Quintinie never lost his love of pears, stating, "It must be confessed that, among all fruits in this place, nature does not show anything so beautiful nor so noble as this pear. It is pear that makes the greatest honor on the table."

From the gardens of Versailles and other great houses, pear varieties radiated throughout Europe. The market gardens surrounding cities such as Paris grew pears in the Versailles style, in which the trees were trained to hug garden walls, creating a valuable crop that took up little space. People from all walks of life spent years trialing new cultivars with the elusive but valued textures prized by the aristocracy. In this environment of frenzied breeding and experimentation rose a man poised to challenge both de La Quintinie and the king himself as the most pear-obsessed orchardist to ever live. His name was Jean Baptiste Van Mons, and he is now known as the Edison of Pears.[40]

Jean Baptiste Van Mons was born in Brussels in 1765, and he lived to be a physicist, chemist, botanist, horticulturalist and pomologist. In his early years, he desired a career in politics, but he lacked the subtle touch required to thrive and stay alive in the cut and thrust of French political life during the revolution. In 1790, he was arrested for treason, and during a three-month stint in a dark and flooded cell, he decided that the life of the mind might suit him better. He went on to become the most prolific pear breeder in history, producing

---

40 Technically Edison should be known as the Van Mons of electricity as he was born later, but history isn't always fair.

forty superior cultivars, including the Bosc and the Anjou. He shared his methods widely and exported cuttings to the far corners of the world. His success came from selective breeding and patience. His method was intensive yet simple. "To sow, to re-sow, to sow again, to sow perpetually, in short to do nothing but sow, is the practice to be pursued, and which cannot be departed from; and in short this is the whole secret of the art I have employed."

Van Mons was one of the first breeders to notice the importance of incorporating a diverse gene selection into his trees. He noticed that the old classic varieties dropped off in quality and vigor over the years, suggesting that each species has a lifespan. He found through trial and error that the usefulness of a cultivar can be extended by an infusion from a wild variety. We now know this isn't exactly true; what he was observing was the vulnerability of clones to disease and pests, and breeding in wild resistance provided much needed immunity. Van Mons produced and named over 800 seedlings to gather his forty or so "stars," a record aided by his illustrious side career as one of history's greatest pear thieves. He built his collection voraciously and offered owners of prized cultivars high sums for their trees. If he was turned down, he would return in the night with his crew and steal the entire tree. As a well-known professor, he became a bit of a pear celebrity, and his new varieties sparked waves of pear fever. This fever reached new heights in England and America.

It's not hard to fathom why everyone became so excited about pears and why the pears began to epitomize elegance in the upper strata of society. They've been described as a symbol of the ethereal and were given as gifts, sometimes in great numbers. They were exchanged by lovers as a sign of desire. The "partridge in a pear tree" from the Christmas carol "Twelve Days of Christmas" is the ultimate expression of that desire, though it is an inconvenient gift for both giver and receiver. Many great collections were destroyed during the French Revolution, but England's monasteries and great houses continued to propagate new varieties of pear, and the merchant class began planting what were called "impyards," orchards of trees grown from seed that might or might not prove useful. Planting pear seed is a lottery ticket. The resulting tree will usually be poor but could be excellent. The supply of pears too bitter or tough to eat helped fuel the revival of perry, as imp pears were used as feedstock for cider presses.

The nineteenth century saw the number of pear cultivars explode. With easy railway travel available, trading pear cultivars became a major hobby, and thousands of new varieties were named by enthusiastic orchardists who ranged from farmers to priests and lawyers to nobles. Some pear growers became local celebrities. The London Horticultural Society became a critical record keeper, tasting and logging new and promising discoveries. In 1816, they were presented with what would become the most popular pear of all time: the Williams Bon Chrétien, which was soon renamed Bartlett. It was quickly given its own pomona, or fruit portrait. The crafting of pomona developed as orchardists struggled to tell the ever-increasing number of cultivars apart. Books of fruit paintings became a popular accessory, and a fashion of framing striking pomona for display began. As for the Bartlett, this new cultivar was sent off to North America.

In the New World, the pear found an ideal home. The rich soils and crisp, cold winters of the American colony spawned a wave of new pears. North America experienced several shortages of fruit as populations grew faster than orchards could be established, leading to mass attempts to bring new cultivars to the New World. Boston became the center of a "made in America" pear fever. Once again, the quest was on for that ideal pear, free of graininess, with the texture of cream or butter. Merchants and lawyers grew pears on their suburban farms, crossing European cultivars. The elite of Boston flocked to tasting parties. The Massachusetts Horticultural Society socialized and exchanged gossip over wedges of fruit. They held an exhibition each year, and by 1852 it highlighted 310 different pears. The best pears were talked about, admired and sold for lavish sums. Henry David Thoreau wrote: "They are named after emperors and kings and queens and dukes and duchesses. I fear I shall have to wait till we get to pears with American names, which a republican can swallow."

Pear madness is reflected in the writing of Thomas De Voe, the butcher we met in the exploration of the passenger pigeon. He discussed many pear cultivars, noting that only a few commanded a high price. As he walked the great markets of the East Coast, he described Bartletts, Doyennes, Sugar Pears, Bloodgood, Brandywine, Seckels, Buffam, Vicar of Wakefield and multiple beurres. The pear season in New York began in June, but De Voe lamented that the best pears were only available from August to October. A prime Bartlett could command a price of a dollar a pear — for many this was roughly ten hours' wages. De Voe also liked to eat the local Seckel pear, one of my own favorites. It was introduced to New York by a man named "Dutch Jacob," who gathered them from a single tree in the New Jersey woods, eventually to be propagated by a Mr. Seckel. These pears, scarcely bigger than a plum, can still be found in eastern and midwestern grocery stores and markets.

The glamor of the pear, along with its ability to withstand travel after it has been picked, led to a global fruit trade that poured pears into the great cities of the Western world year-round, often wrapped in colored paper and swaddled in cotton. And into this new global pear trade came a pear cultivar that finally captured perfectly the long-sought texture of the superb pear, a pear one could spread with a knife: the Bonne du Puits Ansault.

There are thousands of lost pears, and most of them are not remembered or missed. However, the Ansault is a cultivar that presents us with a puzzle. Raised in an impyard in the nurseries of M. André Leroy in Angers France, the Ansault was a marvel. When the misshapen tree fruited for the first time in 1863, the flesh of its fruit was perfect. Knowing a winner when he saw it, André propagated the tree in 1865, and the American Pomological Society listed the variety in 1877, once it was proven the trees could be propagated. The name was shortened in 1883. In *The Pears of New York*, written in 1917, U.P. Hendrick wrote, "the flesh is notable, and is described by the word buttery, so common in pear parlance, rather better than any other pear. The rich sweet flavor, and distinct but delicate perfume contribute to make the fruits of highest quality." The pear itself wasn't perfect. It was medium to large and oblate, yellow in color when ripe and covered with russet. The flesh, however, was magical. It was white, juicy, tender and aromatic, and its arrival was met with excitement when it ripened in early autumn. At the University of Tennessee's Agricultural Experimental Station in 1890, they praised the fine juicy flesh and noted the tree was irregular but extremely vigorous. Upon first encountering the pear, Henry Williams of the American Pomological Association remarked that it was "one of the most delicious pears from abroad in many years." One would expect such a wonder to be popular today, found in gardens and orchards, prized by chefs and widely available in stores. Alas, it is not. The Ansault vanished.

What happened to the Ansault? It is listed as extinct or missing in pear catalogs, when it is listed at all. We have several excellent paintings of the pear and a collection of rave reviews.

That's it. The Ansault did have a flaw — Hendrick noted the trees, so irregular and misshapen, were not suitable for orchard use. But in an earlier era, farmers would have worked on the trees, preserving the buttery flesh and excellent taste while breeding in hardier stock. This did not happen. By the late nineteenth century, the world was shifting to commercial orchards, particularly in California, where pears were grown in the central valley in a new way. Railways brought nursery stock in bulk, and Bartlett, Bosc and Anjou pears blanketed the newly irrigated landscape. Great canneries captured the excess harvest, changing the way that America ate fruit. An icon of this era is Del Monte's fruit cocktail of pears, peaches and cherries, introduced in 1938. The sweet preparation stripped some of the glamor from fruit but could be released from its can at a moment's notice, whatever the season.

People stopped planting the Ansault, and nurseries stopped propagating it. Remnant trees died in forgotten orchards or were cut down as cities expanded into farm country. Pear trees are not as long-lived as their cousin the apple, so it is unlikely at this point that an Ansault tree will ever be discovered in some forgotten orchard corner. This is a shame. I'd like to spread an Ansault pear onto toast with a knife and see what all the fuss was all about.

Chapter Nine

LIFE IS SHORT,
WE MUST HURRY

I was brooding. A month had passed, and I was still tired, sore and unable to travel to pursue extinct foods. I was especially missing the extinction dinners. Thankfully, Dan sensed my disappointment and trekked back to the farm for a pear-centric culinary interlude on a much smaller scale. He had somehow sweet-talked my mother into giving up her kitchen for an afternoon and arrived carrying a lovely selection of pears. He brought Bartlett, Anjou, Bosc and Comice, arranging them in an artful pyramid on the long kitchen counter.

"No Seckel pears for you, alas. I looked around, but they aren't available anywhere, I'm afraid."

"These are wonderful. What are we doing with them?"

"I thought we could prepare pears a few different ways. I want to make something a little unusual," Dan said, as he continued to unpack ingredients.

"But what on earth is this for? It has . . . things . . . in it." I held up a menacing bottle of murky brown liquid.

He smiled, took the bottle and swirled its cloudy contents.

"I know you can't travel right now, so I thought we could visit ancient Rome through cuisine. Now let me do the work."

Dan took command of the kitchen, evicted the cat from the counter and began making "pears patina." The Romans ate pears in a wide variety of ways, including as dishes that served as foundations for their mensa secunda, or second meal, the ancestor of our modern-day dessert course. These follow-up courses included familiar items such as fruit, olives and cheeses, or perhaps an egg dish.

Roman dinner parties were long affairs. Sometimes the mensa secunda didn't appear until dawn. However, we were going to have dessert first. Dan used Bosc pears, as they are firm and stand up well to handling. To make a Roman patina, Dan grated the pears finely and mixed them with pepper, cumin, honey and a little ice wine (the Romans used passim, or straw wine, a wine made from raisins; ice wine is similar as the frozen grapes have an intense sweetness). He added oil, then grabbed the bottle of sinister liquid. He popped the lid and an unmistakable stench filled the kitchen. It was garum, the sauce made from fermented fish entrails, beloved by the Romans.

"No," I said. "Do not ruin my dessert with that."

"It's a critical ingredient!"

"I've been too sick. I can't handle fermented fish right now."

After some bickering, we compromised and made two batches, one with garum and one delightfully garum-free. To each batch of grated spiced pears, we added eggs and then baked the resulting mixture for twenty minutes at a medium heat. The result was surprisingly modern; the pears shone through, along with the honey and complex spicing. Well, for one batch, at least. The batch with garum tasted of a fish store, or of low tide, or of a bait stand. Even Dan pushed his plate aside.

"Maybe we aren't as much like the Romans as I thought after all."

Dan managed to find four cultivars of pear for our snacking, the same number available to early Roman writers. What could we learn from the great contraction in crop diversity that unfolded in the twentieth century? The losses are anthropocentric in their nature, as the vanished cultivars were created by humans and, ultimately, lost by humans. The twentieth century saw massive shifts in agriculture from a regionally based industry in which evolved landraces were used to provide variety and extend availability to a global system in which one or two hybrid cultivars were grown in vast monocultures. We didn't even pick winners based on flavor. We focused on shelf life, uniformity and durability during transport.

This contraction reached its nadir in North America in the 1970s and 1980s. The grocery stores of my childhood were barren places. The lettuce, all of the lettuce, was iceberg. There was one sort of cucumber, the green ones that terrify cats. Oranges were all the same, as were bananas.[41] Peppers were either green or red, and neither variety was at all spicy. And apples were largely divided between Red Delicious and Granny Smith. I suppose the latter is edible, sort of. But the former, to me at least, was the stuff of nightmares. By the 1970s, the Red Delicious was mealy and dry, with a bitter skin and flesh almost totally devoid of any flavor. I was disappointed by them so often that I'm still suspicious of apples in general.

It wasn't always so. The first Delicious tree was a random imp that appeared in 1880, on the farm of Jesse Hiatt in Peru, Iowa. It was described at the time as a round fruit of surpassing sweetness and a yellowish hue. Stark Brothers Nursery and

---

41   This is still true of bananas.

Orchards began to market the tree, and one of their early scions (trees established to grow grafting material) grew a single limb that bore deep red apples. From this limb, we have produced more apple trees than from any other limb in history. By the 1980s, when I was taking the Red Delicious apples from my lunch and tossing them into the woods, this single variety made up three-quarters of the harvest in Washington State. And why not? They are uniform and have a tremendously long shelf life.

Luckily, a new trend was about to sweep North America. We were about to rediscover the magic of taste.

The 1980s saw a sharp increase in culinary complexity in North America and around the globe, radiating from multiple centers of origin. Worried about the loss of their culinary culture, the Japanese embraced the chisan-chisho (produce local, consume local) movement. The Slow Food movement, founded in Italy to protest the expansion of multinational fast food outlets at the expense of local cuisine, spread across Europe. And in North America, visionaries such as chef Alice Waters of Berkeley's Chez Panisse were crafting California cuisine using a dizzying array of produce from hundreds of small farms. North America was ready for better-tasting products and more choice.

Better apple cultivars reappeared. The Red Delicious apple, which Sarah Yager called the largest compost maker in the country in a 2014 *Atlantic Monthly* article, now makes up only one-quarter of Washington State's apple harvest, and it is even less popular in other apple-producing regions. It is a minor cultivar in China, which focuses on the Fuji, a crisp and flavorful apple. Consumers have embraced new-to-us tastes and, to a lesser extent, are also embracing the seasonality that helps build a diverse agricultural sector. The return of local, seasonal fruit is in part linked to the movements mentioned above, but also to the unexpected return to popularity of local farmers' markets.

Seasonality, the consumption of foods during the time of year in which they are ready for harvest, has lingered in part because cultural memory associates certain foods with a time of year.

Traditionally, we find seasonality in every culture that is far enough from the equator to experience clearly defined seasons, and a Cornell University study showed that North Americans are very likely to consume certain foods when they are in season, such as greens, berries, pumpkins and corn. My own work suggests we have positive memories associated with seasonal foods but also that their existence can improve health outcomes. Local foods in season taste good, encouraging us to eat more of them, and these fresher foods contain higher levels of vitamins and other nutrients than their aging, imported supermarket counterparts.

I finally started to feel like myself again. Newly up and about, I returned to the Granville Island Public Market, eager to enjoy the best of both the regional and global food systems. There was still fresh local fruit, including the last of the berries. There were blackberries and the first apples of the fall. I could buy, if I wished, dozens of types of lettuce and a wide range of greens unknown in North America even thirty years ago. I could pick up gai lan, a Chinese broccoli cultivar, or rue, an herb as old as the Romans, with delicate leaves and a strong almost soapy scent. There was fresh shiso, a tender Japanese mint that tastes wonderful in lemonade.

It wasn't always so. I still recall the wonder of first trying romaine lettuce. My parents took me to a "cutting edge" restaurant and the waiter made Caesar salad tableside. He took the big wooden bowl and rubbed it with a garlic clove, and then mixed a dressing artfully. I remember him cracking a raw egg into the mixture and finishing the tossed dish with Romano cheese and anchovies. That was pretty exotic stuff for western Canada in 1980.

I moved through the market, dodging the visual arts students snapping photos of the food. I found a few "pink lemonade" lemons, which have naturally pink flesh. I grabbed them, along with the shiso, to slice up and make into a lemonade later. A pie in mind, I also bought some Meyer lemons. A hybrid cross of the citron and a mandarin/pomelo cultivar, the Meyer is sweet and lush with a distinctive mild citrus flavor and slightly orange flesh. They were introduced to the United States in 1908 by Frank Meyer (we will come back to him). The Meyer was made popular by chef Alice Waters in the 1970s and further promoted by Martha Stewart a few decades later. How did Meyer find a new lemon? Where, ultimately, do new fruits come from? That question leads us straight back to the Mountains of Heaven, the Tian Shan. Except this time, we will focus on *Malus pumila*: the apple.

Imagine a treasure hunt. The earth is covered in interesting plants and animals, and some are unbelievably useful. New foods and new medicines wait somewhere over the horizon, still to be discovered. Other wild plants we know well. They are the ancestors of our current crops, and we turn to these wild relations when we need to breed a new cultivar to resist a disease or pest. I called this wealth of biodiversity a library in the previous chapter, and for a good reason; it has much to teach us even now.

As the world's biodiversity declines, we lose the ability to both repair existing crops and create new ones. It is difficult to pinpoint exactly how bad a problem this is, as biodiversity is spread unevenly across the globe. For example, alpine zones[42] cover about 3 percent of the earth's land surface but are home

---

42 These zones are found above the tree line and below the snow line.

to an unusual number of species. Half of the world's biodiversity hotspots are on mountains. Of the twenty plant species that supply 80 percent of the world's food, seven originate from the mountain regions.

We can't be sure how much of this primary diversity we are losing because of this uneven distribution. However, we do know that the earth has lost 10 percent of its tropical forest, another hotspot for biodiversity, in the last twenty-five years alone. And climate change is pushing species into new ranges, ever farther from the equator, as plants migrate to keep up with their preferred climatic conditions.

In the 1920s and 1930s, when a great deal more of the earth's primary forest still stood, Russian botanist Nikolai Vavilov traveled the world to better understand why some areas of the earth are so lush with diversity. Born into a merchant family in Moscow, he grew up listening to his father's stories of life in a poor rural village where crop failures and rationing were common. Vavilov remembered these lessons. Driven to improve the security of the world's crops, he attended the Moscow Agricultural Institute and began an adventurous series of world travels to map the planet's food crops. As his career advanced, he took a post in Leningrad where he led the Lenin All-Union Academy of Agricultural Sciences. He worked to improve wheat and corn crops and pioneered the identification of wild ancestors of crops in order to combine their genes with domesticated relatives, tracing crops to a small number of special areas.

Vavilov realized that some areas of the planet, particularly mountainous areas, contained a vast diversity of niches, little bioregions sometimes no larger than a valley or cliff face. Evolution ensured that plants and animals would adapt to each of these niches, making certain a wondrous diversity would thrive. In his honor, we sometimes call the most biodiverse regions of the globe

Vavilov Zones. On each trip abroad, he collected seeds from a new region of the globe, creating the largest collection of plant genetic material ever assembled. Vavilov's success rested on his ability to take a team of researchers into remote regions and quickly and thoroughly gather material in adverse conditions. He lived by his favorite motto: "Life is short: we must hurry."

In 1929, Vavilov centered his efforts on the apple. Today, apples are the third most popular fruit on earth, behind the mango and the banana, and they play an important symbolic role in almost every culture and religion. Yet until Vavilov strolled into what is now Almaty, Kazakhstan, near the foothills of the Tian Shan, the apple's origin was lost. The town's name translates as "where the apples are," and even today on the nearby foothills of the Mountains of Heaven, thickets of apple trees hang heavily with wild fruit. Vavilov recognized the region as the birthplace of the apple, adding that knowledge to his growing understanding of where the world's crops each originated. Vavilov found wondrous apple trees a hundred feet tall, and dwarf ones standing waist high. Some of the apples were as big as cantaloupes, others no bigger than cherries. Many were inedible, but some were absolute wonders. Several tasted of anise, a flavor I've yet to encounter in a commercial apple. All of these apples are offspring of *Malus sieversii*, the parent tree of the apple. Like pears, each apple seed grows an entirely new cultivar. Vavilov traced the modern apple to a sprawling tangle of forest, and in that tangle he documented the ancestors of 150 other food crops.

You might recall I suggested that the Tian Shan could be the source of the Eden story. This is because no other region has spawned so many major crops. Ultimately, Vavilov described twelve such centers of biodiversity, tracing our food crops to these key areas. There is one in South Asia. There is one in

Ethiopia, one in the spine of South America and one in India. The wild ancestors in these zones gave us our most important crops, and most of these regions, including the Tian Shan, are threatened today. The Soviets cut up to 80 percent of the wild fruit forests down for wood, and though the losses have slowed in recent times, they still continue as the region develops. The last of the wild forests are now preserved in Ile-Alatau National Park, a place I would dearly love to visit so that I might eat an apple that tastes of anise. These forests in eastern Kazakhstan are so important that the USDA has collected over one hundred thousand seeds from the region.

Vavilov's personal story is a sad one. He placed science before politics and managed to get into a fight over pea genetics, a rather unlikely crime. Vavilov believed the understanding of genetic trait inheritance developed by Austrian scientist and monk Gregor Mendel was largely correct. However, a former student of Vavilov, Trofim Lysenko, believed that a contrary theory proposed by Soviet scientists was correct. Lysenko became a favorite of Josef Stalin, and Vavilov's denunciation of Lysenko led to his arrest while he was on an expedition in Ukraine. He was sent to Siberia, where he died of starvation in a gulag at the age of fifty-five. Life is short: we must hurry.

Vavilov's story doesn't end there, however. While he was in Serbia, his great seed collection remained in Leningrad a city under German siege for twenty-eight months during the Great Patriotic War (the Second World War). The Soviets had, in a fit of short-sightedness, evacuated the art from the Hermitage but not the quarter million samples of food crop diversity, which were arguably a much more valuable treasure. Vavilov's old team of scientists understood the importance of the collection and moved them to the basement for protection from the hungry population. Standing guard over a giant buffet of plant matter, nine of the scientists died of starvation before the siege was ended. The seeds lived on, and Vavilov was publicly rehabilitated during the Soviet Union's period of "de-Stalinization." He is now hailed as a hero of Soviet science and lauded by scientists worldwide. Lysenko retained his post after the death of Stalin, but he was widely denounced and largely forgotten in his old age. The refusal of Lysenko and his comrades to accept Mendel's theories contributed to decades of crop shortfalls in the Soviet Union.

I wanted to meet a living, breathing fruit hunter. I sat down with Tom Baumann at Krause Berry Farm, an hour's drive southeast from Vancouver and a suitable venue for the fruit-obsessed. The U-Pick fields were finished for the season, but the corn stand bustled with smiling people in city shoes towing packs of sunburnt children. Customers lined up for the waffle bar and sampled local wines in the replica old-time western saloon. People stocked up on frozen berries and related products. Blueberries, raspberries, strawberries, blackberries. And in the Porch Restaurant, people enjoyed the house specialty: an extraordinarily tall strawberry pie. The pie's crust holds a thick layer of custard and is topped with a mountain of strawberries held in place with a jelly-like glaze. The whole affair is topped with clouds of whipped cream. The staff take a special training session on how to cut the pie without breaking it. I watched my slice jiggle tantalizingly on my plate. Across from me (and my pie), Tom sipped his coffee.

Tom Baumann wears several hats: professor, agricultural expert and farmer. However, he is also a fruit hunter, working on the front lines of culinary exploration. Tom holds master's degrees from German and Canadian universities and is always good for a culinary wonder. He grows miracle berries (*Synsepalum dulcificum*) for his students, an African fruit that chemically alters the function of our taste buds for a short time so that one's brain registers sour tastes as sweet. The last time I wandered past his greenhouses, they were full of papaya. He loves exotic and tropical fruits, and he has strong opinions on fruit flavors.

Tom follows a long tradition of explorers. As early as 1500 BCE, Queen Hatshepsut of Egypt sent a team along South Africa's eastern coast to find new and exciting fruit. William Dampier, a pirate turned botanist, was commissioned by King William III to hunt fruit around the world, and he published an adventure book in 1697, describing his travels in search of pirate gold and exciting snacks. Vavilov blazed his own trail around the world, and Frank Meyer of Meyer lemon fame made repeated trips into the most remote parts of China in search of the next great flavor. No stranger to the perils of plant hunting, Frank Meyer vanished from a steamer in transit between Wuhan and Nanjing in 1918. Tom conducted similar adventures. Back in suburban Canada, I settled in to hear about travel and fruit.

I mentioned to Tom that I was writing about lost cultivars. He winced and started in on a familiar problem: the loss of landraces.

"The loss is painful. So many cultivars lost. It makes me sick," Tom said.

"Me too. I read about these lost fruit cultivars, and I wonder what they were like."

Tom pounded the table, sending my pie wobbling. "Super-crops spread around the world with the patents held by big companies. Western crops are brought into functioning agricultural systems to 'save' farmers, and the result is more pesticides, more fertilizers, new diseases and soil damage. We need to go back to landraces. We are losing the key to sustainable farming."

After agreeing wholeheartedly in between bites of pie, I asked Tom about whether he hunted for new fruits to help counter the loss of old cultivars. And how did he get interested in such an adventurous line of work in the first place? In his case, the passion was long in the making. He became interested in fruit on his great aunt's farm in Germany, where he was picking berries by the age of five and driving the tractor by the age of seven. He toured farms with his father and continued picking berries for money while he was in university, where he wrote a master's thesis on the mechanical harvesting of raspberries. This work brought him to the town of Abbotsford in western Canada, and he enjoyed it so much there that he convinced his whole family to move to the region. He quickly advanced in his government research and consulting work and eventually took his current position at the University of the Fraser Valley as a berry expert in the department of agriculture.

"But," he paused, looking longingly south at the mountains, "fruit hunters always want what they can't have locally."

In his case, this led to a love of the tropics, where he could locate rare breeds of fruit such as strawberry papayas and exotic mangoes in all colors of the rainbow. He explored fruit markets in Hawaii, finding unusual breeds growing on small farms and in people's yards. He is particularly enamored with the allspice and ackee fruit in Jamaica, and he makes regular trips to Florida to study citrus varieties. Tom keeps a private greenhouse of delicate tropical plants carefully protected from the Canadian winters. I listened in wonder. And I thought my apple and pear trees were a lot of work.

I ask Tom the big question: are there really a lot of fruits left out there to bring to the global market?

"Hundreds, at least. Maybe thousands. Entire species, and high-quality ones. Some are still in the jungles and forests, some you find at markets in rural villages."

Tom sees the future of fruit emerging from several poorly cataloged regions, such as pockets of Africa, particularly West

Africa; Papua New Guinea, where hundreds of fruits haven't even been cataloged; and rural Indonesia, Malaysia and China. Many fruits of the Indian subcontinent are largely unknown in the west. He paints me a picture of new flavors, new cuisines, unknown fruit adventures. Spend time in any of these places and you might find something entirely new to Western tastes.

"You know, there is a lot here to draw upon locally as well."

That surprised me. How could British Columbia possibly have culinary secrets to yield? Tom began with an example, describing a fruit I'd never experienced. *Lonicera caerulea*, the haskap or blue honeysuckle, is a large berry native to the cool temperate regions of North America, including the boreal forests of Canada. It is a deciduous shrub that grows about two meters tall, with gentle waxy pale grayish-green leaves. It has a pale dusty blue skin, the flowers are yellowish white, and the fruit is rectangular in shape and between the size of a grape and a blueberry. The word haskap comes from the Indigenous Ainu people of northern Japan, who have enjoyed the berry for centuries. The haskap plant thrives happily in temperatures as low as minus fifty degrees Celsius, a handy trait in a country where temperatures in its northern regions can drop to forty below zero.[43] They ripen even earlier than strawberries and work well in pastries, jams, juice, ice cream, yogurt and candy and are considered to be a superfood, rich in micronutrients and antioxidants. Tom has been working for more than a decade to foster a haskap industry in British Columbia, creating cultivars that thrive in the more temperate climates found around Abbotsford and that are easier to harvest than the wild plants. Taming the haskap is slow, methodical work. He thinks they have a great color and

---

43 I experienced this level of cold once in Calgary. It was enough to encourage me to shift my research towards the equator.

outstanding antioxidant properties, and he believes haskap could easily develop into a profitable addition to local farm fields.

Tom leaned back and promised to invite me to a haskap tasting.

"There are a lot of native plants here that might work as commercial crops. The wild space is still intact; the material is there to find." He laments a lack of government funding for such programs. Taking a wild crop and making it bigger, more flavorful and more reliable takes years of work. "The Indigenous Peoples of these regions grew hundreds of crops using various agricultural techniques. We just didn't see them as crops. It's a huge loss."

I sighed. When Europeans colonized British Columbia, they discounted local agriculture and actively prevented Indigenous people from cultivating and harvesting their local foods.

As I mop up the last of my pie, Tom leaves me with a question. With global trade, everyone wants the same crop, which limits local varieties. Yet the future of small growers is tied to interest in unusual foods. It isn't clear which system will ultimately dominate. How can we preserve the lost foods that remain?

As he leaves, Tom muses about the Ansault pear. It might, he suggests, still be hiding out there. Pear trees live a reasonably long time under ideal conditions, and someone might have taken a cutting of an Ansault, keeping the cultivar alive. Some fruit hunters specialize in rescuing old varieties; somewhere, someone might be looking for the Ansault, and it might still be there to be found.

A few weeks later, Tom invited me to a haskap tasting. His group had turned out haskap jelly and a lovely crisp made with frozen berries topped with brown sugar and rolled oats. The haskap reminds me of the Saskatoon berry. They are juicy and both sweet and tart, with a complex flavor, a tiny bit of waxiness and a touch of astringency. Both berries are a little like blueberries, a fruit I like more and more as I get older. I'd eat haskap berries if they were more widely available. I wondered if they would navigate the hurdles to commercialization, but for the moment, I was content to have had the pleasure of experiencing a new fruit.

After my meeting with Tom, I kept thinking about the potential fruit crops hiding in my own backyard. As children, my friends and I would spend hours playing in the woods, and we would often eat the berries that we had been told were safe. There were so many: blackberries, blackcaps, dewberries, huckleberries, salmonberries, salal berries. There were even tiny little North American wild strawberries. But what other amazing things were hiding in the rainforest on the edge of town, and why weren't we already growing those crops? Why, in short, are the mainstays of our supermarkets the classic grains, vegetables and fruits from Europe? Our fruit baskets still link directly back to the foothills of Tian Shan.

This isn't so for want of variety. Before global travel, regions housed very different collections of plant foods. Marco Polo wrote excitedly about the fruits of Asia, wistfully complaining that he had no way of knowing what the laden trees were bearing and whether they were safe to eat. Early settlers in North America were also faced with an exotic and alien bounty. The Vikings named the area of North America they explored "Vineland" after the wild grapes found there. Centuries later, the rootstock of North America's grapes would save the European wine industry from an insect pest known as phylloxera, as the North American varieties were immune.

Settlers tend to bring familiar foods along with them. Plant explorers scour the world for useful crops. These two forces, the transfer of crops that occurs as humans migrate and the active exploration for new and exciting flavors, led to the greatest transfer of botanical material in human history: the Columbian Exchange.

For practical purposes, Eurasia and the Americas might as well have been two different planets. Once the final land ties between the hemispheres vanished as the continents separated and sea level rose, plants and animals were free to diverge on different evolutionary paths. Though some species are found globally, many are found only in one hemisphere or the other. However, as the age of exploration dawned, this was about to change. Humans, in effect, re-established the land bridges between the continents through shiploads of diseased and dirty sailors rather than through geological processes. The exchange of plants, animals, people and diseases between the two continents is called the Columbian Exchange, and it caused a lasting and profound reordering of the earth's species that is still playing out.

In the late fifteenth and sixteenth centuries, a flood of plants, animals, culture, technologies and human populations crossed the Atlantic and navigated the Indian Ocean between Asia and Europe. Wondrous new crops spread around the globe, and deadly diseases inadvertently hitched rides to new regions. Diseases from Europe had a particularly dire impact on Indigenous Peoples of the Americas, as they had no immunity.

The term Columbian Exchange was coined by American historian Alfred Crosby in 1972. Crosby saw that something unprecedented had occurred when shipping opened up the Atlantic. Some of the changes to European cuisine are obvious: the potato was taken from Peru and introduced to Europe in the sixteenth century and supported by rulers such as Catherine the Great, changing the diets of millions of peasants. Corn from Central America came to Portugal and influenced the cuisine around the entire Mediterranean basin. The tomato was imported to Europe from South America as an ornamental, and due to its similarity to the poisonous leaves and fruit of the potato,[44] was considered to be inedible. However, in the nineteenth century, chefs in Naples began to use what is now a keystone of Italy's cuisine. It's hard to imagine Italy without the tomato, but it is a relative newcomer. Meanwhile, chilies crossed the Atlantic to Europe, then continued to travel eastward along the spice route, changing the cuisines of China and India forever and displacing local plants that also provided heat to dishes.

Important crops also flowed in the other direction. Coffee from Ethiopia and sugar from India transformed the landscapes of Central America and the Caribbean. Citrus from the Mediterranean came to Florida, bananas from South Asia to South America, and in North America, wheat from the steppes of Eurasia blanketed the prairies. North American foods fell to the wayside, save for blueberries, cranberries, turkey, maple syrup and a few other minor crops and animals. Meanwhile, European animals dominated, including the horse, the dog, pigs, cattle, sheep, goats, honeybees, cats and chickens.[45] Plants poured across the Atlantic. North America gained almonds, apples, apricots, asparagus, banana, barley, beets, brassicas, carrots, citrus, cucumbers, chickpeas, coffee, figs, eggplant, garlic, ginger, leeks, lentils, lettuce, mangoes, olives, onions, peaches, pears, peas, rice,

---

44 The green leaves and fruit of the potato plant contain solanine, a nerve toxin that causes headaches, vomiting and even paralysis. This toxin can also develop in the tubers of the plant, so it's best to toss potatoes with green spots.

45 Some accounts indicate that explorers from China brought chickens across the Pacific before 1492 and that the birds were already thriving in South America when the first Europeans arrived. We can't say for sure.

rye, soybean, wheat and yams. Europe gained guava, allspice, amaranth, avocado, bell pepper, cashew and chili, cocoa and cranberry, squash, sunflowers, corn, papayas and peanuts, beans, pecans, pineapples, potatoes, pumpkins, quinoa, tobacco, tomato and vanilla. Cuisine on both sides of the ocean was irreversibly altered, though the changes in North America were overshadowed by the profound cultural impact of colonization.

This was not an even exchange. Europeans ravaged North America, killing 85 to 90 percent of the Indigenous people present in the Americas in the first 100 years after contact, through violence, displacement or disease. Carefully tended fields in forests and river deltas fell fallow. I was curious to know more about these plants. Growing up, I'd learned a little about the plant foods of West Coast Indigenous Peoples, but there was a lot I didn't know. I decided to see what I could learn about the plant foods hiding in the woods around me.

My first stop was *Ethnology of the Kwakiutl* by German-American anthropologist Franz Boas. The book is a rare source of first-hand accounts, as it presents data collected by the Tlingit scholar George Hunt. Hunt didn't have to travel far to gather his research, as his wife was Kwakwaka'wakw (then known as Kwakiutl by Europeans). She and her friends provided an oral history of the food practices of the region, highlighting key plant foods. She paints a wondrous picture. One of the most important plants and a key food was springbank clover, which was gardened in semi-wild patches in river deltas. The thick rhizomes were dug and stored for winter in cedar boxes. Clover was grown in patches along with cinquefoil plants, and these roots were supplemented by foraged sea milkwort, fern root, wild carrots and lilies. The root of the lupine was recorded as making the harvester profoundly drunk if eaten raw but providing a tasty meal if cooked. The coastal peoples also ate a wide variety of berries, including many of the ones my friends and I used to find in the woods. These included elder berries, salal berries, currants, huckleberries, salmonberries and blueberries. George Hunt also mentions Qot!xolē berries, but I've not been able to put an English name to these. If they still exist, they are not widely known.

Locals boiled berries in bentwood boxes and then dried them into cakes to store for winter. They were sometimes mixed with fish oils to form a type of pemmican, and often elder berries, which are rich in pectin, were used to thicken the cakes. The clover roots were steamed or boiled and then mashed with fish oil. The wild carrots of the Pacific coast were *Conioselinum pacificum*, or hemlock-parsley. My grandfather used to strictly forbid me from hunting the strong-tasting roots, as they are very similar in appearance to the highly poisonous water hemlock, which can kill even in very small doses. In any case, when Boas went into the field with Hunt, he reported the wild carrots gave him such bad diarrhea that he learned to decline them. I remained curious about the lupine that induced drunkenness — the species in question was *Lupinus littoralis*, or seashore lupine. The rhizomes are a meter long and very sweet, but they must be cooked. Raw they contain toxic alkaloids, and the "drunkenness" they cause can easily be fatal.

I finished my exploration of my local environment with more questions than answers. Were some of the foods listed by George Hunt and his wife extinct? Were some of the berries I remember eating as a child now harder to find as our urban areas continued to expand? Would we even notice if some of these marginal species disappeared? While we talked over pie, Tom Baumann lamented the loss of a university program to study these plants. Perhaps it was time to rejuvenate it. Renewed interest in Indigenous cuisines is helping to raise awareness of local species. At the Haida restaurant Salmon n' Bannock in Vancouver, I had a lovely salal berry compote, and I've encountered other wild berries in dining rooms around the city as well. However, I couldn't find anyone carrying on the tradition of tending to springbank clover, once a key starchy food shared among large numbers of dinner guests. I did find some seed companies who carry the seeds, and I plan to give some space to it in my garden, along with my dewberries.

We are at a crossroads in the protection of our remaining wild crops. We could lose this biodiversity if we don't protect it, or we could ensure it endures, providing us with wonderful new foods and a biological repository for strengthening our existing crops. We can enjoy an endless summer of the same few cultivars, but why not also enjoy a seasonally limited but diverse array of fruit including those indigenous to our regions? We can enjoy the best both systems have to offer.

We are also working to protect our biodiversity. One of the most critical elements of this effort is the collection of genetic material from both wild ancestors and landraces; the work done by Vavilov and others continues today. One of the more intensive efforts is the creation of a backup copy of material held in the world's many seedbanks, a collection known as the Svalbard Global Seed Vault or the "doomsday vault." Located on one of earth's most remote archipelagos, the vault utilizes the cold climate to provide secure storage far from war and conflict. Even a global crisis is unlikely to spread to remote Svalbard, leaving a backup copy of our agricultural wealth awaiting survivors, if they can make the trip. This might sound rather gloomy, but the seed collections of Afghanistan and Iraq have been lost during conflict, and the collections in the Philippines were damaged recently by flooding and then fire. Keeping a spare copy makes good sense, backing up 1700 individual collections.

Far from society's struggles, our collected seeds sleep beneath the permafrost.

A much less apocalyptic approach can be found in the Slow Food "Ark of Taste," founded by Carlo Petrini in Italy in 1986 to protect local food and traditional cooking in the face of globalization. Petrini and others were jarred into action by the opening of a McDonald's near Rome's Spanish Steps, an intrusion that represented, in their minds, everything wrong with global food systems.[46] There are now over one hundred thousand members of Slow Food worldwide, divided into regional convivia (groups) that promote local farmers and chefs and encourage the preservation of regional flavors. They even run a University of Gastronomic Sciences in Piedmont, Italy.

The Ark of Taste project has been particularly important in the preservation of regional products. Hundreds of products from over fifty countries have been added to the list, including fruit and vegetable cultivars and breeds of animals, and their list includes resources for those people who want to grow or buy the products. Unlike seedbanks, the Ark of Taste aims to protect local specialties by drawing attention to their possible extinction and encouraging the cultivation and production of these foods as part of living traditions. Curious, I decided to check into the Canadian entries in the Ark that meet their five criteria: products that possess a distinctive quality in terms of taste; are linked to local memory and identity; are environmentally, socially, economically and historically based in a region; are produced in limited quantities; and are at risk of extinction. The Canadian entries cross a wide spectrum: the Chantecler chicken,

---

46 I leave judgment to the reader; personally, I enjoy the little fruit pies made by McDonald's, as they come in interesting regional variations. The coconut pie served in Hawaii is particularly good.

the Tamworth pig, a melon grown only in Montreal, the Gravenstein apple, and Red Fife wheat. Also included are Bay of Fundy dulse, the Saskatoon berry, highbush cranberries and the camas lily bulb. Tom would approve. There are even several pears on the list, including the Jesuit pear, a tall tree producing small sweet pears, planted by French settlers in Windsor and Detroit in the 1700s.

As I finished up my notes on fruit and vegetable cultivar extinction, I paid a visit to a small, spindly tree in the corner of the orchard. It is a pear imp, sprouted from a stray seed from an overlooked piece of fruit. The odds are that the fruit will be sandy, bitter and astringent. But I maintain it anyway, pruning it and shaping it while I wait for it to bear fruit. Psychologist Erich Fromm coined a term in 1964: biophilia, or the love of living things. I feel that exact emotion when I look at the irregular leaves of my little tree. And besides, maybe, just maybe, the tree will produce something sublime, with flesh you can spread with a knife.

Back in the city, I touched base with Dan as we prepared to head off on the next leg of my extinction journey. We were combining forces and fieldwork. After a few months of staying put, I was itching to be on the move. But first, I wanted to give one last moment to pears, and make Dan poire belle Hélène. This classic French dessert was created by Georges Auguste Escoffier, the miraculous French chef, restaurateur and culinary writer who updated the heavier grande cuisine created by legendary chef Marie-Antoine Carême. Escoffier made his dishes lighter and brighter, and he perfected a kitchen system that could feed the hundreds of guests at the grand hotels of the late nineteenth century, a system still used in many large restaurants today. He developed the five mother sauces of French cuisine and established cooking as a respectable profession. A great showman, he would approve of the media reach of today's chefs. A century later, his *Guide Culinaire* is still an important reference in many kitchens, including my own.

Poire belle Hélène was recipe 4685 in Escoffier's book, invented in 1864 and named after an operetta by Jacques Offenbach. But when I first tasted the dish, I knew none of that. I was eighteen, and I was in Paris. I still knew nearly nothing of food. I was in France to look at art, sort of, a restless spirit in search of . . . something. Whatever I was looking for, it wasn't in my ragged hotel room in Pigalle, and so I headed out into the rain and prowled the glistening cobblestones and settled at a street café with marble tables. Swimming in my first ever bout of jet lag, I ordered poire belle Hélène. Pears, vanilla ice cream, warm chocolate. Each ingredient was better than anything I could imagine. The pear was perfectly ripe. The ice cream was smooth and intensely flavored. The chocolate was like velvet. Together it was a perfect harmony of flavor. And for that moment, everything was perfection. I began to forget about art, instead concentrating on the ethereal wondrous world of food. Thanks Escoffier.

Dan and I chatted as I poached a couple of fresh Bartlett pears in sugar syrup with vanilla. I sat them aside to cool and scooped vanilla ice cream into a pair of chilled dishes. Dan melted some good dark chocolate, and the room filled with a complex fruity and floral smell. We poured the chocolate over the ice cream and pears. It was still, after all of these years, perfection.[47]

"That really is wonderful," Dan said, grinning.

I concentrated on eating my ice cream before it melted. Life is short, after all. We must hurry.

---

47   The original contained candied violets.

Chapter Ten

THE SCRAMBLED
PARADISE

"Dan, there's some sort of lizard eating my pie."

The creature squatted on its little legs. Its skin was a vivid neon green with red markings. There were blue highlights around its eyes that made it look like it was wearing a particularly bright shade of eyeliner. It blinked at me and then returned to licking my breakfast. Dan put down the camera lens he was cleaning and peered at the little jewel-toned animal.

"It's a gecko," he said. "A gold dust day gecko. *Phelsuma laticauda*. Aww, look at that tiny tongue! It likes the sugar."

The gecko was lapping contentedly at my slice of lilikoi[48] cream pie. I gently guided it away with the back of my hand, took a forkful of pie from the non-licked side of the slice and gazed out at the sheets and sheets of rain. We were in Hilo, an enchanted, ramshackle town on the big island of Hawaii. I liked the town instinctively; it sported a laid-back pirate vibe amid

---

48 Lilikoi is Hawaiian passionfruit. It makes an excellent cream pie.

a lush jungle landscape. Flowers tumbled over every fence and the buildings leaned against each other in a scenic state of disrepair. There was little traffic and the people were friendly and relaxed. The vegetation was impossibly green and the wooden buildings were painted in bright colors. A gentle decay hung over everything and they had kombucha on tap. Biodiversity was everywhere and fruit hung on trees in alleys and yards.

The islands of Hawaii are a researcher's dream. They are the most remote landmasses on earth for their size and are also geologically young. They formed as the earth's crust moved lazily across a hot spot in the mantle at a rate of about four inches a year, new islands budding from the sea floor in a long chain. The active volcanos are still building new land and new islands, and the older islands are sinking back into the sea. My pie and I were on the newest of the islands, the Big Island of Hawaii, formally Hawaii County. It formed only 700,000 years ago and it is still growing as its active volcano pumps lava into the sea. The six main Hawaiian Islands get most of the attention, but there are 132 islands, atolls and seamounts stretching back towards Asia like a trail of stepping stones. A new seamount, Lōihi, is rising off of the coast of the Big Island and could break the surface in the next 10,000 years or so, a new paradise ready for lilikoi, geckos and researchers. But for now, here in Hilo, we were at the end of the line.

Dan and I were on Hawaii for two different reasons: he was there because island ecosystems are sometimes simple, and I was there because island cuisines are complex. As ecosystems, islands offer up miniature and bounded worlds to study. However, for social scientists, islands are crossroads, drawing diverse human cultures together where they mix in new and unexpected ways.

I was in Hilo with a small team of researchers studying food culture and diverse agriculture, and Dan was there along with a team of students and a mountain of gear to study frogs. Tiny frogs. Loud frogs. We'd pooled our resources and rented a tin-roofed house near town. Our trip, however, was beset by rain. Dan was fighting a losing battle to keep his night vision cameras dry, and I watched as my notebooks swelled with moisture. The frogs were happy, I suppose, and at least it was warm.

The big island of Hawaii has sharply defined ecological niches depending on altitude and location, and the great looming bulk of the volcanos cause the jet stream to lift, cool and drop large quantities of rain on the windward side of the island, creating clearly demarcated dry and rainy sides. As the farms and frogs were on the rainy side, so was I. Hawaii is an island of black sand beaches, lush jungle, cool temperate forest, grassland, hot dry scrublands, cloud forests perfect for coffee growing and, far above all, a harsh land of fire and occasional snow. There are five volcanos on the Big Island and three of them are listed as active. One of them, Kīlauea, has been erupting steadily since 1983. One evening, the whole team traveled to see the glowing lake of lava in Volcano National Park, and I'm glad we did. The great cauldron of molten rock has since drained through rifts and vents to rampage across Puna District as part of the 2018 rift zone eruption, burying some of the farms I studied while making its way to the ocean and emptying into the water in a cloud of toxic fog. The night I was there, however, the lava lake was still filled to the rim, great gouts of the planet's innards fountaining under the stars.

The first explorers to reach these islands found a very different place than we know today. The Polynesians were astounding seafarers, mastering the art of locating islands across vast expanses of water. Their navigators passed on their secret techniques to the next generation in the form of song. They wove and crafted island maps and enjoyed high status in their society. They watched the water for seaweed and followed sea birds. They sniffed the air and paid particular attention to clouds, as islands warm the air above them, causing a trail of cloud to leeward. They had a variety of tools, including star maps.

The Polynesians used sturdy outrigger canoes on their voyages and likely made exploratory trips in fleets, but even traveling together couldn't have entirely tamed the fearful truth that when they set out to start a new colony, they were often paddling into the Pacific with the possibility of failing to find habitable land. Their feats of navigation still boggle the mind. Hawaii is four thousand kilometers from the Society Islands, with little in between save for Kiribati, and that island group is off to the east. Despite this vast distance, the Polynesians pulled ashore on the Hawaiian Islands somewhere between 400 CE and 1200 CE, perhaps first as visitors, but eventually they stayed.

The islands they found, while beautiful, were less lush than today. The Hawaiian Islands are the most remote islands on earth for their size and are hard to reach for non-human species as well. When the islands burst from the ocean in a fountain of fire and steam, they were completely free of any sort of life. The oldest of the islands, Kaua'i, has been above the water for about five million years, and in that time about 270 species have arrived. Most flew there, some floated through the air currents and about one-quarter of the total drifted in on the tide. The islands were bereft of mammals entirely before Polynesian contact, save for one species of bat. A large number of ferns arrived, as their spores can stay airborne for a long time. Other plants hitched a ride in the stomachs of birds. Once there, evolution further diversified the species to fill specific niches. By the time the Polynesians arrived, there were 956 plant and animal species on the islands. There were no freshwater fish, no amphibians and no reptiles. There were grasses, flowers and flowering trees and a limited array of fungi. The newly arrived Polynesians found very little food. They ate some of the fern roots and shoots, and they harvested wild sweet potato and yam as well. They found a few berries, including 'akala, a thornless raspberry found nowhere else, and 'ōhelo 'ai, a small red berry similar to a blueberry. The 'ohi'a 'ai, or mountain apple, was one of the few local fruits that can be easily eaten raw, and it is still popular today. They also found several seaweeds. If this doesn't sound like a lot of food, it isn't, and it is unlikely that a poorly prepared colony could have survived on the islands. The Polynesians, however, were very well prepared. They brought their own lunch.

The Polynesians didn't set out to a new home without careful planning. They brought along a set of beloved plants, known as canoe plants, on every exploratory voyage. The canoe plants were chosen for durability, medicinal uses and nutrition, and included staples such as taro (arguably the most important plant of the bunch), banana, lime, coconut, bamboo, turmeric, sweet potato, noni fruit and arrowroot. They also brought pigs, dogs and a fowl similar to the chicken, which must have livened up life on board their boats. Once established on a new island, they created fishponds and elaborate water systems to move rain from the rainy side of the islands to the dry side. This was particularly important for the main crop, taro, or *Colocasia esculenta*. The plant is grown for its starchy corm and is thought to come from South India and Southeast Asia, though we have spread it so widely it is hard to tell. It is a tropical perennial and a nutritious food source that can be left in the ground until needed. It is one of only three common crops that grows in standing water.[49] The plants have air spaces in their stems that allow them to exchange oxygen, but the water must flow to allow growth, and

---

49 Along with rice and lotus.

so taro fields, called lo'i in Hawaii, must be constantly irrigated. Creating such fields initially is a lot of work, but it paid off in two ways: pretty much effortless weed control and much higher taro yields. The corms contain oxalic acid (likely to prevent creatures such as humans from eating them), and so taro must be well cooked to break down the toxin. The Hawaiians steamed it in pit ovens called imu and then mashed it and fermented it into poi, a distinctive sour purple paste that formed the cornerstone of the Hawaiian diet before European contact. Hawaii still produces six million pounds of taro a year, and demand is growing. Even McDonald's offers taro in Hawaii, in the form of a dessert pie.[50]

The Hawaiians practiced extremely advanced land management based on a stewardship model in which the islands were owned by the gods. It was managed by an administrative class known as the ali'i who directed the workers, the maka'āinana, and the entire system was designed to protect the sensitive ecosystems of the islands from exhaustion. The islands were divided into ahupua'a, wedge-shaped zones that ran from the beaches to the tops of the mountains. Collaboration was critical, and water was shared out as a group exercise, and the water transport systems were managed centrally. High altitude forests were off limits for most forms of harvest, and a complicated system of rules dictated who could eat what and when each food could be harvested. Women were not allowed access to many of the most interesting foods, and men and women were not allowed to eat together until after European contact.

We can't say with any certainty how many people lived in Hawaii before European contact, but it is possible their advanced system of agriculture supported at least several hundred thousand

---

50 It's wonderful.

and possibly as many as a million people. This style of growing allowed for generous allotments of free time. Hawaii's rich culture of song, story and dance was balanced on a backbone of nutritious crops, particularly the taro corms and the creamy poi they provided. Each ahupua'a grew taro, ideally in lo'i or in the shade of upland forests. Taro was so central to Hawaiian culture that it played a key role in their mythology. They treated the plant as an ancestor and told a story in which Wakea, the Father of Heaven, was overcome with desire for his youngest daughter, Papahānaumoku, the Daughter of Earth. Their first child, Haloa-naka (which means "trembling long stalk"), was stillborn, and they buried the corm-shaped body at the corner of the house, where it sprouted into the first taro plant. Their second child, a boy named Haloa, is considered to be the ancestor of all Hawaiian people and was charged to look after Haloa-naka for all time. In return, the taro would nourish them. Today one can find taro baked into tasty bread, fried into chips or made into the ubiquitous poi.

The rain stopped with a sudden rustle of wind, and the sun burst through, shrouding the town in steam. It was time to go eat some Hawaiian creole. I find the long history of Hawaii's food interesting, but I was on the island to document post-contact cuisine. Hawaii was isolated from the rest of the Pacific Rim for nearly 500 years, but as the age of sea travel developed, the islands became the crossroads of the Pacific. British explorer James Cook arrived in 1778, and a mere five years later, King Kamehameha I used European military technology to unify the islands into the Kingdom of Hawaii. Once unified, the islands focused on feeding all of the hungry sailors passing through, exporting Hawaiian agricultural products to the world. Growing crops for export became a major activity on the islands and radically remade the precontact landscape. Americans came to set up sugar and pineapple plantations, and immigrants from Japan, China and the Philippines arrived to work in the fields. By 1896, 25 percent of the population on the big island was of Japanese descent, and the last sugar plantation didn't close until 1996. The Spanish introduced papaya and pineapple, and macadamia nuts were introduced from Australia. All of these crops were grown for shipping abroad, but they brought new groups to the islands at the same time. The coming together of various cultures in the Hawaiian Islands helped to create one of the most interesting sorts of cuisines, a long-term mixing of cultural elements that we call a creole. From the Latin *creo*, "to create," a creole involves the mingling of cuisines in an area where multiple cultures coexist. A creole develops over decades, sometimes centuries.[51]

I hit the road with my research assistant and a mountain of camera gear, and we made a first stop at Hilo Lunch, a classic Hawaiian okazuya, or side-dish, house. These deli-like restaurants were once common, serving boxes of mixed dishes from large platters for takeaway. Today, few okazuya remain, and those that do are in neighborhoods where families settled after leaving the plantations. They are very busy in the morning, filled with locals grabbing a lunch for the coming workday. Construction workers jostle with customers in business attire, and they all crowd in to choose a starch, which can be musabi (rice balls), rice, macaroni salad, chow fun (a stir fry of beef, bean sprouts and noodles) or even a Hawaiian version of sushi such as spam musabi (sheet sushi made with the canned meat that is ubiquitous in the Pacific Islands). On top of this base, one adds classics such as shoyo pork, sweet potato tempura, poke, Japanese pickle

---

51 A creole is different than a fusion, which occurs when a chef mixes cuisines that are not necessarily his own or endemic to the region.

and others. All of this goes into a takeaway box. My research assistant and I both ordered a large box and filled them with a wide variety of tasty looking dishes.

We, however, were not going to wait until noon. As far as we were concerned, this was brunch okazuya. We pulled over at a beach and dug in. The food was very filling, which was a bit of a problem as we had a lot more to eat over the course of the day. I particularly enjoyed the mix of macaroni salad and potato salad, but the density of the food did put a dent in my appetite. We headed north along the coast, marveling at the views and worrying slightly about the reddish color of the waves cresting on the shore, as it was tinted by the soil lost during the last day's storm. Hawaii's farms struggle with erosion, and water was still cascading from the forest and across the road.

We pulled into Honokaa and prepared for another stomach-challenging meal, our first encounter with the Hawaiian plate lunch. The plate lunch shares much with the okazuya and is also a staple for working Hawaiians. It combines the Japanese bento with the American lunch truck, designed to deliver cheap and plentiful calories in a tasty package. As I was thinking about taro, I decided to tackle the taro loco moco at Tex Lunch. It isn't a trivial meal. Loco moco is a plate of white rice topped with a meat or meat substitute, a fried egg and brown gravy. And yes, it's filling. The "meat" can be spam, kalua pork, teriyaki, seafood or taro (but is often a hamburger patty). The dish was supposedly created in Hilo in 1949, at the Lincoln Inn for hungry surfers, and it is quick, satisfying and delightfully tasty. We struggled into the car in a state of food-induced torpor.

"I can't eat any more today," my assistant groaned as we pulled back onto the highway.

I thought for a moment, realizing I likely *could* eat more. Maybe that was why I was a professor of food. Maybe that was also why I'm a bit heavier than I should be. Perhaps, I thought, the rest of the day should be dedicated to fruit? Maybe just a little for dessert. Mangoes were ripe, and there is something magical about a place were so much bounty hangs heavily on every tree. But this bounty, this buffet from around the world, is not the whole story.

Hawaii is a scrambled paradise. What we see now on the islands is an ecological creole, the result of centuries of plant and animal invasion. And this frantic mixing of species highlights one of the critical lessons we can learn from islands: they are ground zero for extinction.

There are two critical factors driving extinction on islands, and the first of these is their vulnerability to invasive species. In the case of Hawaii, extinction began almost as soon as the Polynesians arrived. Very quickly all but one of the native predator birds were killed off, including the world's only flightless ibis. The nēnē goose survived, but only thanks to intensive intervention after the mid-twentieth century, when the population had crashed to little more than a few dozen. The large flightless birds and land crabs vanished quickly, and though the Hawaiians ate some of these species, they were also killed by one of the foods the Polynesians brought along with them: the pigs. These animals quickly spread into the wild where they made a quick snack of birds' eggs. In total, archeological digs suggest that forty bird species had vanished long before the Europeans arrived. Hawaii contains 0.2 percent of the land area of the United States, yet one-third of the plants and birds that appear on the country's endangered species list are endemic to Hawaii. Globally, the situation is similar. Since the dawn of the seventeenth century, 67 percent of mammal extinctions, 80 percent of bird extinctions and 95 percent of reptile extinctions have taken place on islands.

The ecological history of Hawaii can be written as a series of invasions. Plants and animals began arriving soon after the islands formed, but a full 44 percent of species on the island of Hawaii are invaders that arrived after European contact. However, the Polynesians brought the first truly horrid invasive species to the islands, likely without being aware they were doing so — the Polynesian or Pacific rat, *Rattus exulans*. This unfortunate stowaway originated in Southeast Asia and made a habit of grabbing a boat for the horizon every time a group of human explorers felt the itch to put to sea. Once arrived, the rats attacked the unprepared bird populations of their new home. Rats also feed upon vegetation and quickly destroyed lowland palm forests throughout the islands. The lou'lu is a particularly pretty fan palm, and the only large stand of it is on a rat-free islet, Huelo, off of Molokai. The government is attempting to eliminate rats from the islet of Lihue to protect birds, but as of the time of writing, the rats are still winning. As anyone who has tried to eliminate rats can attest, once they've arrived, they are very hard to remove.

The great sugar plantations of Hawaii helped to satisfy the world's sweet tooth, but they exacted a high price upon the land as they exhausted soil and reduced biodiversity. The sugar planters also provided ideal habitat for the rats, who liked to eat the growing sugar cane. They nested in the maze of stalks, and when the planters burnt the field stubble, waves of rats would pour out and move on to the next conquest. Unfortunately, the planters retaliated by introducing the Indian mongoose in 1883, violating a key rule of invasive species: don't attempt to control them with another invasive. A carnivore about the size of a small cat, the mongoose does eat rodents. It also eats birds, eggs and other animals. The mongoose population increased rapidly after their introduction, but it and the rat are active at different times of the day so, in the end, the impact of the mongoose on rat populations was low. Though the sugar is long gone, the mongoose is widespread on all but two of the main islands, and it was the mongoose that drove the population of the endemic nēnē goose to the brink of extinction.

Smaller invaders can be just as damaging. Hawaii was too far from the mainland to be populated by mosquitos, allowing the Polynesians to lounge in the open in the evening without hearing that high singing buzz in their ears. Sadly, this didn't last. The sailing ship *Wellington* from San Blas, Mexico, arrived in 1826 at the port of Lahaina, and while cleaning their water barrels, unloaded larvae of *Culex quinquefasciatus*, the southern house mosquito. Soon the evening was filled with the insects, and once again the primary damage was to bird populations: the mosquitos carried avian malaria. Half of lowland bird species are now extinct in the islands, thanks in large part to mosquitos.

The problem is made worse by the pigs introduced by the Polynesians. Turned loose upon the islands, the pigs quickly became feral and severely damaged the rare fern forests on the islands. These forests are magical places; the tree-sized ferns tower overhead in a riot of green and mist, and as they sit on lava soil, the forests are well drained so there isn't a lot of mosquito habitat. The pigs, however, like to topple the ferns in order to eat the pith of the trees. The hollows in the fallen logs fill with water, thus providing a handy home for mosquitos.

Invasions from the plant world can be just as damaging, and many of the most destructive plants to come to the island were brought there on purpose, including the strawberry guava. These were introduced in 1825 for their fruit and as a source of vitamin C, and they took to the islands ferociously. They form shady thickets with dense mats of feeder roots, pushing out local endemic plants. The strawberry guava is an excellent example of what botanists call a transformer species; they shape the forest to their liking. The seeds can survive in the digestive tracts of birds, and the plant now covers hundreds of thousands of acres of land in Hawaii. Currently, the state government is considering releasing an insect from Brazil that controls the strawberry guava in its home range. Let's hope it doesn't come with even more unintended consequences.

The strawberry guava was introduced at a time when governments were actively searching the world for useful plants to import for economic gain. In fact, there were entire branches of government established to scour the world for useful plants and bring them home. In the United States, the Office of Seed and Plant Introduction within the USDA was established in 1898, with a sum of $20,000 allocated by Congress to be used to secure plants from abroad. Director David Fairchild sent scientist explorers around the world, including Frank Meyer, and over the next half-century they introduced 200,000 species and cultivars to the United States. Some of these plants were indeed very useful, such as hard winter wheat and the soybean, but others have filled our fields and forests with a green invasion. A recent study found that 80 percent of woody invaders in the United States were released deliberately with good intentions. To date, the United States alone has made over a quarter million introductions.

This brings me to Dan's frog. His team was studying the coquí, a group of frog species in the genus *Eleutherodactylus*. They are native to Puerto Rico, where they are a beloved national symbol and, in a sad twist, facing population decline. They are tiny frogs and rather unexceptional, at least until the sun goes down. The males then scream their name over and over, "co-*quí*, co-*quí*, co-*quí*," filling the forest with popping and whistling.

I suggest the reader take a moment to pop on to the internet and listen to the call of the coquí to set the mood. Loud, aren't they? Their call can reach seventy to eighty decibels, about the same as a lawn mower. They sing to mate and they sing to mark their territory, filling the tropical air with their strange alien ballad.

Before the arrival of the coquī, the Hawaiian forest was quiet at night, and Hawaiians in search of a good night's sleep were likely happy with that state of affairs. However, in the 1980s, a few stray coquī made the journey to the island of Hawaii, likely in some plant stock. Though they are beloved in Puerto Rico, they face there a series of predators that keep their populations in check. Snakes in particular love a meal of coquī. But Hawaii has no snakes, and the first few coquī found a paradise on the island, complete with plenty of insects to eat and lots of damp places to hide. This frog has no tadpole stage, a critical advantage on an island with few ponds. So they came and sang their mating song, and soon those first few voices were joined by many, many more. One count on the Big Island found 90,000 frogs in a single acre of forest. No wonder the night isn't quiet any more. The mayor of Hilo declared the country's first "frog emergency" in 2005.

It isn't yet clear what impact the coquī may be having on the Hawaiian ecosystem. Often the full repercussions of such a major invasion aren't apparent for decades. There is some worry the frogs are competing with birds and bats for insects, but we aren't sure. On the human scale, however, the coquī is hitting the Big Island where it hurts: the real estate market. People move to the island for the quiet and mild climate, and they don't want to keep their windows closed to block out the sound of screaming frogs. Real estate disclosure forms, the ones that usually identify structural issues and such, now have a box that buyers must tick to acknowledge they have been made aware of a coquī infestation. In zones still free of the frog, neighbors prowl the darkened streets, listening for the distinctive sound. Other teams practice "spray and pray," showering the dark woods with citric acid, which is reasonably safe for the environment but can kill the coquī frogs and their eggs. It's a big island, though, and the chance of totally removing a species of frog the size of a quarter is unlikely. Meanwhile, people are beginning to adjust to the noise. Personally, I found it soothing as long as the windows were partly closed.

As the trip progressed, we all adapted to working frantically between bursts of rain. As we wrapped up our research, Dan and I decided an afternoon off was in order, and we trooped off for some shave ice. Shave ice is made by scraping "snow" from a block of ice with a blade and shaping the result into a cone, which is then saturated in flavored syrups and condensed milk. The result is airy yet satisfying, bright with local flavors such as guava, pineapple, lychee and coconut. The shave ice stand also sold crack seed, a category of candy that also made its way to Hawaii with Chinese farmers. Crack seed is preserved fruit that has been split open with the seed exposed and then coated in sugar, salt and spices. The flavor ranges from the very sweet, to sour, to salty. I liked the dry plums rolled in anise, which carry a strong pucker factor.

I was learning a lot about Hawaiian creole as I tasted my way across the island, but I was also getting a crash refresher course from Dan in island biogeography, the study of species composition and richness on islands. Islands are microcosms of the larger world, tiny capsules of life in the vastness of the world's oceans. Many early botanists and biologists recognized the special nature of islands; Darwin formulated his most important thinking while in the Galapagos. But formalizing our understanding of these unique ecosystems occurred later, when in 1967, Robert MacArthur and Edward O. Wilson wrote their book, *Theory of Island Biogeography.* Their goal was to predict the number of species to be found on an island and to determine how the size of the island and the distance to other landmasses influence this number. They also wanted to understand why islands tended to have ten times as many species for each doubling in area. What, they wondered, was so important about size? They began this thought experiment with empty islands (a newly emerged Hawaii, for example), then calculated how often a new species would immigrate to that empty island and then how often island species would go extinct. The ratio of these two factors is known as species turnover.

MacArthur and Wilson predicted that the species richness, the number of different species represented in an ecological community, would stabilize over time at a number that is related to the size of the island and to the distance to other land masses. Larger islands have more species, as the population of each species can be larger, and larger populations are less likely to become extinct. Distance is a factor, as remote islands are less likely to be populated by a large number of species; it is simply harder for species to reach them. If an island species population is close enough to another landmass with similar species, occasionally a new individual will arrive ashore, a factor known as the rescue effect because the new arrivals strengthen existing populations. So, over time, an island reaches an equilibrium.

Their *Theory of Island Biogeography* also notes a strange property called endemism, which means unique to a place or region. Consider Darwin, who noticed that the finches on the Galapagos are slightly different on each island. He realized that each species of finch had adapted to that particular island. The older the island, the more endemism occurs. If we go all the way back to the dodo, recall that its ancestor flew to the island of Mauritius. With each generation, the dodo adapted to its environment. With no predators, it lost the ability to fly, and its beak grew large enough to crack the nuts and tough seeds found on the island. As the same circumstances were found nowhere else, the dodo was found nowhere else.

Although the Hawaiian Islands are young, and older islands have higher rates of endemism, Hawaiian forests still support many species found only there. Another odd effect of life on an island is that large species tend to grow smaller, and some small species grow much larger. The Hawaiian tree snail, for example, is as large as a rabbit and colorful. It is threatened by habitat loss and by invasion.

Another critical element of island biogeography is known as metapopulation theory, which is a long word for a simple concept. Think about the Hawaiian Islands for a moment. Each island is a "patch" of habitat in a large ocean, and as each patch is relatively small, the population of each species living there is small. Random fluctuations in population due to disease or an environmental change can quite easily drive species extinct on any one island. However, if populations remain on the other islands, they will likely repopulate the empty patch.

In short, metapopulation theory argues that it is better to have several small patches of habitat rather than just one, as long as they are close together. Better for a species to live on an archipelago than on a lone island. This concept was developed as an extension to the original theory in 1969, posited by ecologist Richard Levins, but it wasn't really understood until continental habitat also began to become fragmented.

How bad is island extinction exactly? A few extra examples help illustrate just how serious species loss has been since humans learned to cross large bodies of water by boat. Turtles, one of the oldest species of animals still in existence, fared particularly poorly against hungry sailors. The island of Pinta lost its giant tortoise, the Galapagos lost four of its fifteen species, Réunion lost its giant tortoise and Mauritius lost two of its tortoise species as well. They were very easy to catch and they stayed alive aboard ships, becoming an important food source on long voyages.

The great auk of the North Atlantic also fell prey to hungry sailors. It stood nearly three feet tall and weighed about ten pounds, and it nested in large groups on small rocky islands with easy access to fish. Near Newfoundland, a colony of nearly 100,000 nested on Funk Island, on an area little bigger than a quarter of a square kilometer. They had no predators and were flightless, and they were predictably hunted on a large scale for food, eggs and feathers. Early explorers including Jacques Cartier skimped on provisions, safe in the knowledge that on the return home from North America, they could load the decks with auks, eggs and similar creatures. They captured them by simply herding them on board. It is likely they also introduced rats to the small islands where the auks nested, with predictably depressing results. Even by the 1800s, sailors guessed that the auks wouldn't survive. The final colony, on the island of Elday, near Iceland, was destroyed on June 3, 1844.

We can also learn from the terrible ecological destruction that happened on the once verdant Easter Island. The Polynesians arrived between 800 and 1200 CE and flourished on the small but fertile patch of land, calling themselves and their island Rapa Nui. They farmed and raised chickens and built ocean-going boats out of the tall local timber, including the Easter Island palm. By the seventeenth century, we believe there were 15,000 people on the island, and they are known worldwide for their moai, the giant stone heads they carved from volcanic rock and erected around the island. But by 1722, when Europeans first visited the islands, the forests had been destroyed and the local population had plummeted to two or three thousand people. By this time, the island had lost forty species, including five kinds of land bird. We think the Polynesians brought rats here too, and the rodents decimated both birds and palms. The *Paschalococos disperta*, or the Easter Island palm, was critical to the culture of the island, as without it the Polynesians couldn't build their boats. Trapped in a dying ecosystem, the culture devolved into warfare, and only a few hundred islanders survived. Even today, the ecosystem of Easter Island is a shadow of what it once was.

The fight to preserve island ecosystems is in full swing in New Zealand. On my first trip through Auckland's airport, I was questioned closely about any biological material I might be bringing onto the island, as all around me groups of backpackers were giving up their camping gear for inspection and cleaning. Travelers emptied their pockets of wayward food items and scraped their boots of alien dirt. New Zealanders have a right to be concerned and cautious, as the island's ecosystems grew splendid in their isolation. The Polynesians noticed the long white clouds that indicated the presence of a significant island only 700 years ago, and when the Māori landed their canoes on New Zealand's beaches, they found a world dominated by ferns and birds, many of which are found nowhere else. There were 245 species on the islands before contact, and seventy-one were endemic. Much of this wondrous variety is still present on the islands, but sadly, at least one-third of New Zealand's bird and bat species were driven to extinction after contact, and another third are now endangered or exiled to small outlying islands. Only 10 percent of the great fern forests remain, once habitat to a zoo's worth of birds and dominated by nine truly large species of flightless birds, the moa. I recall the first time I saw the skeleton of a moa — I was in the British Museum, and the giant creature loomed over us in a corner.

"It looks like Big Bird," I muttered to no one in particular. It was, indeed, a big bird. The largest, which were always rather rare, were as tall as 4.8 meters. They were forest birds, emerging around a million years ago. They ate herbs and berries and largely lived at higher elevations. Their only predator was the Haast's eagle, a massive bird with a wingspan of up to three meters that is also now extinct.

The moa was easy and tasty prey for the Māori, and they likely drove the species to extinction in only a century or so, roasting the birds in their own version of the pit oven, the hāngi. No European ever made a confirmed sighting of a living moa and most didn't believe the Māori's oral accounts of the giant bird. In 1889, a settler in Poverty Bay, New Zealand, finally sent a bone home to England where it found its way to biologist Richard Owen, who compared it to a number of other species before concluding reluctantly that the birds had indeed existed (he was skeptical that such a large bird could exist). Owen helped launch the British Museum of Natural History and is responsible for the moa's skeletal presence there.[52] One clear lesson? It pays to be a flightless bird on an island, until it doesn't. The moa was so large it could graze the forests without much fear or need to take to the air, until the arrival of hungry humans.

I took two lessons away from my time in Hawaii. First, islands are particularly vulnerable to species invasion, and the tougher, adaptable species often win. Second, and related, the small populations of endemic island species are very easy to drive to extinction through hunting, competition and/or habitat loss.

These two lessons have implications for all species. While these issues are critical for islands around the world, there is

___
52   He also coined the term "dinosaur."

also a larger and more sinister implication. Continental species are only sheltered from these two interlocking effects as long as their continental habitat is largely undisturbed. But of course, as we've learned, the continents are not undisturbed. Forty percent of the earth's landmass is being used for farming and grazing, and another 4 percent is covered by expanding urban areas. In the age of the Anthropocene, the continental ecosystems are breaking into archipelagos comprised of small patches of remnant nature. We are in effect making new islands through a process known as habitat fragmentation, patches of intact ecosystems surrounded by modified habitats and anthropogenic boundaries. Habitat fragmentation is one of the main causes of extinction, for the very reasons suggested by island biogeography. Smaller habitat areas can sustain fewer species and fewer individuals of each species. In addition, what are barriers to some species, such as highways and areas of human habitation, can provide pathways for the spread of invasive species.

However, we can also use lessons from islands to do a better job of managing fragmentation. Large patches are better than small patches, and clustered groups of many patches are better than lone patches. Ultimately, islands might teach us how to preserve biodiversity, including culinary biodiversity, on the continents as well.

"You'll like this one," Dan said, grinning. He'd banished me from our rental house, leaving me to wander the town. His team had agreed to work up the next extinction dinner, based entirely on invasive species.

"I'm proud of the wild boar. We roasted it in a pit out back. I think we lost our damage deposit, but we'll take the owner some leftovers and hope for the best."

The pig dominated the small table, but other invasive crops were ready as well. There was guava tart and fresh papaya. Dan had grilled some lovely pineapple to a crunchy caramel brown. The students had whipped up some sort of coconut beverage that smelled suspiciously of rum. Small dishes of macadamia nuts dotted the table. And there was poi, purple and glistening.

"Did you make poi?"

"No. Too much work. I tried but the acid burnt my hands. There are little toxic hairs all over the corms. We bought it ready-made, properly fermented. I buried my failed attempt in the yard."

I smiled and pretended not to hear the last part of his statement.

Poi looks like uncooked cake batter for a shockingly purple cake. The flavor, though, is surprising. Eaten raw it is sweet, but the cooked and mashed corms quickly begin to ferment, developing a complex sour overtone that tastes well on its own or with other dishes. The fermentation is a common *Lactobacillus* fermentation assisted by natural yeasts and *Geotrichum*, a common soil fungus. There is a lot going on in that purple goo. To be honest, the wild pork was a little gamey for my taste, but the fruit and poi tasted just right, sitting nicely on the side dishes, the loco moco, the shave ice and everything else I'd eaten over the past week.

"No frogs, Dan?"

He looked up from the pork. "Not this time. Too small, really. Maybe toxic, and you know . . . I've rather grown to like them."

The meal was over, and the dishes done, our equipment packed into travel cases for the next day's flight back to the mainland. Dan and I decided one more walk was in order. With our work complete, it was time to sample *Piper methysticum*, or Hawaiian 'awa. Named for the Tongan word for bitter, the juice of the root of the 'awa (or kava, depending on the island) has been used for millennia as the intoxicant of choice in Polynesia and Melanesia. It was one of the canoe plants, and I imagine the Polynesians were extra careful to ensure that it survived the journey. It thrives in well-drained volcanic soils and requires both shade and heavy rainfall.

Piper methysticum is an unusual plant as it is cultivated entirely by propagation from cuttings. Female flowers are very rare and there is no known pollinator and no formation of fruit, even with hand pollination. Throughout Polynesia kava is lovingly cultivated, prepared and drunk in the evening. Community meetings happen over kava. Political conversations happen over kava. The peppery drink with the taste of dirty water is experiencing a resurgence, recovering from a period during which it was discouraged by Christian missionaries. On some islands where prohibition lasted too long, their cultivars are now extinct. Without the kava farmers to clone and spread the crop, the last plants lived their lives out and the species vanished. However, on Hawaii, kava persisted, cultivated around taro patches and mountain clearings and prepared fresh for consumption. As the plants age, the root develops high concentrations of kavalactones, which alter human brain chemistry to relax muscles and create a mild euphoria. So-called noble cultivars have particularly pleasant effects with no negative side effects. The roots are harvested after at least four years of growth and are then prepared by pounding the roots into a wet paste. The juices seep out and the beverage can be shared out of a large communal container. Individual servings are doled out in coconut shells and quickly knocked back, as savoring the flavor is not the point.

Dan and I procured a few shells of kava from Kava Dave, the friendly and extremely laid-back proprietor of Bayfront Kava bar. A retired orange juice chemist, Dave now spends his time growing and selling the sacred liquid. And his kava wasn't dirty water at all; it was clean and peppery. After a couple of shells, I became very aware of my surroundings. I became aware of the stool beneath me and the ceiling fan overhead. I became aware of the frogs chirping in the distance. I felt present in Dave's brightly colored bar, which was not quite indoors and not quite outdoors. I began touching the deep green plants that grew around the space. I could hear the conversation about fruit Dan and Dave were having a few feet away from me, but I felt as if I were a great distance away. I felt warm and happy.

Kava has sedative, anesthetic and euphoriant properties, and I was, not surprisingly, happy and relaxed and feeling no pain. Technically, the kavalactone was inhibiting the reuptake of norepinephrine and dopamine in my brain, allowing my mind to slowly fill with happy chemicals. I excused myself and drifted back to the house, falling into bed and into a world of brightly colored dreams filled with taro and kava and delicate birds, turtles on black sand and coffee beans on the bush.

So much to lose, I thought as I drifted. Too much to lose and so little time to save it. Outside in the garden, the frogs screamed.

Section Four

THE
TWILIGHT
GARDEN

Chapter Eleven

HONEY AND ROSES

We picked our way across the sandstone ledges of Botanical Beach, a rugged, rocky landscape jutting into the waters that wash the shores of British Columbia. The sun shone brightly, but the wind whipped the Pacific into a froth, peppering us with spray. There would be no wading in the water here; the ocean was wondrously cold. It was also filled with delicacies. We were at the beach on a chilly autumn day to learn some of the secrets of the foods found in the intertidal zone.

Botanical Beach's pools have a long history of attracting inquisitive professors. Marine biologist Josephine Tilden from the University of Minnesota came to British Columbia's west coast in 1900; she was so taken with the rich sea life to be found in the sandstone hollows of Botanical Beach that she established a marine station here. For seven years, students traveled by steamship from Victoria to nearby Port Renfrew and then picked their way down the coast on a long, slippery trail through the forest. Tilden was a world expert in the study of the life that lives on the fringe between land and sea, and her experiments at Botanical Beach helped to establish our understanding of marine biology. She was the first female scientist on the university's staff and was happy to exchange the chauvinism of her day-to-day work life on campus for the camaraderie she shared with a dedicated group of students out in the field. They spent their summers examining sea stars, anemones, barnacles, snails and mussels. Eventually the university balked at paying to maintain a field station in another country, and Tilden left the university after a long battle with her department chair. She took her samples with her, setting up a lab on the ground floor of her home in Minnesota. British Columbia's algae and shellfish helped her to establish a deeper understanding of the world's mysterious oceans.

Over a century later, we still have a lot to learn.

"These blue mussels are delicious. They grow on the rocks here in the lower part of the tidal zone. In the winter months, they are safe to eat, and I like to steam them over a wood fire. I put them right into coals and cover them with wet seaweed," explained April, an old friend who works as a chef in Victoria.

We were finally taking a long-postponed trip to photograph some of the local tidal delicacies. We'd originally hoped to visit in the spring, when one can sometimes find ka'aw, an Indigenous delicacy of herring eggs on long strands of sea kelp. My appendix had intervened, and April graciously took a rain check and gave me a crash course in shellfish instead, as ka'aw is only available when the herring spawn.

"If you tap these with a spoon, the healthy ones will close up tight. I pick medium-sized mussels."

I snapped a few pictures, struggling to keep the salt spray off of my lens by timing my shots between wave crashes.

"We can eat most of the seaweeds found here," April continued.

"The purple weed growing on the lowest part of the beach is called dulse. I might pick a little for later."

"I studied dulse on the East Coast in New Brunswick. I like it dried and powdered as a substitute for salt."

"Yes. It's salty and tangy at the same time. I'll gather enough to accompany dinner." April said as she gingerly worked her way closer to the waves and filled a small bag with sprouts of dulse, *Palmaria palmata*.

My stomach growled noticeably. "I'm pretty hungry now."

"Maybe it's time for a little lunch."

We retreated to the edge of the beach where there was some shelter from the wind behind a series of logs and rocks. Wild roses grew along the fringes of the forest, their branches now swollen with hips, the hard, knobby fruit of the rose. The Indigenous Peoples of the region harvested rose hips and boiled them into a tea or cooked them into a jelly, and they are still used as a source of nutrients today. I watched a bumblebee nestle into a late rose bloom, release a cloud of pollen and travel on. Roses are not fussy. They are pollinated by bees, by butterflies or by moths. Even the wind will do in a pinch.

The potential extinction of pollinators is one of the greatest threats to our global food systems. Since completing my study of fruit, I'd been noticing bees. I'd been looking for them as I passed patches of flowers, watching them go about their work. And I've been worrying about them. Around the world, our bees are in trouble.

We unpacked a luxurious spread of sandwiches, olives and fruit, the food complemented by the scent of the roses. Every now and then, the wind would fall, and the last of the season's flowers would fill with bumblebees, fuzzily flitting about their work. We dug in, chatting about shellfish as we ate. As we finished up the last few olives, the sun slid behind a cloud. I shivered, burrowing deep into my coat. April frowned.

"I think we should move on. I know a place you will really enjoy, and it's indoors."

I nodded, trying to look nonchalant, and began packing up our picnic. The bees continued their work, racing to gather pollen before the winter.

We pulled over at a tidy farm and made our way down a crushed gravel path lined with lush herbs and flowers. The air was alive with buzzing insects. I watched the bees fly from the herb garden to the hives, tracing their neatly ordered bee lines, intent on making the best of this cool, dry day. Soon we were inside, perched on a stool at Tugwell Creek Honey Farm. They are British Columbia's oldest maker of mead, the ancient alcoholic beverage brewed with water and honey, fermented with the honey's own yeasts. Owner Robert Liptrot has spent his entire life among bees, helping with his first hive as a child on Vancouver's East Side. He's been working with mead for nearly four decades, and he and his partner have over a hundred hives on their farm near Sooke, British Columbia. Inside the low-ceilinged tasting room, we began tasting a series of amber pours, from dry and light double-fermented mead to heavily sweet and fruity dessert meads. After a few sips, a pleasant warmth drove away the last traces of the Pacific Ocean's chill. I could taste the heat and the blossoms, and for a moment I forgot about the approaching winter entirely.

Our love affair with alcohol spans millennia and touches most of the globe, and our alcohols are deeply tied to landscape. Imagine a sake sipped in a Japanese onsen on a snowy evening. Or wine slumbering in long cellars beneath the rolling hills of Bordeaux, France. Imagine whiskey from the moors of Scotland, sipped by the fireside in a snug pub. The list could fill a book,[53] but before those other libations, we started with mead. It is a magical drink fit for gods and heroes; it is the drink of royalty.

Before mead, there must be honey, and before honey, there must be bees. Honeybees are of the genus *Apis*, Latin for bee. There are seven different honeybee species and forty-four subspecies. They all produce honey, but they are very different creatures. *Apis dorsata*, of the subgenus *Megapis*, are giant, open-nesting bees, while *Apis florae* and *Apis andreniformis*, of the subgenus *Micrapis*, are dwarf, single-combed honeybees. But it is *Apis mellifera*, the western honeybee, that we know best. They build large colonies and create delicious surpluses of honey, one of the most concentrated sources of sugar in the natural world. For much of human history, we have been entranced by bees.

Bees came of age in a world rich with flowers. They evolved from short-tongued wasps during the Cretaceous period, roughly 130 million years ago, on the landmass known as Gondwana, which later split into the continents as we now know them. Bees were carried along for the ride. They became attuned to the needs of pollen-producing plants, growing fuzzier (to trap pollen) and longer tongued (to reach nectar). Honeybees appeared roughly thirty-five million years ago, developing their complicated social structure and advanced nest building. We think most bees came from South Asia originally, but not our favored *Apis mellifera*. They arose in North Africa and divided off from the other honeybee species a mere one million years ago.

Bees have a lot of relatives. There are roughly 19,000 "bee-like" species that are found in all regions of the world. However, only four thousand of them produce honey and only the species in *Apis* store honey in concentrated combs of wax. About 500

---

53 A long, pleasant book.

species of stingless bees, meliponines, also make honey that they store in little "pots" they make from wax. Gathering and extracting these tiny blobs of honey is difficult, though not impossible. The Mayans produced such *Melipona* honey as a luxury product for the upper classes. Even today a very small amount of this honey, said to be superior to that made by the common honeybees, can still be found. The effort involved is prohibitive, and the number of *Melipona* colonies kept by bee keepers in South and Central America has fallen by 90 percent in the last decades.

In contrast, the common honeybee makes sweet food in bulk. They live in colonies of up to 60,000 bees, consisting of a single queen, a variable number of workers and a few thousand male drones. The queen leaves the hive for a single mating run, storing enough sperm inside her to last a lifetime. Honeybees exhibit a complex division of labor, tasks divided according to age and colony needs. Some bees gather nectar, some bees make wax. Some tend the young and some guard the hive. There are about a dozen roles in all. Worker bees travel thousands of kilometers to produce a kilogram of honey, making individual flights of up to three kilometers to gather nectar, pollen and water. Each hive controls about eight thousand acres of territory and has its own distinct pheromone fingerprint. The bees that don't forage stay home to build the wax hive, clean up and guard it, and of course to convert nectar into honey. The bees' defining feature is cooperation.

The bees of *Apis mellifera* are important in part because of their temperament. They make an overabundance of honey and are more docile than African and Asian species. All of the honeybees have a complicated dance language, communicating emotions and instructions. Individual worker bees live about six weeks, but hives can persist for centuries. They are a superorganism, acting as one, dancing through pollen-filled summer afternoons. Summer is critical to the bee, and they aren't slacking as they dance. Bees must make honey in summer as they cannot fly once temperatures fall below ten degrees Celsius, and to survive winter, the colony forms a tight ball within the comb, sipping honey to generate heat.

Bees turn nectar into honey by regurgitating it into wax cells, then fanning it to evaporate extra water until its moisture content is 17 to 18 percent. It is about 38 percent fructose, 31 percent glucose and 7 percent maltose and also contains trace elements and nutrients that give honey its distinctive flavor. It is a super-cooled liquid and will sometimes solidify unexpectedly into a translucent glass. If this happens to the honey on your table, you can simply warm it, the same technique used by bees to keep their own reserves liquid. Even in winter, their hives are as temperate as a summer's day. And the wax in the hive is made from honey. Worker bees have glands that convert honey to wax, and then they chew the wax until it is soft and can be added to the hive.

Our hunger for honey is ancient. Deep in our past we began to hunt it, braving swarms of stinging insects to rob natural hives. An eight-thousand-year-old rock painting found in the Cuevas de la Araña in Valencia, Spain, depicts a team of honey hunters using a series of ropes to rob a cliff hive. In the painting, a woman cuts honeycomb from the hive and stows it into a gourd while surrounded by very angry bees. Another painting found in India from five thousand years later shows a similar team of honey hunters gathering combs in a cave. In Africa, hunters collaborated with birds known as honey guides. These birds can't survive the stings themselves, so they led humans and ratels (the honey badger) to hives, letting the mammals do the work of securing the honey. However, the badgers and humans have to give the birds a finder's fee; there is an old African story about a greedy honey hunter who cheated his honey birds. The next time he went hunting, they led him not to a hive, but to a leopard.

Given the risk posed by honey hunting, it isn't surprising that we started trying to bring the honey to us. A bee colony, however, isn't truly a domesticated affair. Our expertise lies in becoming the best possible apian landlord. We don't really know who first set up a home for a colony of bees. Perhaps in Africa honey hunters tired of being led to leopards by ungrateful birds began creating bark containers that they would bait with a little honeycomb. What these hunters noticed was that as summer progressed and bees filled their wild nests with honey, a colony would sometimes divide and a new queen would lead a portion of the hive out into the world to form an offshoot of the original colony. If the hunter was ready with a bark hive, this new colony, called a swarm, might settle into a convenient handcrafted home and stick around awhile. Bark hives have been found in archeological digs around the world. The ability to create honey in larger quantities allowed ancient peoples to take advantage of its amazing qualities. Honey keeps almost indefinitely and packs more calories per gram than just about any other food in nature. It's also antibacterial, making honey one of the earliest effective topical medications.

The honey-loving Egyptians were the first group to move beyond the bark hive. They believed bees were messengers from the gods and felt they were so important that Egyptian rulers divided their kingdom into the reed lands of the South and the bee lands of the North. They contained bees using two technologies — they wove nests out of reeds and they made clay jars to offer bees shelter. They learned that smoke causes bees to calm and retreat, greatly reducing the number of stings a beekeeper received while stealing honey. They learned how to take honey without killing the colony by luring workers and queen into a new hive while robbing the old. They placed a small wooden bridge between the two hives and baited the new one with honey. At some point, they learned about the link between bees, flowers and fruit production, and they began to follow the blooms, using barges to move hives of bees up and down the Nile. They decorated their tombs with images of honeycomb and bees, and Ramses III offered a tribute of 21,000 jars of honey to Hapi, the God of the Nile. They used honey for food and medicine but also in beauty products and as an ingredient in the embalming of the dead. They left pots in tombs as meals for the afterlife. Some of those pots, protected in the hot and dry Egyptian desert, are still edible.

The Greeks also adored honey and incorporated bees into their mythology. One of their myths claims that Zeus was in love with a beautiful young woman named Melissa and turned her into a bee so that she could be immortal and that she spent eternity gathering honey that rained down each night from the stars. They believed that bees would lead a seeker to the Oracle of Delphi.

Aristotle, perhaps tired of lost pilgrims wandering into bee-hives, took a more scientific approach. To understand the bee, he took to the olive groves where bees were kept in straw baskets. He too believed honey came from the sky in the form of dew, but he did notice the link between bees and flowers. He decided the bees gathered their wax from the waxy petals of plants. He noticed the importance of the single big bee within the hive and realized that the workers die if they sting. Aristotle also made progress on our understanding of honey as well, confirming the taste varied depending on which flowers the bees were visiting. The Greeks preferred honey from thyme, savory and marjoram, and they paid a sharp premium for the thyme honey from the Attic Mountains. In 400 BCE, Pericles counted 20,000 bee hives on Mount Hymettus near Athens. There were so many hives that they created an apian roadblock and the statesman Solon legislated a minimum distance of 300 feet between hives so that travelers could pass without being stung.

To the Romans, honey was a necessity for a good life, and even the middle class aspired to keep bees any way they could. They attributed the discovery of honey to Baccus, who was the god of mead before he moved on to be the god of wine, and many Romans spent their days drinking mulsum, a simple wine mixed with honey. Virgil studied bees in the lemon groves behind his home, reconfirming the importance of the one large bee in the hive (the hive often failed if it was removed) and linking honey directly to flowers. However, he did not notice the queen was fertile and instead suggested that baby bees germinated in flowers and corpses. That last idea, perhaps borne from observing maggots exploding from rotting meat, led to some unfortunate experiments involving bull corpses and enclosed rooms. This myth appears in the Bible as well; Samson finds a beehive that has generated in the corpse of a lion and raids it for strength.[54]

Though the Romans were still far from understanding the intricacies of the hive, they achieved dramatic increases in honey production. Virgil documented how to position hives to get the best honeys, and in 310 CE, the emperor Diocletian began controlling the price of this important product. Romans ate a great deal of honey, and over half of the recipes in *Apicius* contain it, including his signature appetizer of dormice submerged in

---

54   There is a type of stingless bee called the vulture bee that makes honey from rotting corpses instead of nectar. Other bees keep their distance.

honey. The very name *Apicius*, which is a pseudonym, means "sought by bees" in Latin.

In their detailed studies of bee behavior, Roman naturalists failed to discover pollination. However, they did take advantage of many other properties of the bee. They perfected the purification of bees' wax through boiling the comb in water, and several Roman colonies paid tribute to the emperor in blocks of pure, fragrant beeswax. They used wax to craft candles for lighting, but also used the material for lost-wax casting and sealing, a process that allowed them to make an accurate duplicate object. Their perfection of this technique represented a quantum leap forward in metalworking, allowing the Romans to produce intricate and sophisticated jewelry.

The Romans weaponized the bee's formidable defensive ability. A bee sting is a punishing mixture of the toxic protein melittin, which damages tissue, and a soup of neurotransmitters that invokes a massive fear response in the victim. The Roman legion kept bees in deliberately fragile clay nests and then launched them over walls. They also intercepted tunneling enemies by digging down into the tunnel and dropping in angry hives. Bees were used similarly to repel enemy ships. The hives were catapulted aboard, driving the enemy into the ocean for relief.

Our current relationship with bees descends from Rome. The fall of the empire was accompanied by a steep decline in honey production as the complex Roman systems of agriculture collapsed, but the art and science of beekeeping persisted in the great houses and religious orders around Europe. Many cultivated hives returned to the wild, and medieval honey hunters would tend giant feral bee trees, carefully guarding their locations. From the tenth to sixteenth centuries, the church was the biggest consumer of wax, used both for polishing woodwork and lighting places of worship. The great cathedrals likely smelled of many things during the medieval period,[55] but one of the more heavenly of these was beeswax. By the sixteenth century, beekeeping was a popular pastime in Britain, and most people with land kept bees. The nectar and pollen in upper class gardens was a tempting target for honey poachers. Enterprising people carried hives on wagons and camped on the edges of the great estate gardens of Britain, while their army of fuzzy striped bandits picked the pockets of the gentry's flowers.

Bees were seen as a model for human monarchies, and for several hundred years, it was assumed that the large bee in the hive was a king. This view was finally corrected in 1609, when entomologist Charles Butler published *The Feminine Monarchy*. He lived under the rule of Queen Elizabeth I, which perhaps made the truth more palatable. Today Queen Elizabeth II has both a Royal Botanist and a Royal Beekeeper, who tends the hives at Buckingham Palace that supply the Queen's breakfast tray. From market gardener to monarch, bees and their honey have left their mark on our food system.

Back on the Pacific Rim, we left the meadery and returned to Victoria with a newly purchased bottle of metheglin, a mead made by adding herbs to the fermenting liquid. April made us a simple supper of steamed mussels and kale salad, and we sipped our mead as we watched the sky darken over the ocean. The euphoria from the mead crept over me, though that might have simply been the good food and pleasant company. For dessert, we baked a small wheel of fresh local brie with honey and dried apricots.

---

55 The most powerful members of medieval society were buried beneath the church floor, giving us the phrase "stinking rich."

"You are treating me far too well," I said. "This is such a perfect dish."

April spread a thick blob of brie onto a chunk of crusty bread. "I love cheese and mead because they pair so naturally. The sweetness of the mead goes well with seafood and cheese for sure. This mead and the honey it's made from reflect the landscape. The bees eat fireweed and arbutus blossom. It's a link to the landscape. The cheese too, really. This is a sheep's milk brie, and the sheep feed on the same plants and flowers as the bees."

We drained our glasses, refilled them and dug out more blobs of molten cheese.

Bees contributed food, medicine and wax to human society. All of these were important, but to many ancient writers and scholars, mead was an even greater gift from the gods. If the moisture content of honey rises above 19 percent, something quite remarkable happens. The natural yeast within the honey awakens and begins to consume the dense sugars, producing alcohol. The communities that gathered honey quickly discovered this effect, a first introduction into the world of intoxication. The natural fermentation is rapid, creating one of the simplest and most quickly obtainable alcoholic beverages. Mead can be mixed with fruits and spices, grain or hops, but the basic recipe remains the same. Take honey and just add water. The natural yeast will create an alcohol content of 3 or 4 percent before that same alcohol stops the yeast's growth, leaving plenty of unfermented sugars. The glucose ferments first, but honey also contains fructose, leaving the simplest meads very sweet. Mead creates a mild euphoria along with the more standard intoxication (from the sugar, largely), and that euphoria made mead a staple in every culture that collected honey. French anthropologist Claude Lévi-Strauss went so far as to argue that mead was the marker of a human transition from nature to culture, the first real technology. It certainly was the source of the first real hangover.

We began making mead early. We have pottery shards with traces of mead dating from 7000 BC, and the oldest description of mead, found in the Hindu hymns of the Rigveda, was written about 1500 BCE. The Greeks drank mead before they moved on to wine, and by the fourth century, the Roman agricultural writer Palladius described four common varieties of mead. Aristotle and Pliny the Elder both discuss mead, waxing lyrical over the Greek practice of making mead with late-season honey and then saving the results in amphora for semi-annual orgies.

The first recipe for mead dates from 60 CE, when the Spanish-Roman naturalist Columella wrote that mead could be made by mixing stored rainwater or boiled water with honey in a ratio of roughly two liters of water per kilogram of honey, then aging the mixture in the sun for a week. This is a sound method: the solar radiation kills errant bacteria, allowing the yeast to work unmolested. Pollio Romulus, one of the first people documented to have lived to be a century old, wrote to Julius Caesar, crediting mead both for his longevity and for allowing him to pursue a vibrant sex life despite his extremely advanced age.

Mead became the drink of choice again after the collapse of Roman winemaking. Queen Elizabeth I had her own mead made from a special royal recipe. Farther north, in the lore of Viking ancestors, Odin drank mead made from giant's blood, and young Vikings proclaimed their intent to marry by stealing away to spend a lunar cycle drinking mead in each other's company, giving us the modern term honeymoon.

Modern mead is a little more complicated than the stuff of Greek and Roman banquets, but the technique is roughly the same. We now bottle young mead with hardy champagne yeast that converts fructose into alcohol, creating a stronger and dryer product. A number of classic varieties are still produced, including metheglin, which includes spices or herbs (cloves, cinnamon and hops are all popular); acerglyn, which contains maple syrup; bochet, which uses caramelized honey to create a smoky bouquet; melomel, which includes fruit; and even rhodomel, a very rare mead brewed with rose hips and petals. Honey and roses.

The chain holds true even now. Mead needs honey, and honey requires bees and flowers. Bees, and many other insects like them, are threatened by the changes humanity is inflicting upon the planet.

Chapter Twelve

THE SEX LIFE OF PLANTS

Thirty-five percent of our food species are directly or indirectly dependent upon pollinators. I learned this lesson (if not the exact figure) early. A huge colony of honeybees lived in a hollow tree near our family orchard, its secret recesses stuffed with comb. When the tree blew over in a storm, my uncle trimmed the limbs off of a section of the main trunk and propped it upright in an attempt to save the colony, but the bees didn't stay. They formed a tight ball and headed off for a better home. We did manage to salvage several five-gallon buckets of honey, but that wasn't why we wanted the bees near our orchard. Apple blossoms must be pollinated to set fruit, and 97 percent of the time, that pollination is completed by a bee.

The wild roses blowing in the winds at Botanical Beach and the apple trees shading my hammock are part of a vast family of plants that has flourished by adapting the very successful properties of reproducing sexually by flowering, fruiting and creating seeds. The angiosperms, or flowering plants, are the most diverse group of land plants, with nearly 300,000 identified species. They developed from non-flowering gymnosperms[56] about 225 million years ago in the Triassic Period and were flowering by about 160 million years ago. These plants diversified rapidly in the lower Cretaceous and have dominated entire ecosystems and landscapes ever since. Plant sex, it seems, was a good idea.

Pollination involves the transfer of pollen from the male anther of the plant to the female stigma, and at its simplest, this can involve movement by gravity within the same flower. However, for plants to diversify, they must trade genetic material, and to do so they face a fundamental barrier; they can't stroll over to another plant with a bottle of wine and a smile. They require a matchmaker. The first such mediators were environmental, and wind and water are still common vectors of pollination. Our three biggest food crops, rice, wheat and corn, are all wind pollinated, a process called anemophily. But other critical species have learned to use living pollinators. Several hundred thousand species of animal play this role. The majority are insects, but there are as many as 1,500 species of birds and mammals who also do the job, including the lemur, which holds title as the largest pollinator on earth.

Flowers use scent and color to attract pollinators. Bat-pollinated plants, for example, tend to have white flowers with sweet nectar that bloom at night. Bats can easily see the flowers, enjoy sipping the sweet nectar and transfer pollen as they flit from flower to flower. Bats are important pollinators that feed particularly on commercial crops, including banana and mango. Plants pollinated by hummingbirds produce great quantities of nectar. Some plants smell like rotting meat, drawing the carrion fly in for a landing. Figs use wasps for pollination, trapping

---

56 Conifers for the most part.

the female wasp inside the fruit. The newly hatched wasps then escape the fig through tiny channels chewed open by the male wasp. Other flowers use butterflies, and these plants often create flowers in clusters, creating a platform for the butterflies to land upon. Some tropical plants in Hawaii and Australia require honeycreepers, a small colorful group of bird species, for pollination. And the lemur? This cute creature pollinates the traveler's palm tree. The lemurs pull open the tough flowers and stick their snouts inside, then carry pollen to the next flower on their noses and paws.

Flowering plants and insect pollinators are an example of mutualism, the cooperation between two organisms of different species such that each individual benefits from the actions of the other. The first fossil of a plant reliant on pollination was a fern and dates to the late Carboniferous period. A gymnosperm, the plants didn't require living creatures for pollination, though by the Triassic Period the fern spore was hitching a ride on the legs of passing animals to supplement wind pollination. But it is the angiosperms that perfected pollination.

Bees treat flowers like a one-stop convenience store. The blossoms provide bees with nectar, an energy supply, and with pollen, a source of protein. Bees also stop at flowers to gather oil, fragrance and water droplets. Consider another mutualist, the coral, which collaborates with algae. Or the 50 percent of land plants that rely on fungi in the soil to provide them the trace elements they need.

Remember the rats and mosquitos that invaded Hawaii? They have driven two-thirds of the endemic honeycreeper bird species to extinction on the islands, and those small colorful birds provided pollination and dispersal services for a wide range of local trees and flowers. Without the birds, the plants can't survive. Many of our crops have evolved mutualistic relationships with honeybees to the point where we ourselves also experience mutualism with our buzzing friends.

The extinction of pollinators could have a larger impact on our food system than the extinction of individual food species themselves. And many pollinators are threatened. Bats are struggling with a fungal disease and habitat loss, and the lemurs are struggling with habitat loss. Recent studies have shown a dramatic decline in general insect populations, including flies that pollinate a variety of critical crops. But for overall impact, it is the loss of the bees we must fear. Our food system is carried on their gossamer wings.

How badly do we need bees? The 35 percent of bee-pollinated plants are responsible for about one-quarter of all of our calories, and that one-quarter contains a huge variety of crops that help to make our cuisines nutritious and interesting. As a small sample, bees polinate most fruit, most berries, okra, onions, beets, canola plants, broccoli and the other cruciferous vegetables, peppers, safflower, many of our spices, buckwheat, sesame, beans and potatoes. We'd want for mustard and for vegetables such as carrots that need polination to set seed.

Unexpectedly, meat production needs pollination too, as cattle use alfalfa as winter feed, and chickens eat grains and seeds from pollinated crops. Coffee is partially self-pollinating, but yield would drop about 50 percent without bees. Similarly, chocolate yields would fall. Cotton requires pollination, as do some timber species. Native North American plants don't need honeybees specifically, but they do require other bee species.

Overall, bees are responsible for sixty major crops in the United States alone, and we estimate that honeybees contribute nineteen billion dollars' worth of crop production nationally, while other pollinators contribute another ten billion. These links between crops and pollinators are ancient and continue even in the age of massive farms and monocultures. And it is there, on those monocultural farms stretching from horizon to horizon, that we encounter the problem. Bees thrive on diversity and attachment to place, and modern agriculture creates a very different environment.

Consider the apple. Each apple's seeds have a different genetic makeup than its parents, creating the wondrous variation described earlier. Pollination management is critical to a successful orchard. One usually plants a variety of cultivars to ensure that several different species are in bloom at the same time. Apples aren't picky and are also pollinated by solitary bees and flies, but a hive of honeybees plunked into an orchard greatly increases fruit production. Inadequate pollination leads to small misshapen apples with few seeds.

Apples and pollinators have been working together since their time on the foothills of the Tian Shan Mountains, and both bees and our favorite temperate fruit have played an active role in culinary and agricultural history. Pliny described twenty-three cultivars of apple, which is more than we find in stores today. Romans also valued apple honey, as it carries a strong floral flavor that speaks of the orchard in bloom.

Apples emerged as a critical ancient and medieval fruit. They kept well, could be eaten raw, cooked or juiced, and fermented into both cider and vinegar. Apple orchards are also extremely long-lived. In 1666, Newton observed an apple falling from a tree, spurring his theories of gravitation, and cuttings from that tree still live. That apple, by the way, was the extremely rare variety Flower of Kent. Bees buzzed nearby in woven nests called skeps, and many great houses had niches carved into their walls to shelter and protect these fragile hives. We remember Newton's apple, but we forget that its growth required bees.

Like pears, apples expanded in variety and popularity in North

America, but that expansion required bees to make the crossing to the continents of the Western Hemisphere as well. Bees came to North America early. In 1621, the Virginia Company sent a ship loaded with peacocks and beehives to the settlements, and once ashore, the bees proved the more adaptable cargo. They quickly moved into the flower-filled woods of the continent to set up wild colonies, flying far ahead of the edge of European territory. Only the Rocky Mountains stopped them; bees were introduced to the Pacific states separately. Bees did so well in North America that some of the nomadic pigeon hunters also worked as honey hunters, supplementing their income by exploring forests for caches of honey in wild hives.

Apples found their own in North America. They were planted for cider at first, grown in bulk from seed in vast nurseries hacked out of the forests along river migration routes. New varieties such as the Northern Spy and the McIntosh emerged out of these orchards, and the apple pie became a national symbol. In the heyday of the apple, there were as many as 17,000 varieties available, including lost varieties such as the massive Cullowhee, which was up to twenty-one inches in circumference; the Indahoma, which was deep ruby red and oblong; and the Adam and Eve, which often produced two apples fused together into one double-cored fruit. The USDA created a division of pomology in 1866, by order of President Abraham Lincoln. At their largest, this division employed fifty full-time artists to prepare portraits of the different cultivars of the national fruit. The USDA also encouraged the keeping of bees wherever possible to support the expanding orchard industry.

Apple cultivation wasn't the only thing to come into its own in the United States. Mid-nineteenth century America was also the site for one of the greatest advances in beekeeping. Lorenzo Langstroth was a tutor at Yale and a Protestant minister, but in his spare time he was a tinkerer and a keeper of bees. Lorenzo hated breaking up hives to harvest honey, as so often the colony died before it could resettle in a new home. He had a radical idea: what if the sections of the hive containing honey could be easily removed and replaced? He realized that in nature bees leave corridors in their hives for access, and that if a person created a nest of removable frames that were separated by one bee width, the bees would not connect the frames with wax. He also realized that bees only raise young near the queen, and that one can exclude the queen from sections of the hive as she is so much larger. He built his first hive on October 31, 1851, and his innovative structure is still used today. The first box of frames contains the hive with its queen and brood, and further boxes added above, known as supers, are separated from the first box with a queen excluder, a barrier that allows worker bees but not the larger queen to cross between boxes. These upper supers are then filled with stored wax and honey. A beekeeper can remove frames from these upper boxes without overly disturbing the hive.

Langstroth's invention allowed for beekeeping on a much larger scale, and for the first time, beekeepers could make a living producing honey exclusively. These new hives were also much easier to move than earlier versions, and once bees could be transported simply, farmers began paying beekeepers to truck their hives to pollinator-starved fields.

"Could you hold this for a second?" My farmer friend's[57] phone was ringing insistently. I wondered how she felt about letting

---

57   She wants to remain anonymous. I'm thankful she let me hang out with her bees.

it go to voicemail. She was trying to hand me a frame from a newly opened super, throbbing with hundreds of bees. "Just for a minute. Take this, they won't hurt you."

I took the frame gingerly and tried not to think about the sheer amount of stinging power represented by the life crawling over the cells. The bees were groggy from smoke, but they were still making small forays onto my hands and forearms. They tickled. They were delightfully fuzzy. Beneath them, honey glistened in rows of perfect hexagonal cells. The beekeeper hung up and motioned to me that she was ready to take the frame from me.

I slowly took a deep breath. "Thanks. This frame is pretty heavy. There's a lot of honey in there already."

I carefully passed back the frame and shook a few stray bees back into the open hive with a flick of my hand. Inside, they hummed with frantic activity. These bees didn't travel; the hives belonged to a farmer who grew a wide variety of bee-friendly crops. When they grew bored with vegetables, they could wander across the road and onto the nearby fireweed-covered hills. I watched the beekeeper expertly slide the frame back into the hive and pop the lid into place. The bees settled into their morning routine, perching on the entrance of the hive before heading off into the sun. Soon, most of the workers would be out foraging, and the rest of the bees would be evaporating honey, tending to the young and the queen or doing a little housekeeping. The fall air was nippy, but the afternoon sun might heat the hive enough that the bees would start fanning at the entrances to keep themselves and their home cool.

Back in the honey house, we sampled various flavors and examined large blocks of beeswax destined for a local candle company. Bees are a hobby for my friend, a handy sideline that brings in a little extra money and improves pollination on her farm. She doesn't move her bees for rental and doesn't expand beyond a few hives. She leaves enough honey to support the colony over the winter. Commercial producers take more honey from their hives and often have to supplement the bee's remaining honey stores by feeding bees dishes of corn syrup. This, on the other hand, was old-school beekeeping, the sort of beekeeping that dominated rural landscapes for centuries, though it is no longer the norm.

The modern honeybee gets around. As agriculture shifted to monoculture crops, local pollinating species simply couldn't keep up with demand, as thousands of acres of identical flowers opened at once. Roughly seven decades ago, farmers began paying beekeepers to relocate Langstroth hives during blossom season, but road conditions provided a thorny obstacle. No one, and I mean no one, wants to lose a load of angry bees on a busy highway. To move bees, one needs very good roads.

Just as American industrial monocultures were pushing against the limits of local pollination, they were saved by Dwight D. Eisenhower's National System of Interstate and Defense Highways, commonly known as the Interstate. Created by the Federal Aid Highway Act of 1956, the road system was built over the next four decades, eventually totaling 77,500 kilometers of road, at a cost of roughly half a trillion dollars. In Canada, construction of a transcontinental highway system began in 1950 and was largely completed by 1970. Suddenly food could be shipped cheaply and safely over long distances, and so could bees.

The first mass movement of bees occurred in the late 1950s and early 1960s as Florida expanded citrus production. However, the best-known example remains the largest: the wild and crazy rush to pollinate the almonds of California.

Almonds, like apples, come from the crisp air of the Tian Shan Mountains and are pollinated almost exclusively by bees. Every year in mid-February, the almond trees of California's central valley begin to awaken, unfurling billions of delicate five-pet-aled flowers in shades of white and pink. The almond fields cover 800,000 acres and stretch from Sacramento to Los Angeles, some ninety million trees in total. This forest, though beautiful, is like nothing found in nature. It consists of almond trees and little else. There are roughly thirty varieties of almonds planted in diagonal rows that alternate by cultivar to allow for cross-pollination. But by what pollinators? Bees can't live in a monoculture; the flowers last little more than a week, and for maximum nut production each flower must be visited multiple times. Bees, however, take time to gather enough honey to last a year. Like us, they require a varied diet pulled from hundreds of plant species. This variety provides both a wide range of trace nutrients and as long a feeding season as possible. They can't possibly live on a week-long almond binge. It's the equivalent of a human trying to live for a month on one night at the all-you-can-eat buffet. Even the most earnest of attempts would lead to malnutrition and starvation.

Each year, in order to create three-quarters of the world's supply of almonds for snacking, nut butter, protein bars, almond milk and a growing list of other products, we bring the bees to the trees. Sixteen hundred beekeepers truck in one million boxes of bees, thirty billion bees in all, still sleepy from the winter. For beekeepers, this one move might yield half of their annual income. For almond producers, having at least two hives per acre has raised production from 500 kilograms of nuts per acre in the 1960s to 1,500 kilograms of nuts per acre now. In California's central valley, bee rental is 20 percent of an almond farmer's production cost.

The bees don't stop at almonds. Once the flowers wilt, the bees must move or starve, and so the beekeepers and their bees head to cherry, plum and avocado orchards in California or to apple and cherry orchards in Washington State. As summer begins, the bees move into alfalfa fields on the Great Plains, then on to sunflower and clover fields. Some bees move south to Texas squash fields or Florida citrus groves, or north for blueberries and cranberries. In a great circle, the bees follow the blooms with their roaming beekeepers. As Rowan Jacobsen writes in *Fruitless Fall*, our food system relies on crops supported by middle-aged men with wooden boxes and tin smokers.

This system has begun to fail. For a time, monocultures greatly boosted efficiency and production. Free from the need for local pollination, farmers planted monocultural crops from fence line to fence line. Beekeepers hit the road each spring, making a decent living from bee rental fees and sales of wax and honey. But this mode of operation was intrinsically vulnerable. Putting all of the continent's bees together for a giant week-long almond orgy guaranteed that problems from one hive would spread rapidly through the entire population. And the travel wasn't ideal either. The hives must be sealed for travel, so the bees can't regulate hive temperature, forage or conduct housekeeping. It is amazing that this mass pollination worked for as long as it did. However, in the early years of the twenty-first century, the inevitable happened: the bees started to die.

A hive of bees is a delicate and complicated organism that functions through careful specialization. Each bee has a job, and if those jobs aren't carried out, the whole organism begins to suffer. In the early years of this century, beekeepers began to log an alarming rise in what is called Colony Collapse Disorder, or CCD. Seemingly healthy hives suddenly empty out, leaving behind a confused queen, a few nurse bees and a large store of honey. The problem began to creep into the industrial pollination stocks in the 1970s, but it was still just the odd hive here and there. Numbers of collapsed hives rose in the 1990s, but the turn of the century brought a new intensity to this old problem.

A hive plagued with CCD is worse than useless; the worker bees simply vanish, ending honey production and pollination. And whatever causes CCD, it is contagious. Bees from healthy hives avoid the remaining honey in a CCD hive as if it were under an ancient curse. If a CCD hive is forcibly merged with a healthy hive, the healthy hive will die as well.

The result of the CCD epidemic was immediate. In North America, populations of *Apis mellifera* crashed, and in Europe and the United Kingdom declines were severe, if not quite as catastrophic. Crops worth hundreds of billions of dollars were put into jeopardy as pollination costs rose sharply. With fewer hives available, bees from as far away as Australia were brought in to pollinate California's almonds. Almond pollination in particular became somewhat of an apian suicide mission; in North America, losses from CCD ran as high as 50 to 70 percent of hives, putting beekeepers' livelihoods under threat. No definitive cause has been found, though several causes have been suggested, including Varroa mites (*Varroa destructor*, named for Roman beekeeper Marcus Terentius Varro), neonicotinoids, pathogens, habitat loss, climate change and the large-scale movement of hives for pollination. Likely the answer involves some combination of these, a collection of challenges that stressed bees simply can't fight off.

Colony Collapse Disorder isn't exactly new, but in the past it was rare. The strange condition was first noticed in 1869, when empty hives began popping up in a few scattered areas of North America. Over the decades, the condition was given many names, including spring dwindle, autumn collapse and disappearing disease. Despite these names, the condition doesn't seem to be restricted to a season and also doesn't seem to be a disease exactly. Sometimes bee colonies simply fall apart, for reasons unknown. However, when the disorder exploded around the world in the early twenty-first century, the hunt for a better understanding began. With entire beekeeping operations wiped out in weeks, the future of pollinated crops required us to understand this puzzling condition in which the adult worker bees go missing and no dead bees are left behind to be found. They vanish. Unhatched bees remain, the queen remains, a few nurse bees remain, the honey remains.

Losses in North America have been most severe. The total number of hives is down from 4.5 million in 1980 to 2.89 million in 2017. The number is up slightly thus far in 2018 after years of decline, in part due to ambitious replacement programs. Typical CCD losses are roughly 25 percent per year, though in some regions they rise to 50 percent, leading President Barack Obama to unveil a national strategy for improving the health of the bee population in 2015 that included funding for research and habitat restoration. In Europe, losses were similar, though overall European bees are individually healthier. Asia, however, saw losses of only 10 percent. Asian bees, though harder to work with and less abundant honey producers, seem more resilient.

The modern bee faces a wide range of challenges, which makes understanding CCD difficult. The USDA identified sixty-one potential stressors on modern beehives, which is a lot for any organism to have on its plate. The first of these, Varroa mites, are an old scourge of Asian honeybees, but they didn't come to North America until the 1990s. In Asia, bees know how to target mites within the hives, and when they find them, they quickly kill them and toss them out the front door. And rightly so. The mite is a vampire, digging into brood chambers and sucking the life out of bee larvae, then clamping onto the back of an adult bee and drinking its blood. Mites are particularly insidious as they weaken the colony gradually, leaving the hive open to raids from other healthy colonies, who then can end up bringing home mites along with stolen honey, spreading disease further.

Varroa is the most destructive scourge of honeybees, killing some outright and weakening the immune system of survivors. Mite-infested colonies are less likely to survive the winter, and their queen struggles to reproduce. Varroa might also be getting a boost from Lorenzo Langstroth's hive itself; wild colonies have shown better immunity to mites, and this might be a result of better construction techniques. Bees in modern beehives build their wax cells along lines inscribed by humans on the empty frames while wild hives have a combination of cell sizes. Brood cells are among those made smaller, perhaps allowing nurse bees to hear the mites in the cells.

Mites alone cannot explain CCD, however. Another leading contender is the use of pesticides and fungicides on crops, specifically the neonicotinoids, chemicals somewhat similar to nicotine. A 2013 study conducted at the University of Maryland found colonies contain on average nine different pesticides and fungicides in their pollen. The study also found a correlation between the number of these chemicals present and the number of mites in the colony. These chemicals don't kill the bees outright but rather impair their development and behavior, perhaps interfering with their navigating and chemical signaling, which would explain why hives with CCD are so empty of bees. They become disoriented and can't find their way back to the hive.

Some of these chemicals are used to coat seeds, and they linger in plants and soil. Bees might not be directly exposed, but they gather nectar from millions of flowers and then concentrate it, concentrating pesticides in the process as well. Neonicotinoids have been shown to cause memory problems in bees and in other animals. If these chemicals weaken a bee's immune system, it is more likely to be infected by pathogens including bacteria, which cause infections, and viruses that deform its wings. Action has been taken against neonicotinoids in the European Union, and the European Food Safety Authority has banned three of the chemicals thought to pose a particularly strong risk to honeybees. They have not yet been banned in the United States.

The weather and landscape have also become less friendly to bees. Climate change is a possible factor in CCD, as extreme conditions keep bees inside and, when bees are overheated, they must gather water instead of nectar, reducing their honey stores. Habitat loss is another possible factor. Before industrial agriculture, bees were treated to a diverse buffet of crops and flowers and there was enough wild landscape to provide even more variety. Even farm fields had hedgerows and woodlots, islands of bee-friendly habitat. Bees are like humans and require food from many sources to obtain enough nutrients. As habitat vanishes and with it the variety of available foods, the bees become malnourished, weakening already stressed hives.

The large-scale movement of bees by truck is also a potential factor. Hives are meant to be place-based. Bees are creatures of habit, establishing territories and internal maps of food sources. While in transit, bees are trapped in a jostling hive, and once repositioned they are in a new landscape with decidedly different food sources. Bees transported for pollination are exposed to new viruses and different mites, a challenging environment for any creature. Bees trapped in the hive are very vulnerable.

Wild pollinators weren't spared by CCD, but they responded to the mysterious disorder differently. As domestic CCD prevalence spiked, wild populations collapsed as well, but the diversity of wild populations ensured that sufficient numbers survived to repopulate. Feral honeybee numbers are now at least stable, adjusting for habitat loss, and wild bees are increasingly adept at kicking Varroa mites out of their homes. Even domestic numbers are looking somewhat better as breeders attempt to develop more resilient populations. CCD has peaked somewhat, with colony loss in North America falling from previous highs.

There is variance in the North American numbers as Canada lost only 17 percent of its bees in 2016–17 compared to 21 percent in the U.S. In New Zealand, that number was even lower at 10 percent. Central Europe's numbers are similar to those found in New Zealand. Americans are still doing something very wrong when it comes to the health of pollinators. Beekeepers are struggling to keep their businesses economically viable, but losses on the scale of the last decade represent more than simply a high economic cost. They take an emotional toll as well. Beekeepers are beekeepers because they love bees. They don't want to send their hives off to slaughter beneath the waving pink blossoms of the California almond belt.

In the fight to protect our culinary species from extinction, bees matter. Life without pollination, or at least the culinary parts of life, would be difficult, expensive and much less diverse. We have a few models for what agriculture would look like without pollination. In the case of one of the world's most popular spices, humans must fill the role of the missing pollinator. I love vanilla, and I always have a few high-quality beans marinating in vodka somewhere in the back of my spice cupboard. I'm not alone. Vanilla is the world's most popular flavoring agent and the most expensive spice after saffron.

I got my first look at vanilla farming during my fieldwork in Hawaii County, where I visited the Hawaiian Vanilla Company, a farm run by Jim Reddekopp and his family. As my team and

I braved winding roads and the driving rain on the Hamakua Coast of the Big Island to visit the farm, I felt a building excitement. Reddekopp and his family began growing vanilla orchids in 1998. At the time, no vanilla was grown in Hawaii, but it seemed possible. The climate was mild and humid, and the market was strong. From the large tasting room, we trekked down to his shade structures where the vibrant green vines snaked up support poles. A few pods dotted the vines, looking rather like oversized green beans. These pods exist because of the skill and patience of Jim Reddekopp's wife, Tracy. For vanilla in Hawaii, like vanilla in most of the world, lacks its insect pollinator.

Vanilla is a truly exotic crop. It is produced from orchids of the genus *Vanilla*, mainly from *Vanilla planifolia*, the Mexican vanilla bean. This type is often called Bourbon vanilla, after the island of Réunion (once called Île Bourbon), where it is also grown. A closely related cultivar, *Vanilla tahitensis*, is grown in the South Pacific and is known as Tahitian vanilla. Bourbon vanilla has the highest vanillin content, the aromatic oil that gives vanilla its distinctive flavor.

Vanilla is the only edible orchid out of twenty-five thousand species of these lovely plants, an unassuming deep green vine that grows wild in the tropical lowland forests of southern and eastern Mexico, Central America and the northern parts of South America. The lime green pods wither and turn black on the vine, emitting a weak essence of the beloved bean. We've learned to process these beans to maximize the amount of vanillin recovered, and we learned to use alcohol extraction processes to bring out the flavor more distinctively.

Vanilla, like most orchids, is quite slow growing. Only after its third year of growth does the *Vanilla planifolia* vine flower, fully opening over the course of about two months. Each flower is only completely open for twenty-four hours, and it must be pollinated within eight to twelve hours of blooming or else the flower wilts and drops from the vine and no pods are produced. This is a plant that needs a prompt pollinator.

Vanilla has a rich history. It was first harnessed by the Totonac people of Mexico, who used the beans for incense and medicine, but it was the conquering Aztecs who began processing the beans to produce an additive for food. They named the pods tlilxochitl, which translates roughly as black flower. The Aztecs began to mix vanilla into their drinking chocolate and, when the new flavor caught on, they demanded tribute in the form of vanilla pods from the conquered Totonacs, who bundled them up and sent this rare and fragrant tax to Tenochtitlan, the Aztec capital. The Aztecs were conquered in turn by the Spanish, and Hernán Cortéz took vanilla back to Europe as one of his most prized treasures from the Americas. He also brought the vanilla orchid itself home, but the plants proved tricky to grow so far from their native territory. The first vanilla plant to blossom in Europe belonged the Honourable Charles Grenville, a member of the House of Commons and an avid horticulturalist. He coaxed the orchid into bloom in 1806 at his home on the outskirts of London. However, much to his disappointment, no pods formed on the vines, for the plant was without its pollinator. But what creature was this? And, the Europeans wondered as they contemplated the barren vines, how could they find this mysterious pollinator?

Vanilla has an interesting sex life. Like many plants, it has both male and female parts within the flower. It is even self-fertile (no second vanilla plant is needed), but there is a catch. The anther and stigma are separated by a membrane called the rostellum, and that membrane must be moved if the pollen is to transfer from one chamber of the flower to the other. In nature, bees of the genus *Melipona* can manipulate the rostellum, as can some hummingbirds, but neither of these species is easy to transport to a new environment. This pollination conundrum gave Mexico a 300-year monopoly on vanilla, as the native birds and bees pollinated enough of the flowers in a timely manner to allow large-scale production of pods.

Once the flower is pollinated, a six- to ten-inch pod forms, filled with thousands of tiny black seeds. As the pods whither, they become coated with crystalized needles of vanillin, called givre, which is French for hoarfrost. The intensity of this frosting determines the value of the crop. The pods with their crystals and tiny seeds can then be used to make vanilla sugar or vanilla extract or added directly to a food.

The trouble with vanilla has always been its rarity. By 1819, a series of entrepreneurs attempted to establish vanilla orchids in Réunion, Haiti and Madagascar in the hopes something local might pollinate the flowers. No indigenous pollinator took up the challenge. The problem was finally understood in 1836, when French botanist Charles François Antoine Morren observed pollination by accident while he drank coffee on a patio in Veracruz. He noticed small black bees circling vanilla orchids that grew near his table, and he watched them work their way into the flowers. He returned every day (and we assume had more coffee) and confirmed that pods formed on the vine that had been visited by the bees. However, the botanist couldn't replicate the action of the bees despite his best efforts. That was eventually achieved in 1841 by Edmond Albius, a twelve-year-old slave of French colonist Féréol Bellier Beaumont on the island of Réunion. He used a sliver of bamboo to lift the membrane (known as the rostellum) and then used his thumb to knock pollen from anther to stigma. Albius was freed in 1848 when slavery was outlawed in France's colonies. Despite his incredible contribution to vanilla farming, he died in poverty in 1880.

Today almost all vanilla is produced this way, including the vanilla I saw growing in Hawaii. And this time- and labor-intensive process of hand pollination is expensive. Additionally, any crop that is hand pollinated is rare due to the cost and effort needed to produce it, and as native bee populations in Mexico decline, the future for vanilla seems to be one of careful hand manipulation of one of nature's fussiest flowers. The only reason we carry out this exhausting agricultural act is that artificial substitutes for vanilla do not replicate the complexity of the natural product. Imitations have been made from scent glands from beavers, from pulp mill effluent and through genetic modification of yeast, but ultimately nothing yet beats a true vanilla bean. I use mine liberally in desserts and even slosh some into the odd main course. Those tiny black seeds, and their heavenly smell, are worth the price.

Dan had been keeping a low profile as I explored the world of bees. He was busy writing up his results from his time with the screaming frogs and was also allergic to the sting of *Apis mellifera*. I agreed that his untimely demise due to anaphylaxis was to be avoided, but now that spending time with me and my research wasn't likely to end with a trip to the hospital, he wanted the same thing that all creatures who have ever robbed a hive want: a sweet succulent meal. We met to plan. I was hoping for something less elaborate than the turducken.

"The weather is gorgeous today. How about instead of a dinner, we do an afternoon tea?" I asked. "A pollination tea. If it stays this warm, we could hold it on your patio. All of the foods have to be connected to or marked in some way by pollination."

"I like the idea. But no bees, right? Like, none?"

"Can I invite the beekeeper?"

"Of course. As long as she doesn't bring the bees."

Once we started planning, it became clear that the English tradition of afternoon tea is completely dependent on pollination. Tea itself is a pollinated species; in order to generate new tea plants, the lovely flowers of *Camellia sinensis* must be visited by bees. I asked my friend Katya to choose the tea; in addition to her skill at sourcing vegetarian burgers, she is an expert in the art of turning leaves and hot water into aromatic magic. She picked a lovely *Lapsang souchong*, a black tea dried in the smoke of pinewood fires in the Wuyi region of China's Fujian province. It is one of the oldest black teas and carries a strong smoky flavor. I made cucumber sandwiches with produce from a local greenhouse where the grower uses bumblebees to ensure a good crop. Dan made curried chicken sandwiches. The chicken had been fed on bee-pollinated alfalfa. The vegan version we prepared for Katya was made from soybeans that are self-pollinating, but new research in Australia suggests honeybee pollination increases soybean yield by 40 percent. Dan included raisins in his curry recipe, and they come from the grape, whose pollination is assisted by bees. We also added some fresh grapes to the tiered plates and, instead of the more traditional cakes and scones, we made a pan of baklava using honey from the farm I'd visited. Dan alternated layers of filo with an almond mixture, lavishly slathering each layer with melted butter. When he was done, he poured a hot mixture of honey boiled with spices and lemon over it all. He stared at the food.

"You know, the bees played a big role in this meal."

"It is amazing. I've never been so thankful for bees before."

Afternoon tea is a light meal developed in the 1840s to help members of the upper class survive the long gap between lunch and the late dinners of the time. But today, it is a good excuse for conversation and fun. We had the traditional tea and sandwiches, served with our own take on the sweets, even though I enjoy the classic scone with cream and jam as well. Dan chose a very light mead to go along with the tea, and soon everyone was nibbling and sipping. My beekeeping friend was very fond of the baklava and managed to convince Dan to give up the recipe in exchange for some honey. The local bees buzzed in the lavender, Dan giving them wary side glances.

Later, the dishes washed and the last of the tea gone, I found myself returning to the idea of mutualism. Even some of the crops that aren't directly reliant on bees (the grapes and soy for example) achieve bigger yields when bees are present. Bees also strengthen the ecosystem in general through pollination. Understanding the struggle to safeguard our pollinators changed the way I saw the food system.

Every monoculture we develop looks like it exists independently of nature, a perfect machine for delivering cucumbers or pumpkins or grapes. But this perception isn't true. Nature is a web, held together by keystone species and mutualisms. If we lose the bees, so many fruit, vegetable and other plant crops would soon follow. Very few of these crops would command the needed price to keep them on the world's table through hand pollination, if that were even possible. Most people would find their choices slashed to those plants that can get along without the magic of bees. Even if bees themselves survive, if keeping them becomes too difficult, many of the honey nomads who support the food system will be forced to hang up their bee hoods and find other work. They are passionate about their industry, but they still have to make enough money to survive. The pollination game played in North America works only as long as it is economical to load hives onto trucks and take them on the road.

Bees are a bellwether species. They are an excellent indicator of environmental health in general, for they are sensitive to subtle changes in landscape. Bees are vulnerable because they concentrate chemicals and live and die in a compact hive, and if one bee gets sick they take that sickness home to all of their housemates.

Today, the bees are indicating to us that something is very wrong with the world. We would be wise to listen. If bees go, a number of critical culinary species follow.

On a brighter note, I found myself for the first time in a position to directly help the species I was studying. Bees need habitat with diverse food sources, and so I headed up to my family's orchard to scatter a few sacks of clover among the orchard grass. The puffy white clover flowers would be an excellent food source for the local bees.

Everyone can do a few simple things for them. We can avoid using pesticides, we can plant bee crops and let our lawns go a little wild. And, of course, we can support our local mead maker. My work done, I bundled up, uncorked a bottle of fine dry mead and walked through the fallen leaves down to my hammock in the orchard, where I dreamed of the flowers of distant spring.

Chapter Thirteen

WABI-SABI

During the last gasp of winter, I returned to the public market at Granville Island and settled at a table with a coffee and a newspaper. I have a favorite spot there, a perch in a loft upstairs with a view of both the ocean and the prepared food hall, where I can watch the vendors at work. In the summer it's a challenge to snag my table, as the market is crowded with tourists who flood the food halls. Ten million people visit Granville Island every year, a nod to the growing popularity of culinary destinations. But on a winter weekday, the aisles of stalls feel drowsy. I sipped my coffee, thumbed my newspaper and alternated between watching the sushi vendor prepare rolls and gazing out at the boats on the water. The city was bathed in watery winter light.

Even in this barest of seasons, every stall overflowed with plenty. There were exotic spices from around the world: fresh wasabi root, dried ancho peppers, kaffir lime leaves. There was high-quality seafood, including great red slabs of British

Columbia's iconic smoked salmon. There was even an entire stall dedicated to local honey from last summer's blooms. The produce vendors were offering fresh fruit and vegetables from around the globe, including Australian mangoes picked at the peak of ripeness and shipped north by plane on the day of their harvest. I folded my paper and wandered downstairs to walk the aisles, making a stop at Lee's, where a tray of delicious lemon cake donuts was still warm from the oven. They were shaped and cut by hand, drenched in a fragrant glaze, and then served on a square of wax paper. I bought one to savor as I wandered through the stalls.

I was seeing the market through different eyes now. As I surveyed the stalls, the lessons of the world's extinct foods filled my mind. As I passed Tenderland Meats' rows of perfectly marbled steaks, I thought about the days of the mammoth and the aurochs and how the transition from the Paleolithic to the Neolithic was borne on an inevitable shift away from the hunting of megafauna, as populations of the great animals crashed. It seemed to me that the shift to farming, a set of technologies that at first led to hunger and much poorer health outcomes, was one of necessity, as the great animals that supported our hunting and gathering lifestyle disappeared. I marveled at a neat pile of tenderloin steaks, an expensive luxury courtesy of the last of the great culinary megafauna: the cow. As I write this, cattle ranching continues to expand, accounting for up to 70 percent of rainforest clearing in the Amazon. Those stacks of steaks come at a cost of negative climate impact, high water use and habitat loss. The cow needs rethinking. Cellular agriculture offers one potential solution, or a greater shift to plant-based substitutes might sate our appetites while reducing the ecological price.

A similar story awaits at the cheese stalls, where hundreds of varieties stand in artful display, rich in terroir, that elusive French concept of "taste of place." At Benton Brothers, I took a sample of Humboldt Fog goat cheese from Cypress Grove Dairy in California, with its signature strip of ash running through the body of the cheese. Is such a luxury of choice sustainable? Does the future of food include such a wonderful cheese or a lump of butter from rare Icelandic cattle, or is the future one of industrial dairy operations rapidly expanding in parts of the world where land is cheap and labor costs are low? Will cellular agriculture dot our neighborhoods with vat milk production in the same way as microbrewing has brought us neighborhood beer? Or will new technologies centralize dairy production further? I took another sample to be on the safe side. In 2018, a group of researchers at the University of Guelph in Ontario, Canada, released a study showing that there isn't enough land on earth to supply everyone with a North American diet. Meat and dairy are major parts of the problem.

I stopped in front of Jackson's Poultry. Stacks of chicken breasts waited, prepped for quick cooking. Chicken Kiev, stuffed with herbs and butter. Chicken cordon bleu, stuffed with ham and cheese. Chicken Florentine, filled with spinach and mushrooms. I'd not been conscious of how much chicken is on offer within our food system before, but now I was spotting it everywhere. At university lunches, as a standard option on menus, as a fast food and as a staple of the supermarket. I couldn't look at the neat pyramids of breaded bird without imagining a sky so filled with passenger pigeons that they blotted out the sun. I would like to share the optimism of the scientists working to bring the passenger pigeon back, but could we ever make room again for such a bird? I've returned a few times to the pages of *The Epicurean* to marvel at Ranhofer's elaborate pigeon dishes, and I've imagined lingering over a gilded age dinner, with course after course arriving on silver plates beneath the gaslight.

I moved on through the market, dodging early morning shoppers. The passenger pigeon might be extinct, but the lessons of its loss have direct application to another flocking creature: fish. I stopped at Longliner Seafoods, marveling at the luminescent blocks of ruby red tuna.

The story of culinary extinction leads us inexorably to the oceans. For most of human history, we lacked the technology to seriously impact oceanic species, but we've always benefited from the ocean's bounty. I've saved the oceans for last, though they were never far from my thoughts. In Iceland, I watched pan ice glow blue in the stillness of the harbor over an ocean filled with cod. In Hawaii, I watched the surf pound the black sand. At home on the West Coast, I'd enjoyed a meal plucked from the shoreline.

The ocean is an old friend, and we overlook its health at our peril.

Water covers more than 70 percent of the planet, and the Pacific alone takes up 30 percent of the earth's surface. We estimate that beneath this vast savanna there are between seven hundred thousand and a million species, two-thirds of which are yet to be discovered, named and described. Ocean life is diffuse compared to land-based ecosystems, and only 1 or 2 percent of the earth's biomass is to be found in the oceans. These ecosystems are no less important, though. Ten percent of the world's population makes their living from fisheries, and 4.3 billion people receive at least 15 percent of their protein from the ocean. On average, we each eat a little under twenty kilograms of fish each year, a number that varies widely. Island peoples are still highly reliant on sea products.

Food production in the oceans is evenly split between wild-caught products and aquaculture. The largest category is the finfish. Smaller fish such as herring and anchovy are mainly used for animal feed, and old standards such as the cod end up on our tables. Clams and oysters are the most commonly harvested and farmed mollusks, and the dominant crustacean is the shrimp, though lobster is important regionally. Seaweed, including that produced by mariculture, is an important vegetable product and is also the source of additives used in everything from ice cream to iodized salt. The oceans shaped our cities, almost all of our great market towns are served by water and the oceans still facilitate our modern trade system.

My story also begins on water. My earliest true memory is of the ocean, of a day spent fishing bait herring on my uncle's small wooden salmon boat. He took me out one day and gave me one of my first real tasks as a member of a fishing family; as he pulled the net, he tossed me the glistening silverfish and I placed them into the bait tank. When we had finished, he made me hot chocolate in a battered pot on the tiny oil stove in the cabin. Later, he would use the herring to fish for salmon, as salmon could be turned into money, or dinner, depending on the day. It was an early lesson in a family whose livelihood was pulled from the cold waters. My dad was literally born at sea, one long winter night just off of D'Arcy Island in British Columbia. The lifestyle stuck, and forty years later he built his own fifty-four-foot halibut boat, the *Jaana*. My father chased halibut the way an old-time pigeon hunter chased the flocks.

From our shorefronts to the deepest trenches, the oceans are in crisis. The fonts of all life on earth are now challenged by the changing climate, overfishing and pollution. Climate change is particularly damaging to the oceans. In normal times, they absorb carbon dioxide that is then taken up by sea life and sequestered in limestone. This is, however, a slow process. If carbon dioxide levels in the atmosphere rise too quickly, the ocean acidifies, devastating marine life adapted to a slightly alkaline ocean environment. Crustaceans and mollusks in particular struggle to build their shells in such an environment. The ocean is also warming as it absorbs excess heat trapped by the atmosphere, challenging cold water species such as my own region's iconic salmon. And sea levels are rising as oceanic waters absorb heat and expand and runoff from melting icecaps increases. Rising waters poses an immediate threat to reefs, wetlands and beaches.

Pollution is also a threat to marine life, and oceanic pollution is very difficult to remedy. We can find just about every possible pollutant in the ocean: agricultural runoff, sewage, hormone disrupting medications, petrochemicals, accumulations of heavy metals. There are over one hundred million tons of plastic alone in the oceans, broken down into tiny choking particles through the action of the waves and the sun. There are also over three million shipwrecks in the oceans, many of them unexplored, their cargos slowly leaching into the environment. The topic of oceanic pollution is too large to fully explore here, but a full, meaningful cleanup will take centuries.

The third threat to the oceans is overfishing. We stand on the precipice of a radical decline in the world's fisheries. Thirty percent of the world's commercial fisheries are overfished and another 60 percent are fully fished. About ninety million tons of fish are caught and eaten annually, and another thirty-eight million tons are caught and discarded as bycatch, the fish we accidentally catch but don't want. Another twenty million tons or so is taken illegally. The population of larger fish species is now at about 10 percent of historical maximums, and in smaller bodies of water such as the Mediterranean, almost all fish stocks are overfished.

Once we begin fishing a species commercially, it rapidly declines, suffering an 80 percent reduction in the first fifteen years, on average. This mismanagement is expensive; the Food and Agriculture Organization in the U.S. estimates fisheries decline has cost us two trillion dollars over the last thirty years. A particularly grim study published in 2006 predicted that if we continue to fish as we do now, all of the world's fisheries will have collapsed by 2048.

There is still time to stem the tide of oceanic extinction. In a world of overfishing, extinction rates in oceans, rivers and lakes are surprisingly low compared to terrestrial extinction rates. Over the last 500 years, only 3 percent of extinctions have occurred in a lake or at sea. There are a few reasons for this. The oceans are larger than the land masses, of course. We also haven't been technologically able to access the ocean in the same way as terrestrial biomes until recently. The oldest boat we have ever found, a dugout, was dated to about ten thousand years ago, at the beginning of the Neolithic, though it is likely people were making sea voyages before that. Once we had boats, we still were very limited in our reach. We had to develop keels, rudders, sails, pumps, the ability to determine longitude and the capacity to provision for long voyages. This latter challenge required preserving food and carrying sufficient water, while ensuring a diet that would prevent scurvy and other shipboard diseases. The easiest solution was to stay close to shore.

In ancient times, boats were critical to the success of Greece, Sumer, Egypt and India, but their impact mostly took place in shallow water. Pliny the Elder and Herodotus describe fishing in detail, and the harvesting they describe is small in scale: single lines and small, fragile, handmade nets. With the exception of the whaling industry, it wasn't until after the Second World War that humans gained the ability to really have an impact on the oceanic environment, with factory ships capable of dragging miles of nets through deep water and able to stay at sea for months, processing and freezing fish as they are caught. The harvest of the ocean is at a stage equivalent to the mass hunting of the passenger pigeon once people had railroads and telegraphs. Land extinctions of flocking animals should be considered as foreshadowing of what will likely occur in the oceans if we don't immediately take action to lower our harvesting.

There are a few extinctions in water that give us an idea of the potential for future ocean losses. Recall that islands have a much higher extinction rate than continents, as they are land-forms in miniature. Lakes and rivers are the mirror of islands, pockets of water with unique species living in a contained environment. Most fish extinctions have happened here. The Brisbane River cod, an unusual fish that had features of both freshwater and saltwater cod, was driven to extinction through habitat destruction and overfishing as European settlers strug-gled to secure enough food in the challenging environment of Australia. A similar fate met the gökçe balığı, a type of carp endemic only to Lake Beyşehir in Anatolian Turkey. They were apparently delicious; the name means "heavenly fish." They were often served with a little dusting of powdered sumac. They were declared extinct in 2014. The gravenche suffered the same fate. This freshwater whitefish was found near the bottom of Lake Geneva in Switzerland, where it was one of the most important fish to nineteenth century fisheries. As recently as 1890, they represented up to 70 percent of all of the fish caught in the lake, and they were prized for their mild flavor and excellent firm flesh. They were so prized, in fact, that by the early 1900s, they were gone.

North America's Great Lakes also provide a case study in commercial fisheries depletion. Before European settlement, the lakes brimmed with fish and helped to support advanced cultures such as the Iroquois Confederacy. As Europeans began to populate the region, large commercial seafood runs began, from salmon in Lake Ontario, lake trout in Lake Erie, and whitefish throughout the system. By 1850, twenty thousand tons of fish were landed annually, and this number rose to thirty thousand by the early twentieth century. However, the numbers hid a creeping depletion; as fish grew scarce, fishers employed bigger boats and more advanced technology and shifted their focus from species to species as stocks declined. Both invasive species, such as the sea lamprey parasite, and pollution, particularly the risk of mercury accumulation in whitefish, devastated fish populations and closed fisheries. The fisheries that once supported over ten thousand workers now support only a few hundred fishers, and fish stocks have fallen by as much as 95 percent from their peaks. Extinctions in the system include the blue walleye, the Lake Ontario kiyi, the paddlefish, the gravel chub, the deepwater, blackfin and shortnose cisco populations, and the Lake Ontario Atlantic salmon run. Lake extinctions such as these give us a taste of what might happen in the ocean if we don't curb our appetite for seafood and reverse damage to aquatic ecosystems.

A few oceanic mammals have been driven to extinction as well. The most infamous is the Steller's sea cow, or *Hydrodamalis gigas*. The sea cow was discovered by Europeans in 1741, and even then it was found only around the Commander Islands in the Bering Sea between Alaska and Russia. Adults were up to nine meters long, and the animals carried a lot of fat to survive the extreme cold. It was named for Georg Wilhelm Steller, a naturalist aboard the *St. Peter* on Danish explorer Vitus Bering's Great Northern Expedition. Steller had a lot of time to observe the sea cows because the expedition shipwrecked on Bering Island and was beset by scurvy.

Steller treated the surviving crew with leaves and berries and assisted in harvesting sea cows. He noted how tasty the animal was. The meat was described as being similar to corned beef, though it needed a long cooking time. He noted that the meat was salty by nature and took a long time to spoil, and that the fat had no odor and the sweet milk could be made into butter. For a shipwrecked sailor surviving on maggoty ship's biscuit, a sea cow was a wondrous thing.

Bering died on the island that bears his name, but the survivors managed to build a boat out of their ship's wreckage and return to their expedition's base camp. Russian explorers, whalers and traders followed in the expedition's footsteps, and the Steller's sea cow was extinct only twenty-seven years later.[58] The sea cow is a reminder that, like land megafauna, we can't harvest the behemoths of the oceans without risking their extinction. They sit atop grand ecological pyramids, few in number, long of life and slow to repopulate.

In my lifetime, I've experienced an oceanic abundance that has long since retreated from more populated shores. In another of my childhood memories, I remember clamming. I recall the moonlight, the cold and the sound of the water washing gently on the pebbles of the beach. My uncle held the lantern while my father sunk the clam fork into the pocked mud at the very edge of the tide. My job was to quickly gather the butter clams glinting in the frigid water.[59] At the time, it was just part of life, but when I think on it, what a strange thing to literally pluck a meal from the natural world.

Back at the house, my grandmother would steam the clams on the woodstove and make them into rich winter soups and

---

58 The Steller's Jay, also named on the same expedition, is doing fine.
59 I remember being really cold.

clam cakes she served with a thick sour cream. And she would talk of how much less sea life there was, how as a girl it took mere minutes to jig up a cod for lunch and how she would gather crabs while wading in the shallows.

Today there is even less sea life, and Dungeness crab is forty dollars a pound at the Granville Island market. Global seafood stocks are in freefall. The Scombridae family of food fish, including tuna and bonito, has fallen by 74 percent, and overall sea life populations have plunged on average by 50 percent since 1970. And the impact is not on the sea and its species alone. Mangrove forests are in steep decline because their brackish habitat is being cleared to create ponds for the raising of shrimp to meet North America's insatiable demand for the shellfish.

One-third of commercial fish stocks are now classed as over-exploited. Some of the loss is very specific and directly related to luxury food products. Sea cucumber populations have declined by 98 percent in key fishing areas and 25 percent of shark popula-tions are threatened with extinction as catches for shark fin have increased by 300 percent over the last decades. Around the world, fish populations are in crisis. And as we've learned from our expe-riences on land, smaller populations lead to more extinctions.

Our most iconic fish species are not immune. The next culinary extinction could well be *Thunnus thynnus*, the Atlantic bluefin tuna. I remember my first bite of bluefin. It was the Easter weekend of 1990, and my parents had taken us all for a rare trip to the city and an even rarer trip to an all-you-can-eat brunch at a waterfront hotel. I was entranced. There were doormen. There were baskets of real cotton towels in the wash-rooms. At the buffet, there was a waffle station. (I liked the waffle station very much.) There were steaming bain-maries filled with every imaginable brunch food. We channeled our Viking heritage and pillaged.

The buffet also had a sushi counter. This was before sushi was available at every corner in Vancouver, and my sister and I, true to our upbringing in a fishing family, were horrified at the thought of eating raw fish. But there was something about the tuna, glistening ruby red, protectively tucked under the chilled glass display case. My sister dared me to try it. The chef was remarkably patient, or maybe he saw something in me. He'd watched me work through every dish of the buffet with the methodical intensity of a foodie in training. I like to think he knew what would happen if I would just take that first bite.

Soon I had a quivering ruby square of fish perched on a pillow of rice. The chef showed me how to dip it fish side down into soya sauce. I remember expecting a smell that saturated our boat, the *Jaana*, and a taste that had followed me my whole life. Instead, when I placed the nigiri in my mouth, it was like taking a swim in a summer ocean. It was, and remains, one of the best things I have ever eaten. It was one of those golden moments, a point at which my destiny of a life spent studying food unfolded. The chef, relieved to have a willing customer, even a string-bean teenager in ill-fitting Sunday clothes, took me through his whole display. The akami (red bluefin) of course; otoro (fatty tuna); the rare and now very hard to find awabi (abalone, overharvested and endangered in British Columbia); akagai (ark shell clam), so different from my grandmother's soup; tako (octopus, which I didn't like and still don't); and the strange uni (urchin), which tasted like the lowest of tides. I've been eating sushi ever since. My family, if I recall, was suitably appalled, especially when I began asking for special trips to sushi restaurants.

I don't eat bluefin anymore.

This tuna, a giant that can reach 500 kilograms, is a glorious fish. The Atlantic bluefin is a wild apex predator, the oceanic equivalent of a saber-toothed tiger. It has always been prized by sportfishermen who enjoy the fight of wrestling such a large fish out of the water. By the 1930s, charter boats sailing out of New York and New England offered up the challenge of the hunt, but for years they wasted the meat or sold it for pet food. There was little market locally for raw fish, and the bluefin is tough and tasteless when cooked. The rise and fall of Atlantic bluefin as a commercial food required a transportation innovation, but this time it wasn't a railway. The story of the Atlantic bluefin as a commercial fish began with an airline and the invention of the Styrofoam packing container.

The bluefin has been astonishing sailors and scientists alike for centuries. The fish was first formally described by Linnaeus himself in 1758. These giants cruise the seas, slabs of honed muscle designed for cold, deep water. Mature fish can be over two meters long, and they can live up to half a century, growing quickly but spawning late in life. They can dive to depths of 500 meters and can travel at speeds of 65 kilometers per hour. They feast on smaller animals such as sardines, herring, squid and shrimp. A potentially lucrative market for these fish waited halfway around the world, in Japan, and by the 1960s, Pacific bluefin was selling briskly there. Today, about 80 percent of the global harvest of Pacific, Atlantic and southern bluefin is consumed there, and at Tsukiji Fish Market in Tokyo the price per fish can run into the hundreds of thousands of dollars. Tuna was an early favorite as nigiri sushi and was served as early as the 1840s, when the Pacific bluefin first appeared in Edo's markets. Later, it would be Japan that pioneered the deep-sea fishing and flash-freezing technologies that vastly increased the catch of tuna, and by the 1960s, Pacific bluefin was emerging as a favorite species for sushi. Atlantic bluefin, however, was located on the other side of the world.

The tuna trade between hemispheres began in earnest in the early 1970s when Japan Airlines tasked an employee in the cargo department to find something, anything, to ship from North America to Japan. As manufacturing in Japan was booming, planeload after planeload of electronics was making the journey from Japan to the United States. The planes then had to return empty. Akira Okazaki began hunting for something that needed to be transported quickly (justifying the flight) and that would be highly prized in Japan. His mind turned to tuna, given the premium price it commanded at home, and a Canadian representative of the airline, Wayne MacAlpine, found an untapped stock of fish for him. In Nova Scotia, fishing charter businesses were catching tuna that weighed up to 500 kilograms. And after the photos were taken and the proud tourists headed home, the companies were burying the tuna in landfills.

An ideal business was born. The first few attempts failed as it proved difficult to ship fish without bruising them or having them rot. In 1972, the problem was solved when the first fish were crated in newly designed styrofoam containers shaped to keep them unbruised. These were then packed into a special refrigerated shipping unit and flown to Japan.

The success of the global shipping of bluefin has predictably affected stocks. At first, fishermen rushed to land bluefin, as suddenly they were an extremely lucrative catch. But bite by soy-dipped bite, the supply dwindled. Stocks are down 70 percent in the eastern Atlantic and they are down 80 percent in the western Atlantic. The Atlantic bluefin can't reproduce fast enough to survive such determined predation.

As the species is so valuable, there has been global cooperation to limit the catch. As with most species on the brink, no one actually wants the fish to go extinct. The International Commission for the Conservation of Atlantic Tunas has attempted to enforce quotas, but that has had mixed success. The United Nations has rejected an American-led ban on bluefin tuna trading and fishing, largely due to opposition by Japan. Bluefin is listed by the U.S. Department of National Oceanic and Atmospheric Administration Fisheries Service as a species of concern, and the prospects for the species remain clouded. Since active recovery efforts began in 1998, the stock has grown by about 20 percent.

And the Pacific bluefin? Since the fish first became popular in the 1960s, the population of bluefin in the Pacific has fallen as much as 96 percent.

Can we save the bluefin and still eat it? One potential solution is to treat prized aquatic giants like the aurochs of old and capture them to raise in captivity. This process for the bluefin began in the 1970s in St. Mary's Bay, Nova Scotia, Canada. Fishermen began capturing juvenile fish and containing them in massive pens, where they grew into monsters weighing hundreds of kilograms. This does nothing to protect wild stocks, however, as the fish are captured before breeding and only a few farmers have managed to get them to reproduce in captivity. They are also difficult to feed. Bluefin eat a lot, a problem that is straining stocks of the smaller wild fish that are harvested to feed larger species in captivity.

These challenges are not unique to bluefin aquaculture. Fish farming is heralded as an answer for commercial fishing's sins. Aquaculture is expected to account for 60 percent of fish production by 2030, but there are still critical questions to be answered. One of the most pressing issues is replacing the need to catch wild fish to feed carnivorous farmed fish. Aquaculture companies have turned to algae and land-based feed options such as insects and soy products and have made strides in efficiency as well. It takes 1.4 kilograms of feed to raise 1 kilogram of farmed salmon, an impressive ratio given it takes 10 kilograms of feed to produce one kilogram of beef.

Effluent, liquid waste discharged into a river or sea, from fish farming remains a more difficult problem to solve. Fish aren't meant to be kept in such small areas. They pollute the surrounding waters and sea bottom and transmit disease to wild stocks. In British Columbia, reports have shown wild sockeye salmon have been threatened by sea lice and piscine reovirus from farmed stock. These problems have prompted the British Columbia government to organize the removal of fish farms located on prime wild spawning routes. Land-based fish farming will likely solve many of these issues, but for large carnivorous fish, we are still perfecting non-ocean based aquaculture. For now, moving fish onto the farm isn't a cure-all for the threats to our wild ocean species.

Lost in thought, I walked past the market's tanks of crabs. The struggle to put nigiri onto our plate, caviar onto our spoons and a nice salmon steak onto our grill reveals a flaw with wild fishing. Large fish are megafauna, like the aurochs, and smaller fish are flocking species, like the passenger pigeon. If we aren't careful, oceanic species will suffer the same fate as their terrestrial cousins.

Fish farming is not yet likely to provide long-term answers for large, input-intensive species. Smaller species, however, can be raised quite easily on land. I recently sat down to a lovely meal at a local restaurant, and the chef served up an appetizer of frisée greens, watercress and a little marsh samphire (also known as sea asparagus), topped with fresh, delicious giant shrimp. These shrimp never saw an ocean. They were farmed in a warehouse in the Vancouver suburb of Langley, fifty kilometers from the ocean. Fed with protein produced on land, these shrimp help to spare the world's mangrove forests while still allowing us our seafood appetizer.

I shook myself out of my reverie and walked over to Granville Island Produce. I had to pick up a few supplies for the last extinction dinner with Dan. The first thing I needed were purple carrots. Since exploring the world of lost fruits and vegetables, I'd been eating a wider variety of cultivars. I was still curious about what an Ansault pear might taste like, but in the meantime I wanted to enjoy the recent increase in new and reintroduced cultivars appearing as grocers cater to a more food-conscious public. One of my favorites of these are purple carrots.

Carrots, *Daucus carota sativus*, are a relatively recent addition to our vegetable crispers. They were first cultivated in Afghanistan around 900 CE, and these early carrots had either purple or yellow roots. Wild carrot roots were small, forked and bitter, and the challenge for carrot breeders was to improve shape and to increase both size and sweetness. Europeans began developing white and orange carrots in the 1600s, and a still-popular red carrot was developed in India in the 1700s. The Dutch pioneered the orange carrot, creating the largest and sweetest roots at the time. There is a longstanding story that the orange carrot was favored as the Dutch were ruled by the House of Orange, but there is no solid evidence for such a link. It is more likely that orange carrots spread so well because they produced well-shaped roots with excellent flavor. They pushed out carrots of other colors in the west for nearly four centuries.

Purple carrots never disappeared in Afghanistan, where they were eaten in a number of dishes as well as used as a dye for cloth. Their purple color comes from anthocyanins, micronutrients that are powerful antioxidants. Purple carrots were reintroduced in the West in the first few years of the twentieth century. They first appeared in the United Kingdom, where grocery stores advertised them as an attractive snack for children. However, customers of all ages liked the brightly colored roots, and they are now widely available around the globe, part of what I call the "new" old cultivars. I picked up a big bag and moved on to Chilliwack River Valley Honey. Since my encounter with bees and pollination, I've been cooking with honey more often and I planned to roast the purple carrots and glaze them.

I had one more stop to make. After a little searching, I found what I was looking for, an unusual spice that was to be a final tasting experience on my quest to understand culinary extinction and the future of food. I tucked the tiny jar into my bag. My shopping complete, I treated myself to a plate of Pad Thai. This time, however, I was smart enough to stay inside by the window, safe from the lurking, menacing gulls.

I walked into Dan's kitchen and was greeted by a heavenly aroma. There were multiple pots on the stove, and Dan was whisking up some Yorkshire pudding batter that would need to rest awhile before it went into the oven at the last minute. He looked very pleased with himself. The fireplace in the dining room crackled merrily, and his best dishes were laid out on the table.

"I thought we were just having some carrots and lentils," I said.

He looked up and motioned me over. "Well, I figured we needed some side dishes."

I lifted a few pot lids. "Peas and potatoes?" I asked.

"Side dish."

"There's a roast in the oven. A very large roast."

"Side dish."

"And Yorkshire pudding?"

"Side dish to the side dish, of course."

"And the tart is dessert, I assume."

A lovely pear tart was cooling on the counter, the pastry gently browned and the poached pears artfully arranged in a spiral.

"Exactly. So, let's assemble your lentils and carrots. I'm hungry."

We washed the carrots, chopped them roughly, and tossed them with a little honey, olive oil, black pepper and tarragon. I sprinkled a little sea salt over them and popped them in the oven to roast. Dan fried an onion and we mixed in some black lentils we had cooked earlier. And to the lentils we added the final mystery ingredient of my explorations: asafoetida. As we opened the container, Dan wrinkled his nose.

"Wow. That has quite the punch."

I took a deep whiff. I tried to figure out what it smelled like. Celery, maybe. With onion, maybe green pepper. "It smells a little like Cajun mirepoix, but a lot stronger."

"Yes, maybe with leeks. Interesting," Dan said between sniffs.

We added a few liberal spoonfuls and left the dish to simmer.

Asafoetida is the dried latex from the tap root of members of the *Ferula* genus, herbaceous perennials native to the deserts of Iran and Afghanistan. The plants are silver in color and grow waist high. They are cultivated widely in India, where the gum is known as hing. It is a pungent spice and is used as a condiment, for pickling or to bring out the umami flavor in foods. It is often mixed with turmeric and added to curries, including lentil dishes such as the one Dan and I were making. Very occasionally it is mixed with salt and sprinkled on salad. The hardened latex is available as an amber-like lump or as a preground powder. The odor of our asafoetida was strong enough to make me flinch, but it mellowed rapidly as the dish heated. Even so, it is one of the five pungent[60] foods avoided by Buddhists.

I was sampling asafoetida because of what it is not: silphium. Remember the silphium of Cyrene, the most important of Roman

---

60 Along with onions, garlic, scallions and chives. Asafoetida is considered to
    be in the same category as leeks.

spices? I've saved it as a last digestif of the Lost Feast. Silphium is the ultimate extinct food. It was, by all accounts, incredibly delicious, economically valuable and culturally important. Once the Romans knew the supply was waning, they fretted about its loss and actively tried to protect their favorite plant, to no avail. Despite its popularity, we don't know exactly what silphium was, a relative of asafoetida, we think, but it could have been a different plant altogether. No sample of silphium or its derivative products have ever been found.

We know asafoetida is at least similar to silphium because it was often listed as a substitute for the more expensive, and then vanished, relation. Asafoetida was first brought to the ancient Mediterranean by Alexander the Great, who first encountered it in Persia. It was not a popular substitute, however. Apicius (the perhaps-mythical gourmand of Roman cookbook fame), Pliny the Elder and others all agreed that silphium was far superior. Dioscorides wrote in the first century that asafoetida was both weaker in power and nasty smelling.

But what of silphium? I've mentioned its fantastical origin story, but what we know for fact is that after Cyrenaica was settled in the seventh century BCE by the Greeks, a lively export trade from the region began: of wheat, barley, olives, apples, figs and silphium. Cyrenaica was a microclimate, a series of lush stepped plateaus surrounded by desert. Silphium was described as growing stubbornly in the wilds of the area, spreading over any and all disturbed ground. Pliny the Elder writes that silphium had a stalk like fennel and leaves resembling parsley, and flat, leaf-like seeds that were heart-shaped (in fact, it is possible these seeds inspired our stylized symbol for the heart). Scholars hypothesize from Pliny's description that silphium was likely also of the genus *Ferula*.

Silphium was used for food and as medicine. The stalk of the silphium plant flavored food, appearing in ancient cookbooks as a seasoning used in a variety of ways. It was also consumed for medicinal purposes, leading Pliny to claim that silphium was "reckoned among the most precious gifts presented to us by Nature." It was used to aid digestion and to treat a variety of gastrointestinal ailments.

The resin was even more prized, used to treat colds, aches, pains and even baldness. It was used to cure dog bites and scorpion stings. Taken in drink, Pliny the Elder claims it was effective for "neutralizing the venom of serpents and of poisoned weapons." Like the stalk of the silphium plant, the resin was used in cooking. Even the leaves were used. Silphium leaves were fed to sheep and cattle and were said to give their meat a pleasant flavor. It seems that the leaves also had a similar purgative effect as the stalk. Pliny claims that when the leaves were fed to cattle, "at first it purged them, but afterwards they would grow fat, the flesh being improved in flavor in a most surprising degree."

Cyrenaica grew rich on silphium. It was grown in great, semi-wild plantations near the capital of Cyrene and exported throughout the Mediterranean. It was so critical to the Cyrenian economy that it was pictured on the currency itself — the coins of Cyrenaica all bore the image of silphium. Although highly stylized, this image illustrates a plant with a thick central stalk, with leaves sprouting from this base and clusters of small flowers growing atop it. Although it's difficult to imagine how silphium may have looked growing in the wild, this image bolsters the theory that silphium may be a long-lost cousin of fennel.

As for silphium's taste, it was described as being a little bit like leeks once cooked. It was loved and appeared in a great number of recipes. *Apicius* includes more than 400 recipes, featuring ingredients sourced from across the Roman Empire. Silphium features prominently in these recipes and it appears alongside other popular herbs and spices, such as cumin, cardamom and mint, to season meat and vegetables. Apicius recommended silphium for a wide range of dishes, using it in recipes for chicken, pork, lamb, fish, sausage, lentils, eggs, turnips, pumpkin and other varieties of squash. He also enjoyed it in salads, sprinkling it on melons or sliced raw cucumbers or using it to flavor salad dressings prepared from oil and vinegar. Many of his recipes are still popular today, with silphium often being the only unfamiliar ingredient in dishes that are otherwise consumed around the world. However, some of his recipes would seem more unusual to us, such as spelt prepared with raw eggs and cooked pig's brains, or recipes for flamingo and for dormouse, both seasoned with silphium. The juice or resin of the silphium roots, called laser by the Romans, was recommended for gravies and in sauces for various meat dishes.

Some commentators have suggested that silphium may not actually be extinct, as we can't say for certain what it may have looked like. One hypothesis holds that this lost delicacy may actually be known to us today as a variety of fennel or might still be growing wild. However, Apicius would seem to contradict the first of these theories. Many of his recipes call for both fennel and silphium, and in sporadic comments he distinguishes between the ingredients. To him, they were identifiably different plants. As for the first theory, while possible, the climate around the site of ancient Cyrene, now Libya, has become more arid over the centuries and has been heavily grazed.

Apicius makes it clear that silphium was already disappearing in his own time. While it may have been a common ingredient for the Ancient Greeks, in his lifetime, only the wealthiest Roman gourmands could afford it. Even Apicius himself, who is reputed to have spared no expense in sourcing the most extravagant ingredients, was forced to find ways to economise with the prized silphium plant. In his cookbook, he suggests a method for making a small amount of silphium go a long way: first placing laser (either the juice of the silphium root or, possibly, a sauce or rue made from this juice) in a glass vessel, then immersing pine nuts in this liquid and storing them until they are impregnated with flavor. These nuts would later be crushed into a dish in order to impart the flavor of laser, which was said to have been strong and pungent.

We also know that silphium and asafoetida are not the same plant. As silphium became increasingly scarce, Roman recipes began calling for asafoetida to be used as a substitute. The two plants almost certainly belonged to the same genus and, based on the similarities in their flavor, uses and preparation techniques, asafoetida would appear to be the closest surviving relative of silphium. However, scholars hunting for traces of the lost silphium plant note crucial differences in descriptions of its stalk and roots, and Roman recipes confirm what the scholars were saying: asafoetida was an inferior substitute for the real thing.

As silphium became rare, the rich and powerful horded the spice. Julius Caesar went as far as to cache 700 kilograms (in the form of laser) in the Roman treasury along with the silver and gold. He might have been thinking of a reason beyond the culinary. As delicious as silphium may have been, its usefulness in the kitchen was likely not the primary reason that the plant was so highly valued. While silphium was also widely celebrated for its digestive benefits and other medicinal properties, it had additional uses that were promoted in more clandestine ways.

Silphium is believed to have had contraceptive properties. Sometimes marketed as Cyrenaic juice, the resin from silphium roots was sold for this purpose throughout the Roman Empire. Although we don't know whether or not silphium actually offered protection against pregnancy, stories of its efficacy as a contraceptive helped to spur widespread demand and to raise its price accordingly. Silphium may also have been used as an abortifacient, said to encourage menstruation among the mistresses of Roman noblemen.

Noting a concerning decline in the population of the City of Rome, Emperor Augustus, who ruled Rome at the beginning of the Common Era, passed laws designed to encourage citizens to have more children. For whatever reason silphium remained in high demand among the families of the Roman nobility. Unscrupulous merchants sold adulterated laser to those who could not afford the pure product or even sometimes attempted to pass asafoetida off as silphium to lower-ranking people who were unlikely to be able to identify the difference. Although the myriad adulterants and substitutions may have damaged the reputation of silphium, its resin remained the exemplary form of birth control within the Roman Empire. Nevertheless, authorities could hardly legislate against it; after all, silphium was used to treat countless other ailments and was purported to offer numerous health benefits beyond contraception.

Silphium was important. It was the vanilla of its time. It shouldn't be extinct.

What troubles me about silphium is that it was allowed to vanish even though it was so valued. The Romans had reason to protect it, and the Cyrenians had reason to encourage its growth. According to Theophrastus, it wasn't easy to cultivate, instead spreading naturally in disturbed ground. Its popularity may have led to overharvesting. Although tenant farmers depended on revenues from silphium and thus attempted to manage the land in sustainable ways, many landlords demanded that it be kept in constant production rather than left fallow to restore the soil. The growing taste for meat may also have been to blame, as productive agricultural land was given over to grazing animals rather than growing crops. Pliny the Elder believed that the loss of silphium could be attributed to overgrazing, stating that "the farmers of the revenue who hold the lands there on lease have a notion that it is more profitable to depasture flocks of sheep upon them."

At the same time, the expansion of the ancient city contributed to soil erosion and habitat destruction, possibly offering an early example of species extinction attributable to urban development.

Seven centuries after silphium was said to have sprung from the ground in a black rain, it vanished from the earth. Pliny wrote that within his lifetime, only a single stalk was discovered. It was plucked and sent to the emperor Nero as a curiosity sometime around 54 to 68 CE. And if the Romans could lose silphium, what could we lose? Vanilla? Coffee? The banana? It sounds ludicrous, but these three crops all carry their own weaknesses. When the last stalk of silphium was plucked, there were roughly 300 million people on earth, and each person had a per capita gross domestic product roughly 6 percent of the average of earth's seven billion people today. Using these numbers, humanity today, in the age of the Anthropocene, has a footprint 500 times that of humanity at the height of the Roman Empire. And every day our shadow grows.

In the dining room, at Dan's long oak table, my host poured a merlot. The roast was cooling on the carving board, and I was ready to fill my Yorkshire pudding with gravy. I took a first bite of the lentil dish. The asafoetida still reminded me of celery, but in the background was a hint of leeks. I served up a healthy pile of carrots, glistening with honey.

In between mouthfuls, Dan peppered me with questions about extinction.

"Do you think we will lose more foods? Even with all of our knowledge and technology? I know we are damaging the environment, but we are aware of it, right? The Romans, clever though they were, didn't have the tools we do."

"I'm not sure. It's complicated. I'm worried the number of culinary extinctions is going to rise. We have overharvesting, habitat loss, climate change. And demand is rising constantly. Not everyone on earth can possibly eat the way North Americans eat now."

"True. But you found people working on the resurrection of necrofauna and also all of the cellular agriculture," he said, swirling his wine. "And other people are bringing back old varieties. Taken to a logical conclusion these technologies could allow us to 're-wild' much of the land we farm and graze. And we could be eating foods we can't imagine now."

I looked out the windows into the darkness. "That's true. The Anthropocene is complicated. I'm left with a strong sense of wabi-sabi."

"What is wabi-sabi?" Dan asked, eyebrows raised.

"It's a concept from Zen Buddhism. It's a worldview centered on the acceptance of transience and imperfection. It's also grounded in an appreciation for the natural world. It embraces the idea that nothing lasts, nothing is finished and nothing is perfect. I keep thinking about it."

"So, we should mourn and accept what we've lost and do the best we can to protect what is left?"

"Sort of. And the idea of wabi-sabi suggests that we should love life while balancing that love against the sense of serene sadness that is life's inevitable passing."

"So, dedicate time to protecting vanilla rather than somehow resurrecting silphium?"

The embers glowed in the dining room fireplace. The candles burned low in the holders. Dan shrugged. "Well, I'd still like to try truffling a passenger pigeon. But for now, here's to the lost feast, such as it is."

"To the feast," I said, smiling.

Dan drained his glass and sank into contemplation.

"Okay, let's cut the tart. And I'm opening a bottle of Tokaji. If I have to contemplate the impermanence of life, I'm going to need another drink."

"Dan, I can't argue with that."

Dan went to fetch the tart, and I drained the last of my merlot. A little tipsy, I watched the embers of the dying fire. Silphium might be lost to us, but the future of culinary extinction is still to be written. I placed my glass on the table among the empty plates, my head full of ghosts.

Suggested Readings

I read many wonderful works in the writing of this book. The following is a list of sources for the reader who is interested in a closer look at the topics covered here.

Chapter One

Khosrova, E. *Butter: A Rich History*. Appetite by Random House, 2016. This is the definitive work on all things buttery.

Brillat-Savarin, J.A. *The Physiology of Taste*. Dover Publications, 2012. I like this version of Brillat-Savarin's classic. It is an excellent primer on the roots of food writing and cuisine as an art form.

Chapter Two

Quammen, D. *The Song of the Dodo: Island Biogeography in an Age of Extinctions*. Random House, 2012. This book isn't about the dodo specifically but rather an excellent introduction to island biogeography. It was this book that spurred my interest in island ecosystems and cuisines.

Mayor, A. *The First Fossil Hunters: Dinosaurs, Mammoths, and Myth in Greek and Roman Times*. Princeton University Press, 2011. Mayor's work explodes the misconception that fossils were unknown in ancient times.

Kolbert, E. *The Sixth Extinction: An Unnatural History*. Henry Holt and Company, 2014. *The Sixth Extinction* is the most important work on extinction written. It is an excellent reference and a timely warning as species loss accelerates.

Chapter Three

Martin, P.S., and H.W. Greene. *Twilight of the Mammoths: Ice Age Extinctions and the Rewilding of America*. University of California Press, 2005. For those readers interested in an examination of megafauna extinction, this book provides a lot of detail.

Lott, D.F., and H.W. Greene. *American Bison: A Natural History*. University of California Press, 2002. I love bison, and this is my favorite book about these beautiful animals.

Shapiro, B. *How to Clone a Mammoth: The Science of De-Extinction*. Princeton University Press, 2015. Shapiro's book is a good introduction to the de-extinction movement.

Chapter Four

Hayes, D., and G.B. Hayes. *Cowed: The Hidden Impact of 93 Million Cows on America's Health, Economy, Politics, Culture, and Environment*. W. W. Norton, 2015. Worried about the environmental impact of the cow? This book will stoke that worry.

Smith, A.F. *Hamburger: A Global History*. Reaktion Books, 2008. This is the best of several books on America's favorite food.

Brears, P. *All the King's Cooks: The Tudor Kitchens of King Henry VIII at Hampton Court Palace*. Souvenir Press, 2011. Do you want to dig into Henry's kitchens in the sort of detail that would make the stove advocate proud? This is your book. It is a wonderfully deep dive into Tudor cooking.

Chapter Five

Shapiro, P., and Y.N. Harari. *Clean Meat: How Growing Meat without Animals Will Revolutionize Dinner and the World*. Gallery Books, 2018. This new book is a comprehensive overview of cellular agriculture. I expect more books in this area to appear rapidly.

Chapter Six

Greenberg, J. *A Feathered River across the Sky: The Passenger Pigeon's Flight to Extinction*. Bloomsbury Publishing, 2014. Greenberg's magical book is my favorite exploration of the passenger pigeon. It will stand the test of time as a definitive work.

Lobel, C.R. *Urban Appetites: Food and Culture in Nineteenth-Century New York*. University of Chicago Press, 2014. There are several books written exclusively about Delmonico's restaurant, but this work captures the broader sense of what food was like in eastern North America during the gilded age.

Wray, B., and G. Church. *Rise of the Necrofauna: The Science, Ethics, and Risks of De-Extinction*. Greystone Books, 2017. For readers who want even more writing on de-extinction, this text dives into the philosophical issues of reviving lost species.

Chapter Seven

Lewis, S.L., and M.A. Maslin. *The Human Planet: How We Created the Anthropocene*. Penguin Books Limited, 2018. A small stack of books on the Anthropocene have appeared recently. I found this one to be an approachable look at the concept.

Wulf, A. *The Invention of Nature: Alexander von Humboldt's New World*. Alfred A. Knopf, 2015. For those who want to learn more about the man who picked up an electric eel, this engaging book provides a look at von Humboldt's adventures.

McKenna, M. *Big Chicken: The Incredible Story of How Antibiotics Created Modern Agriculture and Changed the Way the World Eats*. National Geographic Society, 2017. There are surprisingly few books written about the chicken, but McKenna's work gives an engaging and disturbing look at one of our favorite foods.

Chapter Eight

Sethi, S. *Bread, Wine, Chocolate: The Slow Loss of Foods We Love*. HarperCollins, 2015. My love for the foods in the title aside, I found this book to be a great introduction to cultivar loss.

Pollan, M. *The Botany of Desire: A Plant's-Eye View of the World*. Random House, 2002. This is my favorite of Pollan's works and one of the best books ever written about plants.

Morgan, J. *The Book of Pears: The Definitive History and Guide to over 500 Varieties*. Chelsea Green Publishing, 2015. Is there a giant book exclusively about pears? Yes. Yes there is. It is perfect for the enthusiast.

Chapter Nine

Goldstein, J. and D. Brown *Inside the California Food Revolution: Thirty Years That Changed Our Culinary Consciousness.* University of California Press, 2013. California cuisine played a key role in reviving our interest in local cultivars. This book tells that story.

Gollner, A.L. *The Fruit Hunters: A Story of Nature, Adventure, Commerce, and Obsession.* Scribner, 2013. Fruit hunters are fascinating people. Gollner's book remains one of the few dedicated to their stories.

Chapter Ten

Flannery, T. *Among the Islands: Adventures in the Pacific.* Grove Atlantic, 2012. Read with *Song of the Dodo*, this book might inspire an unquenchable thirst for exploration.

Baskin, Y. *A Plague of Rats and Rubbervines: The Growing Threat of Species Invasions.* Island Press, 2013. This remains Dan's favorite book on invasives.

Laudan, R. *The Food of Paradise: Exploring Hawaii's Culinary Heritage.* University of Hawaii Press, 1996. I've included this one cookbook in my recommendations as it is a wonderful book. The text alternates between detailed explanations of Hawaii creole cuisine and dishes that take the reader to the islands.

Chapter Eleven and Twelve

Benjamin, A., and B. McCallum. *A World without Bees.* Random House, 2012. A thorough exploration of the bee crisis.

Nordhaus, H. *The Beekeeper's Lament: How One Man and Half a Billion Honey Bees Help Feed America.* Harper Perennial, 2011.

If you can't believe we drive millions of bees around on trucks, here is there story in detail.

Ecott, T. *Vanilla: Travels in Search of the Ice Cream Orchid*. Grove Atlantic, 2007. There are several books about vanilla but I quite like this one.

Chapter Thirteen

Greenberg, P. *Four Fish: The Future of the Last Wild Food*. Penguin Publishing Group, 2010. Greenburg's book remains one of my favorite explorations of fisheries.

Issenberg, S. *The Sushi Economy: Globalization and the Making of a Modern Delicacy*. Penguin Publishing Group, 2007. This remains my favorite explorations of the bluefin tuna phenomenon.

Ellis, R. *The Empty Ocean*. Island Press, 2013. Thoughtful and sad, Ellis's book gives added detail on oceanic extinctions.

Index

Footnotes are denoted by n *following the page number.*